MUSIC THROUGH THE LOOKING GLASS

MUSIC THROUGH THE LOOKING GLASS

*A very personal kind of
Dictionary of Musicians' Jargon,
Shop-talk and Nicknames;
and a Mine of Information about
Musical Curiosities, Strange Instruments,
Word Origins, Odd Facts,
Orchestral Players' Lore and
Wicked Stories about the
Music Profession*

Fritz Spiegl

Routledge & Kegan Paul
London, Melbourne and Henley

First published in 1984
by Routledge & Kegan Paul plc
14 Leicester Square, London WC2H 7PH, England,
464 St Kilda Road, Melbourne,
Victoria 3004, Australia and
Broadway House, Newtown Road,
Henley-on-Thames, Oxon RG9 1EN,
England

Set in Palatino
by Input Typesetting Ltd, London
and printed in Great Britain by
T. J. Press (Padstow) Ltd

British Library Cataloguing in Publication Data
Spiegl, Fritz
Music through the looking glass.
1. Music——Dictionaries
I Title
780'.3'21   ML100

ISBN 0-7102-0401-9

INTRODUCTION

Every trade or profession, every group of people with common organized interests, every club or school, has its own jargon. It not only speeds communication by the use of abbreviations and shop-talk familiar only to those in the know, but also makes a common bond and identifies them as members of a closed group. Criminals' slang, for example, is designed to be understood by villains but not by those who keep within the law. It is also constantly changed, so as to keep it one step ahead of outsiders: consider the number of words for illicit drugs, their use and their users. Outsiders soon learn that merely to adopt the language of a group will not gain them admission to it: everyone knows the type of foolish man who talks in a bar among, say, real airmen, about 'wizard prangs'; or motor-racing enthusiast who tells the professionals tales about his latest 'shunt', when he means a crash.

'He plays first violin in the Philharmonia . . . .' Anyone with an ear for musical talk will realize at once that this is no musician speaking. A professional would say either 'He plays in the firsts . . .' or 'in the first fiddles . . .' or (as the speaker may well have meant) 'He's the leader of the Philharmonia.' 'She's a concert pianist and played Rachmaninov's piano concerto . . .' does not work either. 'CONCERT PIANIST' is a solecism; and the speaker is evidently under the impression that the piano concerto he knows is the only one Rachmaninov wrote. But 'She played Rach Two', cryptic as it may sound, is immediately clear, in spite of the fact that 'Rach' also wrote a second *symphony*: in which case it might have to be 'She played *in* Rach Two . . .'. To talk about 'Haydn's String Quartet' is, similarly, wrong; but 'Verdi's String Quartet' refers to the one and only which he wrote (or is played). Then again, the musically versed automatically know that 'A Haydn quartet' without further specification means a string quartet; or a composer's name followed by a number, 'Beethoven Eight', the composer's eighth symphony (a practice I have followed in this book when referring to symphonies and treating the many nick-names given to Haydn quartets). But 'They're doing the Flute at the Garden' spells danger. The professional would certainly say it (meaning Mozart's *Magic Flute* at Covent Garden) but the sensitive amateur will avoid it, for it immediately suggests 'side' – like that of the 'wizard prang' pretender mentioned earlier.

The same goes for people's nicknames. Musicians who played for, and therefore knew, Sir Thomas Beecham, would familiarly refer to him as 'Tommy', though none would have said it in his hearing, and certainly not to his face. Coming from a member of the audience it always somehow sounded wrong. In the same way, only intimate friends or close colleagues would talk about 'Slava' when referring to the cellist, Mstislav Rostropovich, and even then not if the other party were unfamiliar with this family nickname.

It is also not recommended that music-lovers adopt the curious and inaccurate terminology of conductors, who are wont to say 'I played Beethoven Five in Vienna . . .'. It is an avoidable figure of speech. They no more *played* it than 'Henry VIII built Nonsuch Palace' or, 'We buried granny last week.'

The jargon and shoptalk of the musical profession is both more complicated and less ephemeral than most others. It is also linguistically more interesting. Music is the only international language, but in order that one may talk about it, terms must be borrowed from many tongues, ranging from Anglo-Saxon to Italian, French and German. A conductor giving the following instructions to his players would be immediately understood: 'I'd like a hairpin up in the fourth bar after F, with the meno just before the pause, where the soloist has an eingang; then it's l'istesso. I make a luftpause, followed by a subito piano a minim before the corona, and the same goes for the vuoto bar just before the end, so don't make a domino anybody: put a pair of spectacles – and a wiggly line might help to remind you that I prepare the rit a bar early, and I'll subdivide. Horns, in the second movement you're in alto, not basso as marked, with the bumpers-up joining in only in the fortes; and please, no cuivrés whatever you do but seconda volta you're tacet. In the oom-cha-chas don't overdo the Viennese lift, and put a bis over the penultimate bar of the cabaletta. Seconds, you're divisi by desk, senza sord. In the solos just relax and you won't get the purlies. Then, tutti strings, on the penultimate bar, keep scrubbing till I take you off with the left hand while the wind and brass hold. And mind the V. S. in your parts: if the outside players turn there won't be such a sudden drop.' To the organist he might say, 'Continuo, please choose an open eight-foot flute with a bit less chiff to it. I'm also getting too many resultant tones. Let's hope you won't have a cipher this time.' And to a percussionist: 'Bass drum, in the Turkish bits I want you to alternate a wooden head on the strong beats with a rute on the offbeat.'

But although they have a smattering of many languages, English orchestral players do not on the whole make natural linguists. Anglicizations and mispronunciations are almost traditional, and so are hobson-jobson formations – the adaptation of foreign terms to their nearest equivalent English sound – some of them time-honoured, like the 'Jingling Johnny', others more recent, like 'sardines' for mutes, from French *sourdines*, or 'queer flute' for the transverse flute, from the German *Querflöte*. There are also many humorously wilful mistranslations or atrocious puns, such as 'The Girl with the Lines of a Horse' for *La fille aux cheveux de lin* and 'Clear the Saloon' for *Claire de lune*. It is not difficult to guess what players call Mozart's *Schlittenfahrt* in English – and it is not 'Sleighride'.

I have tried wherever possible to avoid including in this book those technical terms (some of them appearing above) which may be found in ordinary dictionaries of music or textbooks on harmony and counterpoint. Such books, generally the work of many hands, must try to be objective and to avoid making judgments: like, for example, that which the fifth edition of GROVE made about Telemann ('lack of any earnest ideal . . . a fatal facility naturally inclined to superficiality') which continued to be repeated in other works of reference until people bothered actually to play, and listen to, Telemann's music. In this one-man dictionary, which tries to be both factual and anecdotal, I have felt no such constraints.

A number of my views, for example those on dodecaphonic music, will be found annoyingly subjective by some, and may tell the reader more about my own prejudices than the music itself. But the book was written, so to speak, from the middle of the orchestra, and orchestral players have always been notoriously narrow-minded in their judgment. 'Tom, have you been able to discover a tune yet?' the principal horn of a nineteenth-century English orchestra called to one of the first fiddles. 'I have not', was Tom's reply. The work under rehearsal was Schubert's Great C major Symphony. On the other hand, I have sat in the midst of most of the orchestral works of Schoenberg, Berg and Webern and, like the vast majority of my colleagues, have not yet been able to discover what is traditionally (if undefinably) known as a tune – although their music is now much older than Schubert's was when Tom and his friend had the same difficulty. So my ignorance is not of the same kind as theirs, or that of the musicologist who made his absurd snap judgment in GROVE on poor Telemann.

If I have also been a little hard on conductors it is only because few of them are heroes to their valets, which is what orchestral players are by the very nature of the relationship. Conductors of my own generation and younger are aware of this, and treat their players as indispensable collaborators (if seldom as equals) – unlike the insufferably imperious Toscanini and his like, who would not be tolerated by modern orchestras. The wise conductor of today does not underestimate the education, literacy, and general musical accomplishment of his players; and the old-fashioned conductor who seldom read anything except scores is becoming a relic of the past. Far from being overawed by an international reputation, many a second oboist has been known to question some maestro's instructions, and perhaps quote QUANTZ at him in support of a long or short appoggiatura. Indeed, the kind of conductor most respected by the modern orchestral player is the like of Mazel, Barenboim or Ashkenazy, who have proved themselves as performers, and may play a concerto in one half of the concert and conduct the rest. Stick technique, as Sir Adrian Boult said, is something that can be acquired in an evening, and in truth holds no secrets for orchestral players: most of them know how to start and stop an orchestra and many do conduct efficiently and effectively without harbouring any great ambitions to earn their living by it. Every rehearsal is, after all, a lesson for them, or at any rate a salutary one on how not to conduct.

Conductors are by necessity dictators, albeit benevolent ones to whose authority players willingly submit, if only until the end of the final bar. True orchestral democracy is impossible, let alone musical socialism: for one thing it wastes too much time. The Russians tried it with their PERSIMFANS and duly made idiots of themselves. To the player, the best conductor is simply one more member of the team, albeit one without whom the performance of many works would be impossible or at any rate vastly inferior. But players hold no illusions and worship few heroes. I can honestly say that during some twenty years of playing under all kinds of conductors, from the indisputably great to the totally incompetent, I was only once immediately aware of being in the presence of genius. And that was as a last-moment deputy in the opera pit, when I had not even been told his name, let alone watched him rehearse.

I am grateful to many colleagues and ex-colleagues who made valuable contributions, suggested corrections or constructively criticised the contents of this book, among them Ray Abbott, Richard Adeney, Manfred Arlan, Robert Braga, Julian Budden, Grizelda Cann, Moran Caplat, Jonathan Del Mar, William Flood, Jessica Ford, Barrie Hall, Peter Hall, Hanny Hieger, Richard Hunt, Cherry Isherwood, Arthur Jacobs, Beresford King-Smith, Barbara McGregor, Graham Melville-Mason, Susan Milan, Peter Mountain, Andrew Mussett, Simon Rattle, Christopher Robson, Mark Rowlinson, Christopher Royall, Robert Sells, Ronald Settle, Jeremy Siepmann, Richard Suart, Christopher Tipping, Ben Trovato, Ernest Warburton, Cathy Wearing and Clive Wearing. Special thanks are due to Robert Orledge for reading the proofs and saving me from making several howlers or even DOMINOES: words thus printed in small capital letters are cross-references.

Absolute pitch/relative pitch

Absolute pitch, also known as 'perfect pitch', is the ability to sing, or recognize and name, any note of the scale; and usually the ability also to diagnose minute degrees of sharpness or flatness. It is a great help to conductors, who can genuinely *read* (i.e. actually hear in their mind's ear) the notes they see in a score without playing them on an instrument. The composer values perfect pitch because he can write music without the need for 'trying it out' on the piano, unlike KEYBOARD KNIGHTS. Some of the greatest musicians did not have perfect pitch; and some non-musicians have it without knowing what it is. It can be a mixed blessing, as it makes transposition in singing, or playing a transposing instrument such as the clarinet, more difficult. Opinions vary as to whether it can be acquired by training, but some very young children have a remarkable capacity for remembering pitch. Relative pitch is what the term implies: namely the ability to find any note from another whose identity is known; e.g. hearing a middle C and being able to pitch, say, F sharp.

The Academy

To a painter or sculptor this would mean the Royal Academy of Art, and to an actor the Royal Academy of Dramatic Art; but for the musician 'the academy' is the customary abbreviation of the Royal Academy of Music in either London or Glasgow. More recently some ensembles have revived and translated the old German word *Akademie* (which strictly meant a concert) and used it in the sense of a chamber music ensemble, like the cumbersomely named Academy of St-Martin-in-the-Fields. The original Academy was a place of learning where Plato taught and which was situated in a garden belonging to one Academus.

Accidentals

In written music, signs that temporarily contradict or re-establish the sharps or flats, etc. of a key-signature. Their effect lasts the whole bar through, and their non-observance is a frequent cause of accidents.

Accompagnato

See RECIT

Accompanist

Many of the greatest songs, by Schubert, Beethoven and others, are just as demanding for the pianist, who may feel justifiably aggrieved if he or she is given inferior status, like some REPET(ITEUR) helping the soloist along or following him by a fraction of a note, or has his name printed in smaller letters. The Germans get round the problem by describing the accompanist as *am Klavier*, i.e. 'at the piano'; but the inventive Americans euphemistically call him 'Collaborative Pianist' or 'Associate Artist'. Gerald Moore, in his entertaining book *The Unashamed Accompanist*, describes the delights, rewards and frustrations of working with great singers. Accompanist is a comparatively new word: the first edition of GROVE (1878) had 'accompanyist'. Announcers and newspapermen sometimes find the word troublesome: 'accompapanist' and 'accomanapist' are not uncommon; and in one concert programme there appeared the accidental but apt portmanteau word 'accompianist', which could hardly be bettered.

Acoustic guitar

A tautological misnomer, usually applied by those who consider it normal for a musical instrument to be plugged into an electric socket and amplified beyond human endurance. Acoustic comes from the Greek *akuo*, to hear. Of what use would a soundless guitar be?

Act tune

See CURTAIN ARIA.

Additional accompaniments

The addition of extra instrumental accompaniments to seventeenth- and eighteenth-century choral music was a pastime

Punch, 1896

Fair Accompanist (cheerfully): *"Now you go on, and never mind me! I'll catch you up by-and-by"*

engaged in by many composers and conductors of the nineteenth century as well as a few twentieth-century musicians such as Sir Thomas Beecham, Sir Malcolm Sargent and Sir Henry Wood. It ranged from subtle re-orchestration to wholesale re-composition, and was in part intended to fill out the bare bones of CONTINUO-based music when the art of FIGURED BASS playing fell into disuse. As the harpsichord had become obsolete by the first quarter of the nineteenth century and choral societies grew in numbers, the orchestras that accompanied eighteenth-century oratorios genuinely needed augmentation and reinforcement. But working in an age of practical expediency rather than self-conscious authenticity, writers of additional accompaniments did not hesitate to add all manner of heavy brass as well as anachronistic instruments such as clarinets, serpents and even saxophones. Handel and Bach, having survived longest in the repertoire, suffered most at the hands of the improvers. But it should be said that Mozart, too, recomposed *The Messiah*, Alexander's Feast, *Acis and Galatea* and the *Ode for St Cecilia's Day*; but he did it in a manner unique to him, and with touches of genius of which only he was capable. The English harp-maker J. A. Stumpff reports a conversation with Beethoven in 1824. *Stumpff*: 'Mozart was able to glorify even Handel by adding a new accompaniment to *The Messiah*.' *Beethoven*: 'It would have survived without his help.' Of all the *Messiah* arrangements, Beecham's is the most exuberantly and unselfconsciously absurd – almost a tongue-in-cheek caricature – with piccolos, triangles, cymbals and a full percussion section that only just stops short of using crockery to illustrate the breaking of the potter's vessel. After a performance of Sir Henry Wood's *Messiah* in 1912, the critic of the *Musical Times* said, 'When it was over, not a few in the hall felt wounded.' On the other hand, there were praiseworthy early attempts to steer a middle way. As long ago as 1899 the knowledgeable Sir George GROVE suggested the formation of a Handel oratorio orchestra proportionate to the big choral forces that had remained normal since the eighteenth century (for the idea that such music is 'authentic' only if performed by a small group is a myth): fifty strings, twelve oboes, six bassoons, a pair each of horns, trumpets and kettledrums. And the Royal Choral Society, under Sir Frederick Bridge (1844–1922) used that arrangement until 1922. Additional accompaniments composed by the Austrian conductor and editor Felix Mottl for Bach's *St Matthew Passion* were at one time popular in Britain and were informally nicknamed by orchestral players MOTTLED ARRANGEMENTS.

Adelaide Concerto

A forgery purporting to be a violin concerto by Mozart, written for Princess Adelaide in Versailles, and dated 26 May 1766. The alleged manuscript is said to bear a dedication to the Princess, eldest daughter of Louis XV. The owner of the manuscript and presumed perpetrator of the swindle, a once well-known musician called Casadesus, claimed to have received the manuscript from a Demoiselle Laval de Montmorency, but always refused to show it to anyone, not even the publishers Schott whom he persuaded to print the work under Mozart's name in 1933. The work is indubitably a forgery, and the grounds for its rejection are overwhelming. Here are a few of them. Mozart and his family did not arrive in Versailles until two days later than the date on the 'manuscript'. The alleged dedication is couched in a form alien to Mozart, who never wrote any formal title-page dedications on his autographs. Neither young Mozart nor his sister (nor his father, a first-class snob) refer to Princess Adelaide in their letters or journals, though they methodically list everyone else of importance they were presented to. Furthermore it is inconceivable that Leopold Mozart could have omitted from the THEMATIC CATALOGUE he painstakingly compiled of Wolfgang's early works a concerto composed for a royal personage. The 'autograph' was declared by Casadesus to have been written on two staves – a practice unknown in the entire canon of Mozart's output, for he had certain, unalterable ways of writing his music straight into full score. The internal evidence is equally damning, with passages of genuine – but not genuinely Mozartian – charm mixed with flat-footed plodding of which Mozart was incapable even as a boy. There are, however, some passages and fingerprints relating to Mozart's French ballet music, notably *Les petits riens* of 1778, including a quotation from one of the gavottes from that work; but these were doubtless placed there on purpose in the manner of false clues. Much of the foregoing was known to, and revealed by, EINSTEIN but the swindler never made any attempt to defend himself in law. Nevertheless, the forgery has been given some false credence by the composition of cadenzas by Paul Hindemith; and several recordings of the work have been made by Yehudi Menuhin and others, who must all have been aware that the piece is suppositious.

Ad lib.

A passage so marked, or an instrument that plays it, may be omitted (the opposite being OBBLIGATO). Also, a marking found in EARLY music at places where a player or singer is encouraged to add such ornaments as he may wish.

Aerophor

An invention patented in 1912 by a German, Bernhard Samuels, designed to help wind players cope with long phrases without running out of breath. It consisted of a pair of bellows worked with the foot which supplied air to the player's mouth through a long rubber tube. It was doubtless based on an earlier French patent of 1877: 'an apparatus known as *Aerophore* which enables the miner to carry sufficient fresh air for his own respiration'. How this extra wind supply could be used without the supporting action of the diaphragm, so important in the blowing of brass and wind instruments, is not clear. Even less clear is how the other members of the orchestra managed to play while laughing their heads off. Like many absurd musical inventions the Aerophor (not 'Aerophon[e]' as occasionally misprinted) would have sunk without trace had not Richard Strauss stipulated it in his *Alpensinfonie*, op. 64 (1911–15) as well as his *Festliches Praeludium*, op. 61 (1913). No one has, to my knowledge, witnessed a performance in which the Aerophor was used; and players seem to manage to breathe perfectly well without it. I wonder whether Samuels was aware of a previous invention by 'the late Mr Hogben the surgeon who, being in delicate form, and subject to cough, found that playing the flute affected his breathing . . . so that he found it necessary, in order to continue the gratification which he derived from this instrument, to contrive an *artificial breath* for it. This he accomplished so perfectly and conveniently, that *he could sing and play at the same time.*' (*Gentlemen's Magazine*, September 1815). Unfortunately Dr Hogben's Patent Wind machine met the same fate as Samuels's Aerophor.

Agent

One half of a love-hate relationship. The aspiring young musician may in the first place have difficulty in persuading a concert agent to 'put him on his books', especially if the artist has not won an important international competition or been declared someone's somebody 'of the Year'. When he does find an agent willing to promote him, he will, after initial gratitude for being accepted, probably start to grumble about him: too little work, too much work, too much commission or (a frequent complaint) having to wait too long for his fee. Even if the concert promoters or music club paid the artist's fee to the agent promptly (and some do) the money may spend some considerable time in the agent's bank account, shielding him, not the artist, from inflation and overdraft. The agent's commission may vary between 10 and 40 per cent, though the commonest is 15 per cent. Some agents work a gentle blackmail (well, *grey*mail) system which music clubs do not like but which works to the ultimate benefit of the young artist. 'I will let you have Yehudi Smith', they say of an artist who is much in demand and a sure drawer of audiences, 'if you'll try this young singer Queenie Zukerman we've just discovered.' In French the word *agent* is considered very rude in some connotations, but I have heard performers call their agents by worse names.

Agony pipe

See LICORICE STICK and other nicknames for the clarinet.

AIRO

A new, trendy acronym to conjure with, from **A**coustical **I**nvestigation and **R**esearch **O**rganisation: a system of electrical amplification employed in some concert halls and opera houses with the supposed purpose of making an orchestra sound more like an orchestra. However, I suspect that the idea is to make live music sound as falsely 'perfect' as people come to expect it to be after hearing too many gramophone records, with their artificially controlled, computerized acoustics. Mozart and Mahler appear to have managed quite well without Airo.

Air on the G-String

Old-established misnomer for the slow movement of J. S. Bach's third orchestral overture in D (BWV 1068). The violinist August Wilhelmj (1845–1908) arranged the movement for violin and piano, transposed it nine notes down into C major, and directed that it should be played on the G-string. Thus the movement is still often described as 'the Air on the G-String' even when played in its original orchestral version and not exclusively on that string. See also under G-STRING in its application as an article of dress, or rather undress.

Alberti Bass

The musician's nickname for breaking up the left-hand part of keyboard music into arpeggio segments, i.e. literally 'broken chords'. The notes are usually played in a certain order: low – high – middle – high, etc. The figuration gets its name from its supposed inventor, Domenico Alberti (d. 1740), a composer, singer and harpsichordist who is said to have used this form of accompaniment habitually until, doubtless, it became 'his thing'. Alberti specialized in accompanying himself at the keyboard, then an unusual and noteworthy thing to do in public performance. It would make the attribution to Alberti of such a trick more likely, just as Brahms has been credited with the discovery of the TENOR THUMB. But it is dangerous in music to claim a first time: somebody always comes along and finds an earlier instance. The best-known example of an Alberti Bass is Mozart's Sonata in C major, K545. Clarinets in their lowest register are also good at Alberti figuration: see WOODLES.

Albinoni's Adagio

Tomaso Albinoni (1671–1751) was a prolific Venetian composer who in his time must have written hundreds of adagios. So why do we suddenly saddle him with a piece whose name is bandied about like 'BOCCHERINI'S MINUET' or 'Tchaikovsky's Piano Concerto' by people under the impression that these composers wrote only one of each? The answer may be summarized in the clerihew:

> The Adagio of Albinoni
> is largely phoney:
> a sort of musical risotto
> cooked up by Giazotto.

That is putting it a little strongly. GROVE tells us that Giazotto is an Italian writer on music who produced 'romanticised biographies of various composers'. He certainly romanticized one of Albinoni's adagios, taken and arranged from an unrevealed source: a kind of passacaglia built on a recurring bass. Since 'Albinoni's Adagio' was first heard in the 1970s dozens of recordings of it have, appeared and its popularity not only brought Albinoni the kind of revival earlier enjoyed by Vivaldi but also exerted influence on new (if not always original) music written for television drama series.

Album

'By hook or by crook I'll be first in this book', we used to write in our friends' albums, and they in ours, when we and they were short of the more desirable AUTOGRAPHS of footballers or other celebrities. Now, however, the word *album* (which comes from the Latin word for white, i.e. a book of blank pages) is misused to mean a gramophone record that is not a 'single'. At first it was confined to the pop music industry – disc jockeys and light-music producers – but the misnomer is becoming increasingly accepted in CLASSICAL circles, perhaps because in the old days record companies had to issue sets of seventy-eights in albums (such as would now be called boxed sets) with each SLEEVE made of stout paper and bound into a spine like a book.

Aleatoric (aleatory) music

From the Latin word *alea*, dice: random music, not written down in any notation worthy of the name, though the composer (*composer?*) may provide the players with vague written or even diagrammatic instructions. The rest of the music (*music?*) they make up as they go along. It invariably sounds like it, too: a random, haphazard mess. Music is, after all, the art of *organizing* and combining sounds with skill and imagination into recognizable order, so as to produce a conscious work of art. A dripping tap, the wind whistling through a crack in a door, or the squeaking of a hinge, may be interesting sounds; but if we are to call them *music* then the word needs to be redefined. (And the same goes for a lot of non-aleatory music as well.) Michael Kennedy, in his *Concise Oxford Dictionary of Music*, says, 'The adjective "aleatoric"is a bastard word, to be avoided by those who care for the language'; for as with that other short-lived craze, QUADRAPHONY, the proponents of aleatory music instinctively hit upon the wrong formation. There was a certain vogue for this sort of nonsense during the swinging '60s but it soon went out of fashion again. Beethoven wrote a curiously prophetic passage in a letter to a publisher, in which he speaks of 'A century hence, when there will be no conservatories and everything is left to chance . . . just to tickle the jaded palates of men without any balls . . . so-called great men.' See also AMBULATORY MUSIC.

Alto flute

The proper name for what is generally miscalled BASS FLUTE.

Ambulatory music

Military bandsmen have always played 'on the march' (see DOUBLE-HANDED); but certain contemporary composers now sometimes require civilian musicians (pianists, harpists and drummers excepted) to combine walking with playing. They feel that the practice may lend their music a little added interest – or help relieve boredom by turning performances into 'happenings'. In ambulatory music players are given certain instructions in their PARTS telling them where and when to walk across the platform so as to play with different colleagues, sharing their desk. It is at best a novel and interesting idea making for differing perspectives of sound or, at worst, a foolish fad, calling for almost choreographic production as well as the careful placing of the music, since the ambulating player, not having the benefit of the military bandman's LYRE, has to be sure of finding his music waiting for him at the place he is to visit. In the Clarinet Concerto by Thea Musgrave (b.1928) the soloist has such a part. At the first performance, on 5 February 1969 in the Royal Festival Hall, Gervase de Peyer successfully negotiated the route from section to section without knocking over any music-stands or having an eye poked out by a fiddle-bow. But when he arrived at the desk occupied by his fellow-clarinettists he found no music waiting for him. Instead, there was a piece of paper with the message: 'F*** off!'

American Quartet

Dvořák's Quartet No. 12 in F was known by everyone (including the composer) as the 'Nigger Quartet'. But in the 1960s Negroes decided to call themselves 'blacks' and strove to have the word 'nigger' abolished because of its offensive associations. The word is now officially outlawed in the USA. But as with all censorship, however well-meant, anomalies soon arose, e.g. when Boosey &

Hawkes were refused USA customs clearance for the SCORE AND PARTS of Delius's plantation opera *Koanga*, which makes legitimate, historical use of the word.

Ammoniaphone

In spite of the *-phone* element in the word, this is not a musical instrument but a patented invention by a nineteenth-century quack, Dr Carter Moffat, who claimed that with its help anyone could become a good singer simply by breathing an approximation of Italian air – presumably air close to an Italian sewage-plant if, as the name suggests, the air supplied was redolent of ammonia. The Ammoniaphone was sold by the Medical Battery Company, 52 Oxford Street, London W.

D'amore/d'amour

Italian/French for 'of love', but applied specifically in music to instruments of lower pitch than the standard member of each family: John Evelyn reports in his Diary that he heard a viola d'amore in 1679, 'played by a German, than which I never heard a sweeter sound or more surprising'. Leopold Mozart's treatise on violin-playing of 1756 says, 'It is a distinctive kind of fiddle which sounds particularly charming in the stillness of the evening . . . [but] unfortunately is always out of tune.'* The English never used their own language to describe such mellow instruments but preferred foreign words like *d'amore*, *d'amour*, etc., perhaps for reasons of delicacy, as terms like 'instrument of love' or 'flute of love' were common euphemisms for the sex organs. Bach had great fondness for the *oboe d'amore* (called *Liebesoboe* by the Germans and *hautbois d'amour* by the French, though the Italians have a more prosaic alternative, *oboe luongo*) and used it in many of his works, both religious and secular. Like the *flauto d'amore* it is pitched in A, a minor third lower than the ordinary instrument, and is therefore a transposing instrument. Richard Strauss used the *oboe d'amore* in his *Sinfonia Domestica*, intending no doubt that intimate inferences should be drawn. Holst has it in his *Somerset Rhapsody* and Ravel specifies (but does not always get) one in his *Bolero*. John McCabe lovingly wrote a concerto for the instrument in 1972, with a particularly pretty young soloist in mind who herself delighted in the nickname 'Oboe of Love'. There is also a *clarinetto d'amore* (much the same as the BASSET HORN); but unfortunately no 'bassoon of love'. The bowed guitar, or arpeggione for which Schubert wrote a delightful sonata, also went under the name of *guitarre d'amour*. See also BOUDOIR PIANO.

*When Leopald Mozart appears to complain about the instrument's out-of-tuness, he says in the original German, 'Es leidet viele Verstimmungen', so it seems to me possible that he really meant 'It suffers many SCORDATURE.'

'. . . And so on'

The most useful three words in the vocabulary of the instrumental teacher or lecture-recitalist. When the teacher, demonstrating to a pupil, reaches a difficult passage he himself is unable (or no longer able) to play, he exercises his prerogative of breaking off and, with an airy wave of the hand, says, ' . . . and so on.' The lecture recitalist, usually a retired singer, interrupts his or her song at such a moment to embark on another anecdote.

Anhang

A word Mozart scholars conjure with. It is the German for *appendix* (literally 'hung-on', i.e. something added to the main body of a work) and is much used in the KOECHEL listing of Mozart's works. Some important and often-played pieces of music by Mozart are 'unhung', as the naturalized English pronunciation makes it.

Apotheosis of the dance

Wagner's description of Beethoven No. 7 as 'the apotheosis of the dance' was until recently trotted out with regularity in BBC programme notes. If he meant anything more than that he considered it a great FOOT-TAPPER it could have been that it was 'music fit for a God to dance to' (which is approximately what *apotheosis* means in Greek); and – doubtless to prove his point – he once mounted a table and gyrated his way through an entire (mercifully private) performance by Liszt of the work in a piano transcription. Wagner was by then no longer young and getting decidedly pear-shaped. It must have been a splendid sight. But perhaps not quite so amazing as the impromptu *pas-de-deux* danced in 1875 by Tchaikovsky and Saint-Saëns on the stage of the Moscow Cons-ervatoire. Both were entering middle-age, but they danced the

Wagner watches Liszt play Beethoven

entire ballet *Pygmalion and Galatea*, Saint-Saëns taking the part of Galatea and the SUGAR PLUM FAIRY that of Pygmalion, to the piano accompaniment of Nikolai Rubinstein. Whether they wore the tutu, too, is not recorded.

The Appassionata

A not inapt nickname given to Beethoven's Piano Sonata in F minor, op. 57, by its first publisher, Cranz. What the editor did was simply to superscribe the piece 'An Impassioned Sonata', which indeed it is.

Applause leader

A member of the audience determined to be first in at the end of a work with a solo hand-clap (and possibly a sonorous 'Bravohh!' as well), as though anxious to let the rest of the audience know that *he* (seldom she) knows the score intimately and enjoyed the performance so much that he cannot contain his enthusiasm a moment longer. In truth, applause leaders are a pest, for they spoil quiet endings with their exhibitionist antics. The PROMS usually have several hundred applause leaders, all eager to be first in. See also CLAQUE, CLAP TRAP.

April Fools Concert

A kind of entertainment held on or around All Fools' Day, pioneered by the Liverpool Music Group and registered in 1958 under the Business Names Act as its corporate property.

Arch

Composers from Bach to Bruckner managed extraordinarily well without employing 'arches'. But much music today is often fancifully described (usually by the composers themselves) as 'in the shape of an arch'. Such structures are seldom visible or audible. It is merely one more manifestation of the curious fact that obscure music has to be 'explained' by even more obscure and meaningless verbiage. On the radio these programme notes may take longer to read than the music to perform. See also CELL.

The Archduke

Beethoven's Trio, op. 97 in B flat for violin, cello and piano is so called because of its dedication to Beethoven's pupil and patron, the Archduke Rudolph of Austria, himself a fine pianist and an accomplished composer. He was on genuinely friendly terms with Beethoven, and the composer occasionally managed to forget their disparate stations in life – even addressing him as 'My dear Archduckling' (*Mein liebes Erzherzogerl*). He is said also to have once rapped the Imperial knuckles during a piano lesson. The Archduke carefully preserved all the many letters Beethoven wrote to him; whereas Beethoven probably used his for whatever domestic purpose called for waste paper. Rudolph suffered from rheumatism and epilepsy, which occasionally forced him to send a court official to Beethoven to cancel a lesson because of an attack. The nickname for 'the' Archduke Trio is something of an understatement: the name could equally be applied to the G major Piano Concerto, op. 58, and THE EMPEROR Concerto; the Piano Sonatas op. 81a and op. 106, and the Missa Solemnis, op. 123, to name but a few of the important works Beethoven dedicated to him.

Archer Street

A small street off Windmill Street in the West End of London, where freelance musicians, chiefly those engaged in the light-music trade, used to congregate in the hope of meeting a FIXER able to offer them a GIG. Much of this street trading would take place out of doors, as many players were too poor to afford a drink at a nearby tea-shop. The street figures much in freelance players' folklore.

ARCM

The initials, often added to the names of musicians, stand for Associate of the Royal College of Music. The Royal Academy of Music also has 'associates' (ARAM) but these letters are awarded honorifically. The RAM produces Licentiates (LRAM).

Aria di sorbetto

Literally, 'ice-cream aria'. In eighteenth- and early nineteenth-century operas, an aria given to a subsidiary character and taken by a singer other than a PRIMA DONNA (e.g. Marcellina in Mozart's *Figaro*) during which, in the informal conditions obtaining in Italian opera-houses, ice-cream would be served. Like CURTAIN ARIAS, such songs are not essential to the plot and would be largely ignored by ill-mannered audiences. 'Just one sorbetto. . . .'

Arie antiche

Artists traditionally start celebrity song recitals with a group of songs by older eighteenth-century masters, thus giving the impression of some sort of chronological order to their programme. That, however, is not their purpose. These songs are regarded by singers simply as warming-up pieces to get the vocal cords moving before she (seldom he) embarks on the real fireworks and nineteenth-century music intended to show off her BEL CANTO. *Arie antiche* means 'old songs'. But that would not sound at all good on programmes and in the writings of music critics, who love to interlard their reports with foreign words.

15

The 'armless' affectation

Watch any conductor who is – or thinks he is – anybody, when off-duty or during breaks between rehearsals, and you will observe this curious fad: they wear their jacket draped loosely over the shoulders, sleeves dangling empty and loose. Some of them, including Karajan and Walter Weller, even appear thus half-clad on record covers. Could it be that they don't want anybody to go through their pockets and see how much they earn for a concert?

Armonica

See HARMONICA

Ars Musica

See BUM BASS

Ashton's Enigma Variations

Part of the arrogance of ballet jargon. Sir Frederick Ashton (some say misguidedly) devised a ballet to Elgar's music, which he took certain liberties with, but did not compose.

Associate (Artist)

Euphemistic title awarded to musicians in order to persuade them to accept a slightly inferior position than they may feel they deserve. An associate conductor is generally an assistant conductor, perhaps one who is of an age or of sufficient professional standing not to want to be described as a mere 'assistant' (see also SORCERER'S APPRENTICE). Associate Artist, like COLLABORATIVE PIANIST, is a euphemism for an ACCOMPANIST. Associate Principals in orchestras are generally second-string principals given nominal equal status with the first; perhaps engaged with a view to their eventually replacing the existing principal. The uncomfortable, unhyphenated prefix Co, as in 'coprincipal' is sometimes seen, but for obvious reasons never 'coconductor'.

Attack

The start of a note or chord (see also CHIFF). An attack can be hard or – oxymoronically – soft. For a longer explanation of the technicalities involved in orchestral attack, see under LATE PLAYING.

At the piano

See ACCOMPANIST and COLLABORATIVE PIANIST

Aubrey Winter Version

Aubrey Winter was an English bassoonist, composer and editor of music who prepared many orchestral works for publication by Boosey & Hawkes. His editions were based on a healthy sense of practical pessimism – the ever-present fear of conductors and concert promoters that several important players would at the last moment fail to attend. He therefore filled all available bars' rest so that those present could cover for their absent colleagues by playing all cues. Orchestral players speak of 'Aubrey Winter Versions' even when referring to music thus edited by someone other than Winter.

Auditions

These are an important part of every orchestral musician's life, at the outset of his career when he is looking for work, when he decides to change jobs or, when his career nears its end and his employers decide to review his capabilities in the presence of an MU official with a view to giving him the sack. Auditions may also be held if the positions of LEADER, REPET or PRINCIPAL become vacant and are to be filled from within the orchestra. Initial auditions may involve the performance of a prepared piece, such as a concerto, followed by SIGHT-READING to test the candidate's instantaneous response to unfamiliar music. There is usually a panel of judges which may include the section principal, leader, conductor or manager (even though he may not be a musician but an accountant: everyone working in music *thinks* he knows everything about it). Only very rarely do conductors take auditions alone, for some of them have been known to make a disastrous choice if their interest in a candidate was more than musical: but such tales can be told only in private. 'Blind' auditions are, curiously enough, rare, although the BBC at one time used to test prospective broadcasters behind the curtained glass of the control cubicle, so as not to be swayed by a candidate's attractiveness or lack of it. There are many anecdotes concerning auditions, of which the most famous is that about an over-confident candidate (either a string-player or bassoonist, for reasons which will become clear from the music example below), who came away from his ordeal convinced that he had been successful.

A: *How did you get on?*
B: *Fantastic. Couldn't have gone better.*
A: *Play well?*
B: *Never played better.*
A: *Any sight-reading?*
B: *Easy. Piece of cake.*
A: *What was it?*
B: *Dunno what it was called, but it went*

Autographs

One kind of autograph is the manuscript of a composition in the composer's hand (from Greek *autos*, self and *graphe*, writing); but more popularly, a person's handwritten signature, as collected by autograph hunters. 'Beethoven's last autograph' can therefore mean two different things. Although artists are flattered to be asked for their autograph, they are also often in a hurry. In a Lancashire mill town there must be many 'autographs' purporting to be the signature of the conductor Nikolai Malko (1883–1961) but which are actually in the handwriting of Bob Brown, the then orchestra manager of the RLPO. Malko was anxious to catch his train, so Brown collected the autograph hunters' ALBUMS and signed them in Malko's name. There is an often-told (and probably fabricated) story about Sir Malcolm Sargent: on his being told by the GREEN ROOM attendant at the Royal Festival Hall that there were 'some people waiting for your autograph, Sir Malcolm' Sargent (according to that inveterate teller of anecdotes, Ben Trovato) replied, 'Oh, send in the first half-dozen.' The attendant opened the door, and let in the two waiting small boys. Every artist, every celebrity, comedian or news-reader worthy of being asked to sign his name has a story about being accosted for his autograph by some person, who gets his wish but then expresses disappointment that the celebrity was not the person the auto-graph hunter thought he was. Thus if Rubinstein told this hoary old story (which he did not) he would have reported his fan as saying 'Oh but you ARE Claudio Arrau, aren't you?'

'A work they have made peculiarly their own'

This used to be a stock phrase used by BBC music announcers whenever the BBCSO played certain works, usually by Elgar or Vaughan Williams, and under Sir Adrian Boult.

B. A. C. H.

Many composers used the notes B. A. C. H. as a basis for compositions, as did Bach himself in his last work, *The Art of Fugue* – a fitting signature to his life's work. Beethoven, too, had planned an overture on the notes B. A. C. H. at the time of his death. B. A. C. H. spotting is a favourite pastime among knowledgeable music-lovers. See also B/B FLAT and MUSICAL REBUS.

The Bach Double

The universal name in the profession for J. S. Bach's Concerto in D minor for two violins, strings and continuo (BWV 1043), in spite of the fact that there are other Bach concertos for two solo instruments. The expression goes back to the time when it was the only 'Bach double' in the repertoire. The BBC sometimes uses 'the Bach double violin concerto', suggesting some kind of double-fiddle played by one person.

Back desks

The music-stands farthest away from the conductor (and also by extension the pair of string players sharing each such desk). It is generally assumed that since the leader is supposedly the best player in each string section, those sitting towards the back must be the worst. There is a certain element of practical truth in this; for when it comes to DIVISI solo playing by the first few desks, as in Weber's overture *Euryanthe*, it is obviously desirable that the best players should take the most exposed parts, as the inexperienced may suffer nerves and get the PURLIES. But in a good orchestra every player pulls his weight. Beecham recognized this and always paid an extra fee to his back desk string players, thus attracting better players to positions that appear to have a little less glamour than the leading desks. See also SEATING.

Banda

The Italian word for a band – of robbers as well as musicians. *Banda* has been adopted into English musical jargon because of its frequent appearance in opera scores, where it may mean either a stage-band or one heard offstage, usually a wind band. Stage bands are part of an old operatic tradition, for musicians love dressing up and showing off as much as anyone else. Unfortunately only the most lavish productions can afford to engage players specifically for such a brief appearance (for which they have to get a full fee, plus the statutory 'Dressing-up Allowance' stipulated by the MU): all too often there is a noisy scramble out of the orchestra pit and back again. Glyndebourne has a particularly strong tradition in the use of stage bands, and its producers have always taken care to make the musicians *act* as well as play.

Band/orchestra

Orchestra comes from the Greek word *orcheomai*, to dance; and originally meant the space in a theatre reserved for the musicians accompanying the dancers. The word began to come into English use in the early eighteenth century ('But hark! the full orchestra strike the strings . . .' wrote John Gay in 1720, putting the accent firmly on the *second* syllable in the North British manner, not the first as in the South of England). *Band* (surely to be preferred) remained the standard word for even a full symphony orchestra until well into the twentieth century, and was a favourite of G. B. Shaw in his musical writings.

Bandroom

The place (seldom if ever 'orchestra room') where members of the orchestra change their clothes, relax, grumble, gossip, read or play cards, but seldom practise: see above and below.

Bandroom soloist

An orchestra member, usually a young and inexperienced one, who by constantly practising concertos likes to show off his skills to colleagues or anyone else who happens to be around. Strange as it may seem, practising in bandrooms is not welcomed ('We want some peace and quiet . . .'). The general view is that if a man *has* to practise, let him concentrate on perfecting any difficult orchestral passage, or prepare for his solo appearances, if any, in private. The RLPO used to have a principal horn who became known as 'The GREEN ROOM Passage Soloist', for whenever a visiting conductor was installed in his room (where presumably he, too, wanted some peace and quiet to study his scores) this player would stand outside and rattle off a potpourri of his showiest concerto passages. His motto was 'It pays to Advertise', and he was perfectly open about it, boasting that his unsolicited auditions resulted in several solo engagements. In the hard world of professional music the meek inherit very little. A good recipe for shutting up a bandroom soloist is to go up to him and ask, 'Have you ever considered taking it up *seriously*?' But the most popular thing ever played in a bandroom is still cards.

Bang Gang

A nickname for the percussion section, generally known by its full name – never, *never* 'the kitchen department', which is laymen's talk.

Percussions' eye view of a distant conductor

The Barber

Always refers to Rossini's *Il Barbiere di Seviglia* (1816), never to the much rarer opera of the same name by Paesiello (1782), to *Der Dorfbarbier* (The Village Barber) by Schenk (1796), *Der Barbier von Bagdad* by Cornelius (1858), or to any of the other operatic barbers. But in string players' conversation 'the Barber' may be an informal reference to Samuel Barber's most popular work, his *Adagio for Strings* (1936).

Baritones and Barytons

The baritone is a kind of low bass or high tenor singer; but to a saxophone or brass player 'baritone' means the big E flat instrument, the low tenor or high bass voice of the families which include the soprano, alto, tenor and bass. Then there is the *baryton*, a string instrument of cello size and with viola da gamba qualities, plus some extra strings. The instrument would now be forgotten had it not been a favourite lost cause of Haydn's boss, Prince Nikolaus Esterházy, who asked the composer for some pieces for it. Haydn obliged with several hundred. The instrument and its technique have been revived, and the Esterházy Barytone Trio formed, a group with probably the smallest repertoire, and the largest number of misprints in its name.

Barrel

The detachable small joint at the top end of the clarinet, just below the mouthpiece to which the reed is clamped.

Bass bar

This is not a bar for boozing double-bass players but, in string instruments including the double bass, a strip of wood glued to the underside of the instrument's belly.

Basset horn

Neither a horn nor a relation of the basset hound, but an alto clarinet in the key of F. It has survived chiefly because of the glorious music Mozart wrote for it, most notably in the Gran Partita (Wind Serenade, K361). The word *basset* comes from *bassetto*, which is the Italian diminutive of *basso*; whereas the basset hound gets its name from the French word *basset*, a terrier or earthing-beagle. George Bernard Shaw adopted the pseudonym Corno di Bassetto when he wrote music criticism during the last decade of the nineteenth century. There is also an organ-stop so named which, however, sounds nothing like the real instrument – a common failing of organ-stops.

Bass fiddle

The non-musician's name for the double bass. Players seldom give it the full name but speak of 'the bass'. Other names for the instrument include BUM BASS, BULL FIDDLE, DOGHOUSE, etc. See also BASS VIOL and BLUE-EYED ENGLISH. Double-bass players learn to bear stoically the stock question from the ignorant unmusical: 'How do you get it under your chin?'

Bass flute

Misnomer for the alto flute, pitched in G, a fourth lower than the ordinary flute. There is, however, a real bass flute in C, pitched an octave below the ordinary flute, now used in popular music, and played with a BOEHM'S CRUTCH.

Basso continuo

See FIGURED BASS

Bass viol

The lowest-but-one bass instrument of the viol family, about the size of a cello, and having only the violone (see VIOLA) below it. The violins form a separate instrumental group from the viols, and are not their descendants: both kinds of instruments – viols with frets, violins without – developed side-by-side as different yet related families. But the violins eventually ousted the viols in popularity, having been made fashionable by various French kings. Broadly speaking, the violins remained folk-instruments, the fretted viols art-instruments (in so far as the two streams of music could in the past be separated). But none of this interests British Rail(ways). Their regulations concerning the carrying of large musical instruments reject musical history and call all double basses 'bass viols'.

Bathroom acoustics

A concert hall or other room where music is played and where there is much reverberation and/or echo, depriving the music of its clarity. Journalists now use *acoustics* in the singular, as in 'a good acoustic'. See also BUYING AND SELLING ROOMS.

Bathroom virtuoso

One who gives his best performances in his bathroom, where the acoustics are flatteringly resonant and where one never suffers from CONCERT NERVES.

Baton charge

Jocular name for a conductor's fee, especially if exorbitant. Many of them charge several thousand pounds for a single appearance, which is out of proportion to the fees earned by those who actually play the music and without whom conductors would be useless. Perhaps concert promoters, opera houses and other concert-giving bodies will form some sort of union and agree on a scale of maximum fees, saying, 'Look, maestro, we feel that £1,000 plus your air ticket and a suite in the best hotel is adequate and, moreover, is all we can afford. And you won't get any more from any other society.' Maestro would be only too happy to accept, for if the truth were to be told, most conductors are so eager to climb a rostrum that it would be difficult to prevent them from exhibiting themselves. Some do, in fact, pay for the privilege, engaging first-class orchestras with their own money.

'The baton is always silent'

Common saying among orchestral players, exemplified by a story about Sir Malcolm Sargent, who usually said he 'played' music ('I played *The Dream of Gerontius* before the Queen last week') when he meant 'conduct'. During a recording session he would say to the producer, 'I will play it again and we shall hear what it sounds like.' But one day the players conspired to play a trick on him: as he brought his stick down, *nobody* played. A voice from the back of the orchestra was heard to mutter, as only orchestral players do, 'Let's play *that* one back and hear what *you* sound like.' The same point was made even better, and certainly with more subtlety, when there was a sudden power-failure during a concert by the Vienna Philharmonic in the middle of the last movement of *The Eroica*. The orchestra, knowing every note from memory, continued playing the work without seeing either their music or the conductor, Karl Böhm. Near the end, and still in almost total darkness, one of the wind players said loudly, 'Is he still there? Or has he gone home?'

BBC Philharmonic

New name (1982) of what was for many years the BBC Northern Orchestra, and for many more the BBC Northern Symphony Orchestra; and colloquially 't'Manchester wireless band'. Since the latest change it has been called the 'BBC Enharmonic Orchestra' – i.e. 'different name but the same sound. . .'.

BBCSO

The BBC Symphony Orchestra. But the abbreviation is seldom used in the trade. People within the BBC usually call it 'the Symphony Orchestra', but older professionals still sometimes say 'the Wireless Orchestra'.

BBC Worst of England Orchestra

Nickname for the BBC West of England Orchestra, now defunct. Like its sister combination, the BBC Midland Light Orchestra, it played the kind of light music for which (it was decreed in the late 1970s) there was 'no longer any call', so both were disbanded.

B/B flat

For some reason the neat, simple and alphabetical English way of naming notes, C D E F G A B C (and thus repeated up the scale) does not suit the Germans, who prefer the odd sequence C D E F G A H C their H being our B natural, and their B our B flat. Apart from this single-letter B, they express their sharps and flats with suffixes, adding *-is* for sharps, *-es* for flats, *-isis* for double sharps and *-eses* for double flats. Thus their C sharp is *cis*, their F sharp *fis*, G sharp *gis*, A sharp *ais*, etc.; and their C flat *ces*, their D flat *des*, E flat *es*, F flat *fes*, G flat *ges* and A flat *as*. This is pronounced exactly like the English 'arse', so that Josef Krips

Punch, 1898

Tenor (singing): *"Oh, 'appy, 'appy be thy dreams—"*
Professor: *"Stop, stop! Why don't you sound the H?"*
Tenor: *"It don't go no 'igher than G!"*

(1902–74) caused some consternation when, while rehearsing Schubert's Great C major, he said to the trombones, 'Ze arse a little softer please!' Perhaps the Germans chose this method because of the ease with which one can make up a MUSICAL REBUS of the B. A. C. H. type; and they certainly made plenty. In case you want to write your name in German rebus fashion, as Shostakovich repeatedly did in a convoluted way and Bach, Brahms and Schumann managed to do more simply, here is a complete German scale:

Note	Sharp	Flat	Double Sharp	Double Flat
C	CIS	CES	CISIS	CESES
D	DIS	DES	DISIS	DESES
E	EIS	ES	EISIS	ESES
F	FIS	FES	FISIS	FESES
G	GIS	GES	GISIS	GESES
A	AIS	AS	AISIS	ASAS
H	HIS	B (and HES) ISIS	BES

The possibilities are endless. It could, for example, be postulated that Mozart's aria 'O Isis und Osiris' is addressed to a double sharp and its companion. Scottish DODECAPHONIC composers could write a note-row on B-A-G-G sharp, reading H-A-G-GIS in German. There exists already a Victorian song on the title (and notes) BAG and BAGGAGE.

The Bear

See L'OURS

The Beethoven of the Flute

Sobriquet applied to the Dane, Friedrich Kuhlau (1786–1832), a prolific composer of all kinds of music (including an opera *Lulu* in 1824), and revered by flautists for providing them with hundreds of excellent bravura pieces. During a drunken evening with Kuhlau, Beethoven wrote a jocular canon to the words 'Kühl, nicht lau' ('Cool, not lukewarm'). This is generally taken as having been a slight on Kuhlau and his lukewarm talents. But it has now been established that they got drunk on champagne; so the words of the canon surely refer not to the Dane but to the best temperature for serving the drink. Beethoven is reported to have said to Kuhlau that he himself was 'The Kuhlau of the Orchestra'. Such comparisons, many scattered about this book, include 'The Joachim of the Horn' (which please see), 'The Liszt of the Violin' and 'The Liberace of the Flute/Organ'. The English humorist Beachcomber summed it all up nicely when he declared that 'Wagner was the Puccini of Opera'.

Beethoven's Tenth Symphony

Name given by Hans von Bülow (1830–94) to Brahms's first symphony, a work that caused its composer much heart-searching because he felt that with the death of Beethoven all that could be said in symphonic language had already been said. Bülow's description was therefore both praise for the work and reassurance to Brahms, who suffered from symphonic self-doubt all his life. Bülow, a man with almost as great a reputation for witty sayings as later Sir Thomas Beecham, then went on (as Beecham would not have done) to flog the idea to death by calling Brahms's second, third and fourth symphonies 'Beethoven's eleventh, twelfth and thirteenth'. At one time the whole thing looked like collapsing when it was thought (in 1910) that Fritz Stein had discovered at Jena a real tenth symphony by Beethoven, which was therefore named the 'Jena Symphony'. But that indefatigable discoverer of musical truths and long-lost works, H. C. Robbins Landon, subsequently found the same work correctly attributed to Friedrich Witt (1771–1837); and later another copy, also bearing Witt's name, was brought to light. It was a rather weak imitation of the style of Haydn, so poorly done that no one really believed the attribution – except perhaps Fritz Stein and his publishers, who had a financial interest in the discovery.

The Beethoven Triple

Beethoven's Concerto in C major, op. 56, for violin, cello and piano is usually referred to in this way, or even just 'The Triple'.

Bei Männern

Professionals in all trades habitually abbreviate, as will be seen in many of these pages. In the case of song titles, especially foreign ones, the result is often absurd. *'Bei Männern (welche Liebe fühlen)'* is a case in point. It is like calling Purcell's song 'When I am laid in Earth' (from *Dido and Aeneas*) 'When I am laid'. *'Bei Männern'* is doubly popular, as not only singers speak of it but also cellists, for whom Beethoven wrote a set of Variations (WoO 46) on the theme.

Bel canto

Literally 'beautiful song' or 'beautiful singing' in Italian, but more loosely used in music criticism and general musical jargon to describe a certain characteristic kind of smooth, well-controlled singing, usually in the Italian style. *Belcanto* (the two words are

Bel Canto: Enrico Caruso as the hungry poet and Marcella Sembrich in the role of the consumptive Mimi, in La Bohème. *Caricature by Mayer*

sometimes drawn into one) is in opera often applied in a context that makes nonsense of the composer's intentions, that is, a kind of technical showing-off. It is said that corpulence is an aid towards the perfect *bel canto*. As the American composer Ned Rorem (b. 1923) wrote, '*Bel canto* is to opera what pole-vaulting is to ballet:

the glorification of a performer's prowess and not a creator's imagination.' I suppose the opposite of *bel canto* would be 'can belto'.

Bell

Apart from the obvious meaning of the word (and bells do sometimes figure in the percussion), wind and brass players speak of the bell of their instruments when they mean the flared bit at the end. But so do bassoonists when referring to the non-bell-like end joint at the *top* of the instrument (but the bottom of its register); and players of the ENGLISH HORN when they refer to the bulb-shaped end of theirs.

Bent note

An artificially distorted note, either in pitch or, more rarely, in quality. From jazz usage. See also BLUE NOTE.

Bergerette

The word means 'little shepherdess' in French but is in music applied to a certain kind of song popular in the seventeenth and eighteenth centuries, when the French court set a fashion for playing at nymphs and shepherds. Sex was, of course, at the root of it, for the practice enabled the royal, the noble, or the merely rich, to disport themselves in the fields, wearing little more than nighties and pretending to be simple country folk. The fashion spread to England, too, where at one time every amorous couple that appeared in song was called 'Corydon and Phyllis', 'Alexis and Clio', or 'Amyntas and Chloe' (and incidentally helped to spread the popularity of such names, as well as Celia, Sylvia and Colin, etc.). A collection by Weckerlin of French bergerettes appeared in an illustrated English edition in 1913, of which a copy was at one time to be found in every middle-class nursery or music-room and which helped to keep the bergerette in popular English musical currency. There was another, more specific, kind of bergerette called the BRUNETTE. Both bergerettes and brunettes also appeared in certain sorts of instrumental music of a pastoral or rustic character, perhaps including (or imitating) instruments such as the musette or the bagpipe.

Berufsverbot

One of those German words which have no English equivalent –
for the good reason that the concept it expresses – 'a Prohibition
On Earning One's Living' – never took hold in English-speaking
countries. Between 1933 and 1945 German, Austrian or Jewish
musicians like Kleiber, Kletzki, Korngold, Kurtz, Kreisler, Klemperer, Kern, Kalman, etc. (to name but the Ks) were subjected to
Berufsverbot. After the war the Allies applied it for a time to men
like Karajan (to name one more K) who had been members of the
Nazi party, but the ban was soon lifted.

Best Pair of Nylons

Facetious nickname given by orchestral players to Sir Hubert
Parry's Cantata *Blest Pair of Sirens* (1887) with words from Milton's
At a Solemn Musick. The nickname is more commonly heard in the
North of England, where this splendid work retained its popularity
longer than in the South. Milton's words are delightfully parodied
in an unpublished *Ode to Discord* by C. L. Graves, set to music by
Sir Charles Villiers Stanford (1908), and later by Hugo Cole, a
diatribe against what was considered discordant 'modern' music.

Bible regal

Not a bible and unconnected with kings, but a kind of early
harmonium in use from the fifteenth to the seventeenth centuries:
a small portable organ with single beating reeds, folding like a big
book (hence the bible element in the name) and indeed often made
to look like one. When opened, one cover would reveal a keyboard
and the other a pair of bellows to provide wind for the reeds. It
appears in many old paintings, played with one hand pumping
wind and the other fingering the keys. The origin of the word
regal is said by the *OED* to be 'obscure' but *Regal* in German means
a 'shelf, stand or contraption'.

Biedermeier

Not a suburb in Vienna but a certain, well-defined period of
Austrian (less often German and sometimes Scandinavian) culture.
Bieder means honest, worthy, conventional, upright, conservative,
a little naive perhaps, and rather self-righteous with it; *Meier* is a

common Austro-German surname. *Herr Biedermeier* was the invention of a writer named Ludwig Eichrodt (1827–92) who put satirically philistine opinions into his mouth: a kind of Alf Garnett before his time. Austrians use Biedermeier like the British use 'Victorian' – to describe the spirit of an age and embracing painting and design as well as its music. Biedermeier furniture, for example, is well-constructed but heavy almost to the point of clumsiness. *Gemütlich*, that other Austrian word beloved of critics which also defies translation, is a strong ingredient of Biedermeier.

> The pleasing musical image of a friendly encounter in Biedermeier, Vienna, between the two Franzes – Schubert and Liszt, is regretfully but firmly demolished by Alan Walker in his Liszt biography

Biergartner

Hans von Bülow's self-deprecatory nickname for himself when, in 1892, he had to conduct some concerts in a low-class hall (where beer was served) whereas his rival conductor Felix Weingartner (1863–1942) was enthroned – there is no other word for it – in the Royal Opera House. (*Wein*= wine; *Bier* = beer). The joke occurs in a letter from Bülow (28 January 1892).

Big-box-you-hit-him-he-cry-out

Pidgin for the piano. See also LITTLE-BOX.

The Big Tune

Said of the kind of expansive, spacious, romantic and probably *fortissimo* tune which composers usually leave to the end of a work and then present with a grand, applause-MILKING gesture. The Big Tune may sometimes be found miraculously to fit in perfect counterpoint with a tune previously revealed. A miracle? No, it would thus have been ordained all along, but a clever composer knows how to marshal his ideas. Famous big tunes (which are a late nineteenth-century invention – CLASSICAL composers spurned them) include the endings of several RACH piano concertos, most Mahler symphonies, Britten's *A Young Person's Guide to the Orchestra* and TCHAIK's B flat minor – which however brings in a Big Tune that fits nothing else in the work and has not been heard before.

Bimperl

The Mozart family's dog, referred to many times and with much affection in the Mozart letters, which closely catalogue his tricks and other doings, food intake and excretory habits. He also appears in a single manuscript sketch in Mozart's hand of a fugue subject (surely a worthy companion to Scarlatti's CAT'S FUGUE). Bimperl would have been the Austrian name for 'Little Spot', for *Pimperl* in Austrian dialect (in which the P and B sounds are interchangeable) means a pimple. See also Elgar's beloved dog MINA.

The Bird

Nickname for Haydn's Quartet No. 32 in C major. Not to be confused with THE LARK.

Bis!

French for ENCORE! Without the exclamation-mark, and when written over a bar, or group of bars, of music, *bis* means 'play this bit twice'. See also RÉPÉTEZ!

Bite of the Humble Flea/Blight of the Humble Fee

Facetious spoonerisms of the English name of Rimsky-Korsakov's instrumental interlude in the opera *Tsar Saltan*. *The Flight of the Bumblebee*, or in German *Hummelflug* (*Hummel*, as in the composer's name, means bumble-bee).

The Black Dyke

A Yorkshire brass band formed early in the nineteenth century (not as a brass band but consisting at first of wind and brass). Its proper name is the Black Dyke Mills Band – the mills being the cotton mills in which early northern bandsmen worked. Such industrial bands were formed by benevolent employers who paid for the instruments as well as the gaudy uniforms, and also supplied 'ale, bread and cheese', as an inducement to the men to spend such spare time as they had in wholesome pursuits, not in gin palaces. Many of the big northern choral societies were formed by mill-owners for the same sociological reason. Employers also sought to fill the cotton operatives' minds with music to such an extent that they forgot (or had no time left for) trades union or 'socialist' activities. The Huddersfield Choral Society, for example, had a comprehensive code of regulations laid down in 1842, of which Rule XXVIII declared that 'No person shall be a member of this Society, who frequents . . . the "Socialist Meetings" nor shall the Librarian be allowed to lend any copies of music (knowingly) belonging to this Society to any Socialist, upon pain of expulsion.' The Black Dyke's gramophone records now enjoy an accidental popularity among negro lesbians who labour under a certain misapprehension about the nature of the band's membership.

Black Jack

Nickname given by the BBC PHILHARMONIC to their former resident conductor George Hurst when he held that position in Manchester.

Black looks

A dreaded FLASH speciality. Whenever a player made a mistake during a concert, Sir Malcolm Sargent (1895–1967) would fix him with those dark eyes of his and stare at him for a full fifteen seconds, if necessary turning his head ninety degrees to do so while conducting a passage elsewhere in the orchestra. If the guilty player made a point of avoiding eye-contact to escape the 'black look', he would still get one in, perhaps during another movement or even the next work. On one or two occasions his determination to let a culprit know his displeasure at a mistake (possibly a minor one of which the public would not have been aware) led to his losing his own concentration and making a mistake himself – which always caused much suppressed glee in the orchestra. But Sargent also often offered smiles of praise and encouragement, as when a solo which had given a young player some trouble at rehearsal came off well at the performance. There was once a crisis in an orchestra when owing to a sudden shortage of bassoonists the second player, a blunt Yorkshireman called Albert Entwistle, was asked to play in the HOT SEAT. Being a man without ambition, and also unsure of his ability to tackle the solos, he refused (which his SUB-PRINCIPAL contract entitled him to do). Sargent was getting desperate, as the evening's concert depended on Entwistle's co-operation, and quite uncharacteristically *implored* him to play. Entwistle finally agreed, with words that eventually became a famous quotation: 'Aw raght then. But none o'tha black lewks an' naw messin'!' That was not the end of the story. During the continued rehearsal it turned out that Entwistle's modesty had been well founded and things did not go too well. Sargent was anxious not to offend or un-nerve him, and, with his finger tugging at the inside of his stiff collar (a characteristic gesture signalling discomfiture) he said as gently as possible, 'Er, you know, Mr Entwistle, you are playing *rather* a lot of wrong notes.' The player, now sure that his position was unassailable, replied in a loud voice, 'Ah knaw as well as thee!' On another occasion Entwistle, engaged as a freelance CONTRA player, arrived late for rehearsal with the YSO at Leeds Town Hall, making a great deal of clatter while Maurice Miles was conducting. Miles turned round and said to the intruder, '*Who* are you?' Entwistle drew himself up and replied in his measured Yorkshire tones, 'Mah naem is Albert Entwistle. And who maht *you* be?'

Black notes/White notes

A comparatively modern term for the naturals and sharps of the piano keyboard and, by extension, also of other instruments. For on eighteenth century and earlier keyboards the colours were often the other way round: ivory was scarce and plastic substitutes for it unknown, whereas ebony was comparatively plentiful. Sharps were therefore often white, to save costs. When Sir William Walton (1902–83) composed his *Johannesburg Overture* for some South African celebrations in 1956, quips were heard among orchestral players on the lines of 'He's written it for the white notes only . . .'. But as James Aggrey (1875–1927), the first African principal of a Gold Coast university, said, 'You can play a tune of sorts on the black notes of the piano; you can play a tune of sorts on the white notes. But for real harmony you must use both the black and the white.' See also FLYSHIT for another kind of black notes.

Blackstick

See GOBSTICK and the many other words for the clarinet.

Bleeding chunks

Excerpts from larger works performed in a concert and out of context. The term was invented by Sir Donald Francis Tovey (1875–1940): '. . . bleeding chunks of butcher's meat chopped from Wagner's operas and served up on Wagner Nights as *Waldweben* and *Walkürenritt*' (*Essays in Musical Analysis*). Yet how many concert-goers would know music from Wagner's operas were it not for such bleeding chunks? The term is now also used in non-Wagnerian applications, as when some cinema or television producer arbitrarily takes a few bars of music he has just discovered and uses them as a background noise for his film or programme. Mozart's ELVIRA MADIGAN CONCERTO is a case in point. But the biggest bleeding chunk of all is the Wagner orchestral excerpt known as 'Prelude and Liebestod', for it effectively TOPS AND TAILS the entire opera *Tristan und Isolde*.

Blight of the Humble Fee

See BITE OF THE HUMBLE FLEA

Blow

See SUCK

Blue-Eyed English musical markings

Percy Aldridge Grainger (1882–1961) was a composer of originality and vision – but also a man with many strange qualities and personal quirks, some of them not very nice. His obsessions with what he called 'Blue-eyed English' could have been dismissed as harmlessly silly had they not been, like Hitler's racial prejudice, based on qualities supposedly possessed by blond, blue-eyed nordic people. These ideas led Grainger to banish from the scores of his compositions (or rather, *tonery*), his writings and conversation, all Latin, Greek or foreign-based words. I don't know how well he succeeded in his speech, but his letters are peppered with ugly inventions like *meat-shun-ment* (vegetarianism), *with-suffering* (pity – a direct translation from the German *Mitleid*) and *tone-wright*, which is what he preferred to call himself rather than a composer. His audiences were *concert-hearers* and his string instruments – more engagingly – *fiddles*, *middle fiddles* (i.e. violas), *bass fiddles* for cellos, and *big bass fiddles* for double basses (although the score of *Molly on the Shore* has 'Bouble Basses' – probably a printer's contribution); and he also banished Italian tempo and expression markings. There was, of course, nothing new in this, although the practice has always met with resistance from publishers, who like to keep their products as internationally saleable as possible. Wagner, Mahler and Richard Strauss preferred to mark their scores in German, as Schumann had done before them; but whereas Schumann's are straightforward, Strauss's and Mahler's indications of mood, tempo and dynamics have a literary sophistication that makes them difficult to render in any other language. Beethoven, too, went through a brief Germanic phase while under the influence of a book he had read (see HAMMER-KLAVIER). And when Elgar made his grand ceremonial arrangement of *God Save the King* in 1902 he asked for all markings to be in 'plain English'; the names of the instruments, he declared, 'look *very nice* in English, I think, and *Kettledrums* is a good Handelian-looking word . . . as to *Haut-boys* I feel that Oboes wd. spoil the whole thing . . .' (and to make matters worse, the printer had wilfully modernized Elgar's conscious anglo-archaism *Clarionets* to 'Clarinets', which annoyed the composer). Grainger, however, was not being English but pseudo-nordic, neither patriotic nor literary but plain silly. Here is a list of selected 'Blue-eyed' Graingerisms:

Standard terms	Grainger's 'Blue-eyed English'
solo	to the fore
duo	twosome
trio	threesome
quartet/quintet/sextet, etc.	foursome/fivesome/sixsome, etc.
chamber music	room music
morceau	titbit
intermezzo	between-piece
pizzicato/arco	plucked/bowed
crescendo poco a poco	louden bit by bit
crescendo molto	louden hugely
staccato ma pesante	short and heavy
espressivo e marcato	feelingly and piercingly
espressivo e legato	feelingly and clingingly
legato	smoothly

sonore/molto sonore	rich/very rich
ben marcato	well to the fore
ritardando	slacken
rallentando	slow off
poco meno mosso	very slightly slower
sostenuto	lingeringly
finale	end-piece
appassionato	soulstirring
staccato	short-toned

Blue note

Jazz term, occasionally heard in orchestras, for a slightly 'depressed', i.e. flattened, note. In blues, from which the term comes, this treatment is usually given to the third or seventh notes of the scale, giving the blues one of their strongest characteristics. See also BRIGHTNESS.

Boccherini's Minuet

As absurd a name as would be 'Beethoven's Sonata', 'Haydn's Symphony' and as is 'PACHELBEL'S CANON' and 'ALBINONI'S ADAGIO'. Boccherini's allegedly singular minuet comes from his String Quintet in E major, op. 11 (some editions have op. 13) No. 3 – and is, of course, one of hundreds of minuets written by this composer. Most people could hum its opening – but how many would recognize the TRIO?

Boehm's Crutch

Nothing intimate or relating to lameness, but a small, detachable, T-shaped device invented by a famous flute-designer Theobald Boehm (1794–1881) which was meant to help the player support the instrument by resting it between the player's thumb and first finger of the left hand. The idea was to support the flute on the crutch without impairing the mobility of the finger and thumb. Although Boehm is the father of the modern flute and the inventor of the 'system' that bears his name, his crutch is one of the less successful musical innovations. Few flutes now have one and even fewer players use it when they have. Bassoonists do use a crutch support for their overworked right thumb, but it is not Boehm's and they call it a 'hand rest'.

Boehm System

Theobald Boehm (see above) was a German jeweller and flautist who was dissatisfied with the mechanism of the flutes then in general use. Being a professional metal-worker and amateur musician he was in the perfect situation to do something about changing the existing arrangements, for professional players are necessarily conservative about the system they learnt on when they started to play: having got used to it they cannot then afford to take the time off work to get used to a new system. Boehm had all the leisure he needed in order to re-learn – and also the skill and equipment to experiment with new keys, levers and linkages. Having invented the 'system' (though some say he merely modified an earlier invention by someone called Gordon) he did much the same thing as Bach had done in his FORTY-EIGHT: he composed a set of studies in all keys so as to prove the superiority of his system over the old flute, especially the ability to play in tune even in extreme keys. Although the Boehm system is now almost universal, it includes one or two compromises in the arrangement of the keys for the thumb and, usually, the 'closed G sharp' for the little finger of the left hand. Elements of Boehm's System have also been incorporated into the keywork of the oboe, clarinet and bassoon.

The Boiled Veal

Nickname for the Boyd Neel Orchestra, founded by the medical doctor and (at first) amateur conductor Boyd Neel (1905–82). It was basically a string orchestra of about eighteen players, with additions of wind and brass as required, and gave its first concert at the Aeolian Hall in London in 1933. Together with the Jacques Orchestra (founded by Reginald Jacques (1894–1969)) the Boyd Neel Orchestra led the way in the English revival of chamber orchestral music, especially the performance of baroque works; although Neel's policy was always more forward-looking than that of Jacques. Britten wrote his *Variations on a Theme of Frank Bridge* for the Boyd Neel, and they gave its first performance at the 1937 Salzburg Festival, consolidating their own reputation and establishing Britten's as a composer of international importance.

Boiled voice

A description of a certain type of low contralto sound. Why boiled? Perhaps the term is related to the *OED* definition of *boiled*: 'figuratively speaking, inflamed, in a state of passionate agitation, bursting with passion, etc.' See also FOG HORN, WHITE VOICE.

The Boss

Orchestral players' name for their conductor.

Bottle organ

A possibly unique specimen exists in the Rushworth Collection of Musical Instruments assembled by the firm of Rushworth & Dreaper of Liverpool, now in the city's museum. It works on the principle observed by anyone who has blown across the top of a bottle to produce a musical note. The instrument, by J. S. Kühlewein of Eisleben in Germany, was built in 1798 and has 106 bottles arranged in four horizontal rows rather like wine-racks (Kühlewein, coincidentally, means 'cool wine' or 'wine-cooling' in German). There is also a piano mechanism of fairly standard late eighteenth-century design. The organ sound is produced by means of nozzles that direct a stream of air across each bottle mouth. There are four pedals, one of which couples and uncouples the keyboard to the organ mechanism (to make the instrument into a piano) and another controls the supply of wind. It has a range of five octaves from the bottom F of the classical piano – 62 notes in all. The bottles vary in size from 6¼ inches to a mere ¼ inch and were tuned by having varying quantities of red wax run into them until the required pitch was attained. The bottle organ was a practical instrument, not a frivolous experiment, for it was built for use in a church on the North German island of Heligoland where, it was thought, wooden pipes would be affected by the weather, and where organ tuners were difficult to come by. It should be added that at the first APRIL FOOLS CONCERT in Liverpool in 1952 a kind of human bottle-organ was used for a special arrangement of 'Haydn's Surprise Symphony with Additional Surprises' (later adapted for the first HOFFNUNG concert in London). The performance was directly inspired by the Liverpool Bottle Organ.

Boudoir piano

Absurd name invented by the piano trade for a small grand piano with a rounded bottom end. I have known many pianos in bed-sitting-rooms belonging to students or young professionals but have yet to meet a lady so grand that she sleeps in a 'boudoir' but has nowhere else to keep her piano. There was, however, a Dormitory Pianoforte patented by a Mr Milward in 1866, which in addition to the usual arrangements contained a bed, mattress, wash-basin, jug and looking glass, and a closet for the bedclothes. See also MINIPIANO.

Boulangerie

Occasionally applied to the twentieth-century school of composers taught by the French composer, conductor and teacher, Nadia Boulanger (1887–1979). Among her pupils were Sir Lennox-Berkeley, Walter Piston and Aaron Copland who offered their audiences the rare prospect of an acceptable, and sometimes even smiling, face of CONTEMPORARY music. Some of them, like Jean Françaix, occasionally even produced cheerful modern light music. Critics have often applied to such music phrases like 'confections from Nadia's Boulangerie'.

The bowing of parts

The impressive effect of the unanimous up-and-down movement of the bows of a whole string section or an entire string orchestra is not achieved spontaneously. There are many different ways of bowing – where to use an upbow and where a downbow – and if string players were left to their own devices, unanimity would be lost. Players therefore have to follow their section LEADER's guidance, and that needs the careful preparation of each separate PART. The bowing of parts involves the addition (in pencil, never ballpoint or ink) of upbow and downbow marks at salient points. *Salient* points, because the natural tendency is to make alternate up and down strokes of the bow – playing 'as it comes'. But sometimes each kind comes in series: repeated upbows may produce a lighter effect, repeated downbows allow the player to exert more force. Conductors differ in their views about bowings. Some, like Toscanini, Barbirolli, Rignold, Koussevitzky and others who started as string players, held strong views about their bowings. Many others, like Sargent, Beecham and Boult, who did not play a string instrument, were content to take the leader's or section leader's advice. A good leader will ask for the conductor's requirements, but if he has none, will bow the parts himself in consultation with the other string principals; or at any rate will bow a set of master parts whose marks are then copied into the separate parts by the orchestra LIBRARIAN. Many composers betray an ignorance about string bowings. In the *Duo Concertante* (1931–2) by Stravinsky (1882–1971) written for the violinist Samuel Dushkin, the composer at first indicated an up or down bow mark on every note – a totally unnecessary thing to do except in a nursery fiddle primer, and the equivalent of marking the places where a wind player should exhale after having taken a breath. Stravinsky also wrote some wildly absurd instructions into his wind parts.

The Box

The conductor's rostrum, as in 'Who's on the box tonight?' See also CARVING and PODIUM.

Box of Teeth

See GROAN BOX

Box Set

See ALBUM

The Brahms Double

Brahms's Concerto in A minor, op. 102, for violin, cello and orchestra is always referred to in this abbreviated way. See also BACH DOUBLE and BEETHOVEN TRIPLE.

Break

Apart from the obvious kind of break, or interval in a rehearsal, concert or recording-session (see TAKE FIFTEEN) there are two other sorts. The jazz musician's break, a solo improvisation of predetermined length ('an eight-bar break') which gives him the chance of displaying his prowess (and from which comes the saying, 'Give him a break'); and the break in the register of a voice or instrument:

perhaps where a singer changes from chest voice to head voice, e.g. a tenor from his 'normal' sound to a falsetto register. Wind instruments have a break where the octaves, OVERBLOWING or otherwise clearly defined registers join, or where fingerings are awkward. Both singers and players take great pains and much practice to cross their particular breaks in such a way that the hearer is unaware that one exists.

Breitkopf

Words like 'He's using the Breitkopf parts . . .' are heard wherever CLASSICAL music is played, for the name is almost synonymous with music publishing and goes back to the age of J. S. Bach. The printer Bernhard Christoph Breitkopf (1695–1777) in 1719 founded the Leipzig firm which was sooner or later to publish the music of Telemann, Mattheson, Mozart (father and son), some of the Bachs (though not J. S.), Haydn, Beethoven and Mendelssohn, to name only some (although Breitkopf was originally a book publisher and the first work he issued was a Hebrew Bible). Breitkopf and his sons were joined by Gottfried Härtel at the end of the eighteenth century at about the same time as the introduction of lithography into music printing. Since the last war the firm has undergone an East/West German split: the Leipzig firm is state owned, supported and controlled, the Wiesbaden side (re-formed in the West in 1945 and not connected with its namesake) free to publish what music it pleases, including Elgar and Karl Marx (not *the* Karl Marx but a different one). Both firms use the familiar old Breitkopf music cover, an adaptation of which appears on the cover of this book.

Brighouse and Gastric

Nickname for the Brighouse and Rastrick (Brass) Band.

Brightness

Euphemism for a sharpness in pitch. Musicians don't like to accuse each other of playing out of tune, so one might casually say to another, 'Oh by the way, isn't that F sharp of yours a little on the bright side?' Piano tuners, too (many of whom make a habit of tuning the top octaves a little sharp because pianists are said to like it that way) answer orchestral players' complaints with the 'brightness' euphemism.

British Actors' Equity Association

The full name of the trades union usually known as Equity, to which not only actors but also professional singers belong, at any rate those who sing in opera choruses, concert choruses, SESSIONS or groups that record television jingles. Even cathedral choirs are now fully unionized. See MU.

Brochures

Musicians' advertising brochures are an important by-product of the music industry. But although they help to keep designers, printers, stationers, AGENTS and the Post Office in business they do not do very much for the artist. Brochures usually follow a depressingly predictable form. They are often printed on a glossy, shiny paper that is unpleasing to handle, and carry a text that is always too long and usually boring to read, containing not so much what the prospective engager wants to read about the artist as what the artist likes to read (or write) about himself: for although

Haydn's anti-visiting card ('Gone is all my strength, old and weak am I') with which he used to repel visitors and offers of work

brochure eulogies are written in the third person singular, they are usually written by the artist, and everybody knows it. Phrases like 'has given concerts in Vienna, New York, Majorca, Corfu, etc.' are standard clichés that impress no one: it depends *where* in Vienna, New York, etc., and before whom. Besides, if he really is an artist of such wide international repute everyone will know about him anyway and he will not need a brochure. A photograph is considered essential, and this may be several years old, taken in soft focus – and most likely dramatically lit and posed in a studio rather than taken in action: conductors' pictures thus giving the absurd impression that they are conducting the photographer. Newspaper notices may be quoted, but in a highly selective manner. 'She played with much sensitivity and feeling . . .' could so easily have been followed by the (omitted) qualifying clause '. . . but unfortunately played handfuls of wrong notes when the music became difficult.' Young conductors' claims such as 'Studied with Scherrchen, Klemperer . . .' etc. are meaningless. Scherrchen, for one, did little more for his 'pupils' than allow them to be present at his rehearsals. The mass-mailing of brochures to all music-clubs and other concert-giving organizations is an expensive and largely useless venture, for address lists are notoriously quick to go out of date. Many of the clubs listed in the directories do not engage artists but employ only home-produced talent, and some listed Music Festivals are in fact competitive. The best way in which a young artist can promote his career is to win an international competition, or persuade a television company to give him exposure, or become somebody's musician 'of the Year'.

Broken consort

Consort is a fine old English word for a group of musicians, and one which might well be pressed into service more often than some of the many pretentious or macaronic group titles now so fashionable, like 'Camerata', 'Contrapuncti Musici', 'Musica da Civic Hall Nottinghamiensis' or 'Virtuosi di Budleigh Salterton'. Consorts get broken not through carelessness but when, say, a group of recorders, together making an unbroken consort, is joined by a viol, crumhorn or some other instrument outside its family, or a voice. Not to be confused with broken chords or broken octaves, which really *are* broken, in a manner explained in any dictionary of music.

Broken strings

Strings break during performances and there is nothing a player can do about it except stop and put on a new one. Only Paganini would purposely break string after string (with the help of some special device?) sending his audiences into frenzied enthusiasm by demonstrating his ability to continue on his last remaining one, having, of course, carefully worked out the routine beforehand. If it happens in the orchestra little harm is done apart from loss of concentration: there are plenty of colleagues to cover for the victim. If, however, it happens to the LEADER, he exercises some kind of *droit du seigneur* and simply takes the REPET's instrument, or that of the nearest RANK-AND-FILE player behind him, in exchange for his. The player of lower rank then replaces the string from a spare he keeps in his pocket (or she in her handbag), retunes the fiddle and waits for a suitable moment to hand it back. Afterwards, no doubt, there is some private discussion about replacement or reimbursement, or re-exchange if the spare string was a treasured one. The viola player Robert Braga tells a cautionary tale about the danger of not carrying spare strings. He and the other members of a student string quartet were about to start a concert at a music club, and were poised to play when, snap, the leader's A-string broke. He apologized and left the platform. To his dismay he found he had no spare A-string. From the wings he beckoned to his second, who duly walked off to join him. Their dismay deepened when they discovered that they had no spare between them. Then the viola player, wondering what caused the delay, went off, too. All this was observed by the audience with goodnatured amusement, for English spectators love these little emergencies (which often stimulate the applause greatly). As Braga could not help either, and tying a knot in the broken string proved impossible, they made signs to the cellist to come off as well. After a quick conference they decided the only thing they could do was to pack their instruments, put on their overcoats and quietly steal away. Their music and music stands, which they could ill afford to lose, were left behind.

Brunette

Today's gentlemen may prefer blondes, but fashionable seventeenth- and eighteenth-century French mock-shepherds celebrated brown-haired girls, or *brunettes*, in their BERGERETTES. Learned

French authorities have traced the name to a particular refrain, *Ah, petite Brunette! Ah, tu me fais mourir* in a particular song, *Le beau berger Tirsis*. Songs addressed to brunettes became such a craze in eighteenth-century popular music that they established their own musical style (rather like modern pop songs) and whole volumes of them were published, although in some of the songs the hair colour was taken for granted and merely the girls' general desirability extolled.

BSO

The Bournemouth Symphony Orchestra. It is a comparatively recent name, for the orchestra, which grew from Dan Godfrey's augmented seaside band, was from 1896 the Bournemouth Municipal Orchestra (the oldest CONTRACT ORCHESTRA) until 1954, when it dropped the municipal connotation. It also has a chamber orchestral offshoot with the now fashionable American name, SINFONIETTA. Both orchestras are now under the aegis of the Western Orchestral Society.

Buffo

My Italian Dictionary says *buffo* means 'queer, ridiculous; as in buffoon, comic actor, squall of wind'. When used as a musical term it generally suggests a comic operatic bass singing-role, or is used as an element in the description of an opera as comic, e.g. *opera buffa*. Although there is no reason for denying sopranos, contraltos or tenors the tag, descriptions such as *soprano buffa* are never heard. *Buffone*, incidentally means not only a buffoon in Italian but also a 'breaker of promises'.

Buggery on the Bounty

Nickname for *Billy Budd*, Britten's nautical opera with an all-male cast. The reference is not only to the famous English mutiny against Captain Bligh but also possibly to the scandalous, parodistic 'Buggers' Opera' said to have been written by (?Gilbert and) Sullivan for private performance at a London gentlemen's club. I know at least one person who claims to have seen a score during the 1920s, and he confirmed some of the cast names which I already knew from another source – among them the heroine, 'Felicity F*ckwell' and 'Scrotum, a Wrinkled Old Retainer'. If anyone knows more about this alleged masterpiece I would like to hear from him; and those who refuse to believe that such obscene satire could have been produced by the composer of *The Lost Chord* and *The Light of the World* should read Arthur Jacobs's biography of the composer (1984).*

*Arthur Jacobs suggests that the source for this story might be a work entitled *The Sods' Opera* (by George Sala?) which could well have been sung to G & S tunes.

Bull fiddle

A double bass. Facetious adoption from the jazz usage. See also BUM BASS, DOGHOUSE and the various other cross-references.

Bum bass/Bum fiddle

Bum has for centuries had connotations of the human posterior, buttocks, bottom or arse. Grose's *Dictionary of the Vulgar Tongue* (1811) gives *Bumfiddle*, 'the breech, the backside', and also the punning *Ars Musica*, 'the bumfiddle'. *Bum bass* occurs in Pegge's *Annonymiana* (1809), in a context suggesting that the cello is meant; but it would probably have been a corruption of the German *Brummbass* (i.e. 'growling bass'), a common German nickname for the double bass. There was also a bladder-and-string English folk instrument of the seventeenth century and later, called the *bumbass*. It is worth adding that doctors concerned with the treatment of obesity describe a certain kind of female figure with double bulges as 'violin-hipped'.

Bum note

A note that sounds flawed and ugly, at any rate to the player. See also WOLF.

Bumper-up(per)

An extra player who sits with the section principal and 'bumps up', i.e. joins in during the loud bits, usually while the first player is RESTING. It is chiefly the brass who have bumpers-up, and horn players are most vociferous in persuading managements that they could not possibly make their LIP last without them. Players ask for bumpers-up so as to obtain lip-relief, whereas the conductor wants them so as to raise the decibel count of the music. They are a constant source of friction and irritation. Conductors do not like the spectacle of a whole orchestra playing with the frenzied energy they like to think they have inspired – while one or two brass principals sit back doing nothing. Nor are bumpers-up liked by the rest of the players, especially the strings, who can never take a rest even if their arms are wellnigh breaking off from fatigue.

Busking

This was not at first a musical performing activity. The word probably comes from nautical slang, in which it means 'to cruise about', related to the French *busquer sa fortune*, to seek one's fortune; or Italian *boscare*, 'to prowl, go filching' (or perhaps *buscherio*, 'noise, hubbub, a crowd': is not modern busking done where there is a crowd?) Henry Mayhew's *London Labour and the London Poor* (1851) describes several itinerant musicians as buskers, but also includes among them those 'going into public houses and cutting likenesses of the company', and men 'selling obscene songs' (but who did not necessarily sing them). Since the turn of the twentieth century busking has been exclusively musical: 'busking is the jargon for wandering minstrels – folk who play the perambulating pianos we see in the streets or on the sands – folk who sing from morning till midnight' (*Daily News*, 21 September 1897). Such performances would, of course, be improvised, and only seldom performed from music. Hence the modern, orchestral use of the word, meaning to play extempore or from memory, e.g. someone might say, 'Halfway through the last movement my stand collapsed and the music fell under the platform, so I had to busk the rest.' With the emergence of a splendid duo called the Cambridge Buskers, who have become international recording stars, busking has acquired new connotations of excellence.

Buxtehude

North German composer and organist (1637–1707) of Danish adoption whom Bach admired and went to hear in 1705 in Lübeck, where he had gone on four weeks' leave but stayed about four months. All of which is well known. But here is a curious fact that will not be found in GROVE or any other musical dictionary. When a German talks colloquially of 'the back of beyond', or wants to dismiss some place as obscure, remote, provincial, outlandish or

Sixteenth-century buskers

of no importance, he may invoke Buxtehude: not the composer but the place from which the composer's family hails, which is south-west of Hamburg (rather like an Englishman speaks of 'Timbuctoo'): 'They may compose music like that in Buxtehude, but here in Darmstadt . . . .' Austrians, on the other hand (possibly not aware that there really exists such a place) call it 'Buxtihudri', thereby giving a kind of comic, mock-slavonic connotation to what they consider unfashionably provincial and primitive. Indeed, they used to treat the Czechs as their country-bumpkin cousins.

Buying and selling rooms

A trick resorted to by some fiddle dealers who use a bare, uncurtained and extremely resonant room with BATHROOM ACOUSTICS for customers trying out violins with a view to purchasing them; and a heavily curtained, carpeted and acoustically 'dead' room for those who bring them their violins to sell.

BWV

Abbreviation of *Bachs Werke Verzeichnis* – a THEMATIC CATALOGUE of the works of J. S. Bach, compiled by a man called Schmieder; hence also the so-called 'Schmieder Numbers'. Unlike the Mozart KOECHEL numbers in Koechel's catalogue, BWV numbers are no indication of chronology (an impossibility in the case of Bach's output) but are ordered according to instrumentation.

Cabaletta

A word to conjure with when remarking on the performance of opera stars. It means the concluding, faster section of an aria, the bit designed to wind up the proceedings and whip the audience into enthusiastic applause. Various etymological suggestions have been made, from *cavature*, an extraction, to *cabala*, an intrigue; or even *cavalettu*, a grasshopper (the letters *b* and *v* being often interchangeable in Spanish and Italian). I have a suspicion it may have something to do with a horse – *caballo* – because it marks the moment when a PRIMA DONNA takes the bit between her teeth and gallops towards her OVATION. Indeed, many cabalettas are in an appropriately horsey six-eight rhythm (see also THE HOME STRAIGHT); and arias in the minor key usually go into the major for cabalettas, a sort of galloping major. The term is most often applied to nineteenth-century Italian opera, in which it was a favourite effect. But cabalettas are found in eighteenth-century operas as well; for example in the closing pages of *Dove sono* in Mozart's *Le Nozze di Figaro*.

Cadence

See any dictionary of musical terms, or harmony primer; but don't confuse the cadence with the cadenza, of which it is not a translation.

Calypso

Caribbean art of improvising and singing words and music on a topical subject, generally to the accompaniment of a steel band. The rhythms are like that of the South American samba, with African influence. It is probably the most important musical art-form of Trinidad, where calypso competitions are held somewhat on the model of the Welsh *eisteddfodau*. The musical dictionaries and encyclopaedias fail to tell us where the word comes from:

Calypso was the name of one of the daughters of Atlas, and – perhaps rather inappropriately – the Goddess of Silence.

Canaries

The choristers at Eton College, the English public (i.e. private) school have always had this nickname. 'The Colets and Lord Tenterdens . . . started life as canaries,' wrote A. D. Coleridge in his *Eton in the Forties* (1896). German and Austrian choirboys are called *Spatzen*, i.e. SPARROWS. There is, of course, also a dance called the *canary*, as well as *canary wine* (supposedly from the Canary Islands) with both of which Shakespeare made verbal sport.

Can Belto

See BEL CANTO

Canned music

Recorded music, especially when used in place of live musicians. The MU's motto is 'Keep Music Live' and it frowns on canned music. When it is used in theatre or ballet performances the union may insist on the engagement of live musicians who have to attend the performances without playing but are paid a fee for being there. A kind MU official reports the following conversation:

Voice on Telephone: *I need an orchestra of five musicians for the first three weeks in June at the Empire Theatre. Shows every night except Sunday, plus matinée on Saturday.*

Union Official: *What instruments would you like?*

V. o. T.: *Oh it doesn't matter. Any instrument, so long as they're all paid-up MU members.*

U. O. : *???!!!???*

V. o. T.: *Oh we don't want them to play. The music is canned. All they need to do is come to the theatre, sit in the pit and draw their wages at the end of each week. They don't need to bring any instruments.*

So the official sent along five of his most impoverished members.

In the event they did not even sit in the pit but in the pub next door. Keep Music Live?

Cantilena

The word now used to describe any flowing tune, though in Italy it means a sing-song or a cradle-song. There is an English group with the now so fashionable, foreign, one-word title 'Cantilena', whose members presumably do not seek to send their audiences to sleep.

Capons

The word for castrated cocks, and hence the ancient nickname for eunuchs in general and castrato singers in particular: 'Of a 1000 such capons who addict themselves to their booke, none attaineth to anie perfection, even in musicke (which is their ordinarie profession)' writes an author of 1594. The name was apt, for the loss of natural male hormones often made musical eunuchs, like real capons, grow to a grotesque size. The late Alfred Deller (1912–79), the English countertenor whose artistry led to the revival of the English COCK ALTO, was for some years virtually alone in his field. He was very tall and wore at first a moustache and then a beard, perhaps to still ignorant speculation on the part of those who did not know that his speaking-voice was, of course, perfectly normal and manly. Deller was much in demand on the continent and was one day asked by a member of his French audience, 'Monsieur Dellaire arr you – how do you say in England – eunuch?' He replied, without blinking an eye, 'Well yes, you could say I am. *Unique.*' And it is related that two ladies were once overheard at a concert of his, speculating about his voice. One said, 'How does he sing so *high*?' The other replied knowingly, 'Oh it's because of a small operation men can have done, which makes their voice go up.' Said the first lady: 'And I suppose that's why he has a *beard* – to hide the scar.' Musicians tend to name their neutered tomcats after some of the well-known castrati of the past: Tenducci, Grossi or Senesino, etc. Angus Heriot's fascinating book *The Castrati in Opera* tells how it was done – from partial mutilation to total amputation. The last surviving castrato was Alessandro Moreschi (1858–1922) who lived long enough to make some recordings in 1902 and 1903, the year Pope Pius X abolished the operation. The records reveal Moreschi's technique as lamentable, with an excruciating lack of vocal control such as would fail every elementary critical test if applied to a female soprano of today. As the operation had to be carried out by the age of about six, true musical promise was not always evident (the boy Haydn, incidentally, is said narrowly to have escaped the ordeal); and many castrated boys who were turned into failed capons were put into the priesthood. There was, however, one problem. The Roman church insists that a man can be ordained only if in full possession of his manhood, for where lies the virtue in abstaining from something you do not know or miss? So, according to some authorities, the amputated genitals would be preserved as a kind of insurance against musical failure. And if the need arose for ordination, they were kept in the ordinand's pocket. He would then be, at least theologically, 'in full possession of his manhood'. It is not known when the church started castrating men for musical worship, but a clue may be found in the New Testament, *St Matthew* 19. 14, in which Jesus says, 'For there are some eunuchs, which were so born from their mothers' womb: and there are some eunuchs, which were made eunuchs of men: and there be eunuchs which have made themselves eunuchs for the kingdom of heaven's sake.'

Carthorse

Anagram of ORCHESTRA. There is an old musicians' saying, heard when an orchestra is subjected to a succession of guest conductors, 'In the old days they used to change the horses; now they change the riders.'

Carving

Musicians' nickname for what conductors do. As in 'Who was carving at your concert tonight?' (To which the classic reply could have been, 'Dunno. Didn't look.')

Cats' Clavier

In German, *Katzenklavier*: one of the many invocations of the cat's name to describe discordant music. See below.

Cat's Fugue

The subject of a FUGUE by Domenico Scarlatti supposed to have been suggested to him by his cat when the animal walked on the

Cats' Clavier: A seventeenth-century German engraving after Callot

keyboard of his harpsichord. Cats often do this, especially when one is trying to practise, or else they try to sit in one's lap. But that would have been difficult in Scarlatti's case, for he had no lap. Indeed, he eventually became so fat that he was unable to play CROSSED HANDS. His Cat's Fugue nearly had a worthy companion-piece in Mozart's dog's fugue: see BIMPERL.

Cats' music

A now somewhat outdated term for unpleasant and apparently random musical sounds, much used in the late eighteenth and early nineteenth centuries when first the romantics and then the FUTURISTS began to annoy the classical traditionalists. Among works described as 'cats' music' were Wagner's *Tristan und Isolde* (by Heinrich Dorn in 1870) and Liszt's *Dante Symphony* (by the *Boston Gazette* in 1886). The music critic of the *Boston Evening Transcript* in 1913 reports how the audience began to giggle during a performance of Webern's *Six Orchestral Pieces*: 'The plaintive little meow, like that of a cat with catarrh, was too much, and the audience started off again. From that time on, the pieces were played mostly amid laughter.' But see also DONKEY MUSIC. There are several examples of attempts at writing comic cats' music, most notably 'Rossini's Cat's Duet', which is not by Rossini at all but a posthumous potpourri of tunes taken from his works.

Cats' music by Moritz von Schwind

Cats' Waltz

For once this is not a critical reflection on supposedly discordant music (see above) but the title given to Chopin's op. 34 no. 3, relating to an unsubstantiated story that his cat helped him compose it, just as an earlier cat is said to have helped Scarlatti write his CAT'S FUGUE. See also DOG WALTZ.

Cav and Pag

Universal nickname for the two operas frequently given as a double bill: *Cavalleria Rusticana* by Mascagni and *I Pagliacci* by Leoncavallo.

CBSO

The now usual abbreviation of the City of Birmingham Symphony Orchestra, previously the BSO – Birmingham Symphony Orchestra (founded 1906) – and the CBO – City of Birmingham Orchestra (1920). 'Symphony' was added in 1948. As with the BSO and other municipally aided orchestras it may be noted that when councillors give grants for music (usually with reluctance) they like to see elements like 'Municipal', or 'City of . . .' or 'Borough of . . .' in the title.

Celebrity concert

One for which higher ticket prices are charged. Also GALA CONCERT.

Cell

Not a monk's bedroom, nor a prison; but a common and largely meaningless cliché in the description of *avant-garde* music, as in 'the work is built on a four-note cell'. See also ARCH.

Cellists' faces

Brass players may go purple in the face; oboists (who take in much breath but release very little) sometimes look like having an apoplectic fit; some flautists have screwed-up EMBOUCHURES; many pianists grimace a lot, too. But cellists are the worst. For unexplained reasons many of them make the most dreadful faces when they play, as though they were in pain and hating every note, continually writhing about. Hugo Rignold told of a Polish symphony orchestra he was visiting as guest conductor and whose LEADER wore a most miserable expression, whether playing or RESTING. Rignold (who was sometimes a little sensitive or downright touchy, and often suspected a slight where none was intended) finally asked him why he looked so miserable. Did he not find his conducting satisfactory? Was there anything he could do to make him feel better? 'Nothing personal, maestro,' said the leader. 'It's just that I *HATE* music!'

Cellist's Nipple and other musical ailments

An occupational hazard that may affect female cellists which, together with some of the others described below, has been described in the *British Medical Journal*, which says the cure was probably effected by the purchase of a padded brassière. Female cymbal players may suffer discomfort when they have to stop the clashed pair of cymbals vibrating – for there is only one place in their anatomy against which the sound can be dampened, especially in rapidly repeated clashes such as in Tchaikovsky's Symphony No. 4. Perhaps that is why there are comparatively few female percussionists. Pianists can get *Glissando Thumb* from too frequent use of GLISS; a bad case of *Flautist's Chin* was reported in the same issue of the *BMJ* (not a condition suffered by flute players who talk too much but an inflammation caused by an adverse reaction of silver on the chin). *Clarinettist's Lip* is a particularly painful affliction caused by the pressure of the underlip on the lower teeth: I have seen many a bloodstained reed. There is an old superstition that wind and brass players are prone to piles, but they are no more so than string players, authors or bank managers, or anyone else whose job requires him to do much sitting. *Fiddler's Neck* is an often painful and always ugly discoloration that may be seen under the player's left jaw where the violin is gripped. It is just like a love-bite, and girl violinists report that they often get that I-know-what-*you*-were-doing-last-night look. *Organist's Trousers** is not a medical condition but an extreme shine given to trouser-seats, caused by constant sliding to and fro on the organ bench while pedalling. So to identify a fiddler, look at his or her neck; but to spot an organist, examine his seat. Brass players, especially trumpeters, are prone to emphysema, or barrel-chest; brass and woodwind to piles, as well as the condition known as 'ale gut'.

*Organists get an income tax allowance for frequent trouser replacement.

Cello

Not *'cello*. The apostrophe which denotes the omission of the first part of the word *violoncello* is as outdated as *'though* for 'although'. So is, of course, the word 'violoncello' itself, like PIANOFORTE and CLARIONET.

Chambre Separée

The most famous song from the 1898 Viennese operetta *Der Opernball* (The Opera Ball) by Richard Heuberger (1850–1914). It is called, in the Austro-French then so fashionable, *Im Chambre Separée*, which is usually translated by radio presenters and others as 'in separate rooms'. This is not so much a mistranslation as a misunderstanding of Viennese customs and the discreet facilities obtainable at the turn of the century. It does indeed mean separate rooms – of a rather special kind. For restaurants would provide for their diners not only private rooms but equip them with a bed as well as the more usual eating-house furnishings: what are in

61

English (and a somewhat different context) advertised as Rooms for Private Functions.

Chanson

The French word for a song. See LIED: most of the remarks thereunder are equally applicable to the *chanson*.

Charivari

A regrettably neglected old word for noisy, confused, discordant and generally unpleasant music. Its popularity waned after *Punch* was founded in 1841, with the sub-title 'London Charivari' (in imitation of a Parisian satirical magazine).

La Chasse

Nickname of Haydn's Quartet No. 1 in B flat; not to be confused with THE HUNT by Mozart, although the two works have HORN HARMONIES in common. The name (or nickname) has often been applied to music descriptive of the chase, by composers ranging from Anon. to Le Blanc, Jannequin, Kreisler, Liszt, Mehul, Mondonville, Morin, Mozart, L., Mozart, W. A., and from Paradies and Paganini to Trad. What most of them share are the horn harmonies mentioned earlier, as well as attempts to reproduce in music some of the sounds of the hunt – dogs, guns, horses and hounds – and of course hunting-horns. Haydn's Overture to his opera *La fedeltà premiata* is also known as his Symphony No. 73 in D, 'La Chasse'. The opera, produced at Glyndebourne in 1979, has what is probably the most complicated plot concerning the (amorous) chase but the music is perfectly enchanting, and so were some of the jokes in John Cox's production.

Chief Conductor

Do not be deceived when you read announcements that Maestro Soandsosky is to be appointed 'Chief Conductor' or (military-style) 'Conductor-in-Chief' of this or that symphony orchestra. The title suggests an office, residence nearby and control over the day-to-day artistic running of the orchestra as well as the hiring-and-firing of its members – in other words a 365-day interest in the job. 'Chief' conductorships are nothing of the kind. For conductors

are shameless moonlighters, and the greater their jet-setting poten-
tial the more such lucrative but strictly part-time 'chief' conductorships they will try to fit under their Gucci belts, flitting between
this, that and several other symphony orchestras. A chief
conductor is unlikely to conduct more than half-a-dozen concerts
with each before flying to the next one – which also saves him the
need for learning too great a repertoire. With such a short stay in
each place he is unlikely to leave a personal musical stamp on any
of his orchestras, as Beecham did on the RPO, Barbirolli on the
Hallé, Rignold on the RLPO or Gibson on the SNO. And this state
of affairs is now surely borne out by the increasingly plasticized,
uniformly competent but bland-as-junk-food, quality of orchestral
playing to be heard almost everywhere in the civilized world.
French, German, American (even Japanese) orchestras, once
immediately recognizable by a national style of playing, are now
practically indistinguishable, at least on gramophone records. All
this costs a great deal of money, and if the price of concert tickets
has risen sharply (together with the demand for state subsidies),
it is not because the players' fees have increased in proportion to
inflation. Managements are only too well aware of all this but
try to distract attention from each exorbitant BATON CHARGE by
inventing all kinds of absurd and convoluted titles for their rare
visitors: from *Conductor in Chief* to *Musical Director*, *Artistic Adviser*,
Principal Conductor or (if the truth will out) *Principal Guest
Conductor*. When the appointment draws to a close the incumbents
may be elevated to the status of *Conductor Emeritus* (a meaningless
borrowing from the academic world), *Guest Conductor Laureate* or
even *Conductor for Life*. The last three are useful when the time
comes for tactfully telling a previous 'chief' conductor that he is
no longer as welcome as he used to be. The words 'Elect' or
'Designate' sometimes have to be added, for the music industry
has to do so much long-term planning that a conductor's 'forth-
coming' appointment may have to be announced a full three years
before it takes effect; and by the time it happens audiences may
have forgotten all about it. Stokowski, as stated elsewhere (see
STOKEY), signed a ten-year contract when he was 95, but was
unfortunately unable to honour it.

Chiff

The sound of the initial ATTACK on an organ pipe (at any rate in
flute stops), giving a kind of hard edge almost akin to OVER-

BLOWING, a phenomenon also heard when beginners on the recorder blow a little too hard. The effect can, however, be used subtly and purposefully. The word is onomatopoeic. Plenty of chiff is one of the strongest characteristics of the baroque organ.

Chocolate rustlers

Some members of audiences celebrate their visit to a concert hall with the purchase of a box of chocolates, as is traditional in the cinema and theatre. The sweets are handed round and noisily unwrapped. Theatre actors do not like the custom either, but in the concert hall, where one normally expects to hear no other sounds except that of the music, it is an abomination. See also COUGHERS, and TAPPERS, NODDERS AND TIME-BEATERS.

Chromatic bullock

Nickname given to the ophicleide, or bass bugle (a giant keyed bugle descended from the serpent): from *ophis*, a serpent, + *kleis*, which is Greek for a key or cover, cf. *clef*. The origin of the nickname probably goes back to Berlioz. G. B. Shaw (as 'Corno di Bassetto', see BASSET HORN) certainly quotes it. Mendelssohn, Schumann, Verdi and Wagner all ask for the ophicleide in their scores but seldom get it; for in the modern orchestra its aggressive rasp is usually replaced by the more tame and well-rounded sound of the tuba, which is a pity. A specimen once turned up at rehearsal but proved to be hopelessly sharp, having been made to the older high pitch. The conductor kept asking the player whether he could put things right. The ophicleidist left the stage (as it turned out later) to go to the gents' lavatory and hold it under a cold tap so as to cool the tubing: but when he returned it was just as sharp as before. The conductor again complained, and the player said rather tetchily, 'I'm sorry, but I've passed water through it and that's the best I can do.'

The Chuck Steak Opera

See MOSES

Cigarette papers

The sale of these now depends almost entirely on cannabis-smokers and wind-players. The latter habitually carry a packet in their instrument case – not because many of them smoke but because the thin tissue is used for drying the moisture caused by WATER (i.e. condensed breath) that can collect in a key and make it stick, with often disastrous results: the player may correctly finger a C sharp, but the key obstinately stays closed – and out comes a C natural. For another use of cigarette papers, see CUT.

Cinelli

The Italian word for cymbals: *Tschinellen* (pronounced like 'chin Ellen') is the Germanized version of this pleasantly onomatopoeic word. The Italian's *cinelli* ('chee Nellie') are sometimes colloquially called *piatti*, i.e. plates.

Cipher

Also *cypher*. A word of unknown origin meaning a note that sounds continuously on an organ whether the key is depressed or not, owing to the imperfect closure of a valve or PALLET. The cipher is a constant dread of organists as there is no way of curing it unless the player climbs into the organ. Even when they take their final bow and walk away from the instrument, it still plays that solitary embarrassing note until the wind is turned off.

Circular beat

When a conductor's beat becomes circular (instead of directional, as described under STICK TECHNIQUE) the chances are that he is lost, and hedging his bets by not committing himself to any particular part of the bar. For if he were to give, say, a strong DOWNBEAT anywhere but at the beginning of the bar, he would run the risk of misleading those actually watching him and relying on the directional nature of his beat. That could cause a major mishap, whereas by freewheeling with an indeterminate beat and leaving the players to their own devices, a clever conductor can eventually regain his bearings when he hears (or sees if not conducting from memory) a landmark in the score. But it should be said that some conductors have a naturally unclear beat that is of little help to the players; and such conductors are known as STIRRING-THE-PUDDING CONDUCTORS. Also, that some of the greatest conductors have had the unclearest beats, for the very uncertainty it engenders makes for a softer-edged sound: see LATE PLAYING.

Circular bow

Every string player dreams of this, but he will get one only if he takes up the HURDYGURDY. Jocular references to circular bows may be heard when a conductor asks for BOWINGS that permit too few changes: 'He thinks we've got a circular bow.'

Circular breathing

The alleged ability (claimed by certain oboists) to play continuously, while breathing in through the nose and out through the instrument.

Circus acrobats

A term of abuse seen in music-critical writings, aimed at performers too preoccupied with finger or vocal dexterity and not enough, it is implied, with true musical expression. 'The attraction of the virtuoso for the public is very much like that of the circus for the crowd', wrote Debussy in *Monsieur Croche*. 'There is always the hope that something dangerous may happen: M. Ysaÿe may play the violin with M. Colonne on his shoulders; or M. Pugno may conclude his piece by lifting the piano with his teeth.'

Clap trap

A piece of music with a deceptive or false ending, or with an unexpected silence following a cadence that may mislead the unwary or over enthusiastic concert-goer into prematurely applauding, one of the most embarrassing and humiliating things that can happen to one, especially if others go 'shhhh!' or worse, the conductor turns and glares at the culprit (see also APPLAUSE LEADER). Weber's *Invitation to the Dance* (in the Berlioz orchestration) is a notorious clap trap because almost invariably some members of the audience get carried away by the emphatic JOHN BROWN FINISH of the waltz section. Weingartner's arrangement contains a cunning device to forestall the clap trap: being an experienced conductor he knew about such things. Sibelius 5, with its several isolated chords separated by lengthy silences, sometimes inspires the odd early clapper; and so does the penultimate movement of Tchaikovsky 6. Indeed the Soviets reverse the order of its movements. In order to satisfy the political requirements of the culture commissars, the March is played last, thus totally altering the composer's intentions. They do this not to save embarrassment to premature clappers, but because Tchaikovsky's despairing last movement (whose real meaning has only recently come to light) is considered inimical to ideas of Socialist Optimism.

Claque

The word means a slap or a hand-clap in French, but is also the name of a system, once rife but now almost extinct except in some continental opera-houses, by which artists (or their agents) employed paid groups of clappers. In France especially, each opera house operated an official claque by which well-paid *claqueurs* would encourage the real audience with their own, feigned, enthusiasm. Claques were most highly organized in Vienna and Paris, and there were some excellently-run ones also in Italian houses. Strict rates of pay were laid down everywhere. In Italy (according to a report in the *Musical Times* (1919) the fees ranged from 5 lire for interruptions of *Bene!* or *Bravo!*; 10 lire for 'ordinary applause'; 17 lire for 'more insistent applause' and 50 lire 'for a *BIS* at any cost' – to 'a sum to be negotiated' for 'Wild Enthusiasm'. French *claqueurs* were divided into specialist groups: *rieurs*, who would laugh to emphasize jokes, *pleureurs*, to weep ostentatiously into big handkerchiefs, and *bisseurs*, the most vocal of them all, who would continue to shout *BIS! BIS!!* to demand ENCORES. The ultimate paymasters of the claques were, of course, the artists themselves, and a good deal of bribery went on, too, to get one singer's claque to ruin the performance of another with booing. Every claqueur would bask in the reflected glory of his employer ('We sang well tonight'). Although it now appears to us a totally dishonest way of MILKING THE APPLAUSE, people were perfectly open about it. The Austrian violinist and writer Joseph Wechsberg wrote amusingly about claques in his book, *Looking for a Bluebird*. The *Musical Times* in 1897 reported an enterprising claque leader who, in order to draw attention to the unbounded enthusiasm evoked by a certain singer, engaged a couple of one-armed *claqueurs*, one without the *left* arm and the other without the *right*. Between them they – almost singlehanded – brought the house down 'as by happy inspiration they joined forces in a co-operative hand-clap'.

Clarinettist's Lip

See CELLIST'S NIPPLE

Clarino

Old word for a trumpet, now used to distinguish high trumpet parts from ordinary ones.

Clarionet

The old-fashioned English word and spelling for the clarinet. It survived until well into the twentieth century in poetry and non-musical prose because of its extra syllable; and also in its use by those who like using words that are quaint or archaic. Ambrose Bierce, in *The Devil's Dictionary* (1911), says, 'Clarionet, noun. An instrument of torture operated by a person with cotton in his ears. There are two instruments that are worse than a clarionet – two clarionets.' Bierce therefore either forestalled or copied the well-known saying, 'What could be worse than a flute? – Two flutes.' This summary judgment on the instrument is typical of Bierce's sardonic humour; or else perhaps there were some very bad clarinettists in Ohio, San Franscisco – or in London, where he worked as an American journalist from 1872 to 1876. Soon after the publication of his *Devil's Dictionary* Bierce disappeared without trace in Mexico – perhaps tortured to death by a pair of wild clarionettists. See also BLUE-EYED ENGLISH, ESCAPING GAS, THE OBOE IS AN ILL WIND . . . .

Clart

Common abbreviation, on old band parts, etc. of 'Clarinet'. When a concert was advertised on a poster as 'Conducted by Sir Thomas Beecham, Bart.' a wag annotated the soloist's name to 'Reginald Kell, Clart.'

Classical, Romantic, Baroque, Modern, Authentic, Popular and Light music

Musical styles are given many loose labels. *Classical* should properly be used only for the Haydn/Mozart/Beethoven period; *romantic* for music like Mendelssohn/Schumann/Brahms/Tchaikovsky, etc. (Schubert having a foot in both camps). *Baroque* was originally a term of abuse, from Hispanic *barrocco/barrucco*, meaning 'rough, grotesque, imperfect, whimsical'. Until recently this was applied to the music of J. S. Bach and his contemporaries; but recent musical revivalists have loosened the meaning of *baroque* still further, and it can now cover a multitude of styles – anything up to, say, Brahms, provided it is played on reproduction instruments by smaller forces than usual (which is cheaper, too, so concert promoters and record companies love it). In German-speaking countries *baroque* is the opposite of *rococo* (seldom used in this country) which together with the all-but-forgotten ZOPF covers the Haydn/Mozart period. But *baroque* is not necessarily the same as *authentic* music. Here the revivalists often disagree violently among themselves, arguing endlessly about ornamentation, CONTINUOS, cadenzas, etc., and questioning each others' stout claims to have a direct line to dead composers. Much splendid work has been achieved in the field, and long-lost techniques revived, especially in wind and brass playing. But much of it is flawed by bad intonation, PEARSHAPED NOTES, rough bowing and the often total denial of VIBRATO. Authenticity on its own is no substitute for years of practice towards a perfect technique. *Modern* is an even looser term. Some people admit that by 'modern' they mean the music of Mahler, Bax or Vaughan Williams: perhaps any twentieth-century music not to their taste. Pop music has its own subdivisions (not within the province of this book) though its popularity is artificially stimulated by the publicity industry. Light music, too, is a term much misused, for it can include that of Ketèlbey and Eric Coates as well as Johann Strauss waltzes, Mozart CONTREDANSES and Bach minuets. But *classical* when used as the antithesis to *pop* music is indefensible on any grounds, and is a mark of the totally non-musical.

Clavier/Klavier

The distinction in spelling is useful and might be preserved to mean two different things. Until German spelling was reformed and standardized at the end of the nineteenth and beginning of the twentieth centuries, many words could be written with either a C or a K; as in Carl or Karl, Caffee or Kaffee, Cantor or Kantor, although in earlier times the C spellings were customary. J. S. Bach, for example, wrote a *Clavi(e)rübung* (the e after i was also often omitted). At that time *Clavier* simply meant a keyboard, whether of a harpsichord, spinet, clavichord, organ or the newly invented fortepiano. Thus *Clavi(e)rübung* simply meant 'keyboard practice'. By the time German spelling was modernized and standardized the harpsichord and clavichord had all but disappeared and *Klavier* (now with an obligatory e after the i) had become the standard word for a pianoforte, meaning usually a GRAND, so *Klavierübung* now specifically means *'piano* practice'.

Clear the saloon

Facetious nickname for Debussy's *Clair de lune*, the third movement of his *Suite Bergamasque* for piano.

The Clock Symphony

The title/nickname for Haydn's no. 101 in D is a nineteenth-century invention, but one which has more than a grain of authenticity in it. It supposedly comes from the 'ticking' quavers in the slow movement, which is not implausible. But I think it is far more likely that it refers to the fact that an earlier version of the third movement was played by a mechanical organ-clock (or 'Flute Clock') in 1793, a year before the first performance of the symphony. I therefore suggest that 'Clock Symphony' really meant 'the symphony with the tune the clock used to play'. The instrument, made at ESTERHÁZA by a man called Niemecz, is still in existence and can be heard merrily playing the familiar minuet in a delightfully unfamiliar way.

Co-

See ASSOCIATE

Cobbler's patch

See SCHUSTERFLECK

Cock altos

Nickname for countertenors; current among cathedral choristers and other professional singers, who also call them 'Queens'; more

with reference to pregnant cats than homosexuals. See also
CAPONS.

Collaborative pianist

American euphemism for an ACCOMPANIST. As with many
euphemisms, it is slightly insulting, as it manages to suggest that
such a pianist never plays on his own but is obliged to collaborate
with another musician. Another euphemism for an accompanist
is ASSOCIATE ARTIST.

The College

As with other professions, 'the College' is the standard abbreviation of the Royal College of that particular discipline. For musicians it means the Royal College of Music in London – when
referred to without further explanation and the conversation takes
place in London. But in Manchester the Royal Northern College
of Music (formerly the RMCM) would be meant. 'THE ACADEMY'
could mean the Royal Academy of Music in London, or else the
Royal Scottish Academy of Music in Glasgow; or, more recently,
the Academy of St Martin-in-the-Fields.

The Colon

'Surely, you were joking?' wrote a reader. She was referring to a
newspaper article I had written which mentioned the Colon Opera
House (Teatro Colón) in Buenos Aires. 'Is there really an opera
house named after the lower bowel?' she asked. Of course, there
should have been an acute accent over the second *o* – newspapers
are happy these days to get their words right, never mind the
foreign accents. *Colón* is the Spanish name of the man we call
Columbus, after whom the opera house and many other South
American institutions are named. The first Teatro Colón was built
in 1857 and lasted until 1888, and the present one opened in 1908,
probably the biggest in the world. When we played there with an
English orchestra we found that on the revolving stage, behind
the backdrop, the entire seating arrangements – platforms, chairs
and music-stands and music – had been set up ready for another
orchestra.

Coloratura

' . . . Is a term applied by the Italians to all variations, trillos, diminutions, &c., that can render a song agreeable,' says *Grassineau's Dictionary* (1740). Such ornament would, in the eighteenth century, have been extemporized; but later, as spontaneous ornamentation began to fall into disuse, the term came to mean florid passages written into a song by the composer himself. Hence a *coloratura aria* that would be sung by a *coloratura soprano*, one who specializes in that type of singing. The term is sometimes applied to a MEZZO but never to male singers, though I suppose there could be a 'coloratura COCK ALTO'. The word comes from the Latin *colorare*, to colour, adopted into Italian in the above form and into German as *Koloratur*.

Coming in

English debutantes used to 'come out', and so now do homosexuals. But musicians come *in*. When they do, i.e. make their entry as indicated in the conductor's SCORE and their PART, there is nothing noteworthy about it. Coming in early is called a DOMINO; coming in late may cause confusion if the culprit persists in playing music not intended to be played in that place. But not coming in at all may cause little harm and could even go unnoticed, both by conductor and audience, especially in an AUBREY WINTER ARRANGEMENT; unless, of course, the absence of a SOLO results in a hiatus.

Composing-by-numbers

Derisive nickname for TWELVE-TONE and SERIAL music which, some say, is produced by the strict application of mathematical rules that put notes into a certain numerical order (see also KNITTING-PATTERN MUSIC) and has little if anything to do with artistic creation. This important movement in composition, pioneered by Schoenberg and others round the beginning of the twentieth century, proved extremely influential in a peripheral kind of way, but itself became a musical dead end. Most composers now consider it old hat. There is a curiously prophetic passage in Anton Schindler's book *Beethoven as I knew him* (written a decade or two after the composer's death) in which he confesses himself puzzled by the GROSSE FUGUE: Such music, he writes, 'should belong to that grey future when the relationship of notes will be decided by mathematical computation. Indubitably such combinations must be regarded as the extreme limit of the speculative intellect, and its effect will always remain one of Babelish confusion. One cannot here speak of darkness in contrast to light.' On the other hand, proponents of twelve-note and serial music may feel that the twentieth-century musical public is as unperceptive about their music as Schindler was about the Great Fugue in 1850.

Comps

Complimentary tickets given by managements to performers as a concession, rather as miners get free coal. But when PAPERING THE HOUSE, managers and musicians are positively encouraged to distribute free tickets to their friends and persuade them to come. When Beethoven and his friends were organizing the concert at which his Ninth was first performed they were pestered for comps by many of their acquaintances, including the printer who supplied the advertising leaflets.

Concert Manager/Orchestra Manager

See GEIGER COUNTER

Concert Master

American word, for a LEADER, an uneasy translation from the German *Konzertmeister*.

Concert nerves

Some musicians suffer from them, others do not. Some play better when nervous, others (who perhaps have the makings of a BATHROOM VIRTUOSO) are unable to achieve their best in public. Nerves show themselves in a variety of ways: shortness of breath or a dry mouth – uncomfortable for wind and brass players; sweating of the palms – potentially disastrous for string players; a kind of nervous rigidity of the fingers, which can near-paralyse all musicians and may prevent pianists from passing the thumb under the fingers as well as they can in private. Weakness at the knees – they may even threaten to give way – an affliction suffered by one or two very well-known stand-up soloists; a nervous looseness of the bowels is not unknown, and some players are troubled by horrendous pre-concert flatulence. And for string players, there are, of course, the dreaded PURLIES. The best insurance against concert nerves is *practice*. For if one knows a passage or work so well that one's fingers can apparently play it on their own, and one is able to play it 100 times without mishap, then the likelihood is that it will go well for the 101st time ON THE NIGHT. Some musicians resort to drugs: the so-called beta-blockers have recently been found useful; other sufferers seek courses in psychotherapy, and therapists advertise alleged cures in the musical press. Other players take to drink – which may temporarily relax them, but the need for constantly increased dosages makes for addiction and tragedy: they only *think* they are playing well.

Concert pianist

A solecism that betrays the non-musical, often the unmusical journalist. To the musician a pianist is a pianist, whether he is an amateur or professional, plays in concerts or for his own amusement. If referring to an ACCOMPANIST, chamber music player, soloist, dance band or pub pianist, the knowledgeable speaker can and will specify. I once heard Julian Bream introduced to an amateur who had just taught himself to strum three chords as 'a fellow guitarist'. The hostess was correct. It would have been tautologous to call Bream a 'concert guitarist'. Equally common, tiresome (and ultimately meaningless) is the description 'in concert'. In what else?

Conductor-baiters

There is a certain type of orchestral player who seems unwilling or unable to submit to the conductor's (in any case very temporary) authority, always anxious to remind him that the baton is not a musical instrument and that without the players the conductor would be soundless and useless. He therefore takes every opportunity of baiting the boss. Such baiters are usually instrumental soloists, seldom RANK-AND-FILE or SUB-PRINCIPALS, and never the LEADER: he is thought to have divided loyalties. Rows between leaders and conductors are rare; and in any case, the skilled conductor-baiter does not have rows. On the contrary, he will if anything be excessively courteous, his tactics subtle but understood and enjoyed by his colleagues. A twenty-year-old would-be whiz-kid of the baton is gravely addressed as MAESTRO; or an ageing musicologist, who has spent a lifetime talking about music but seldom gets the chance of standing up before an orchestra, is spoken to in a way that is sure to make him feel even smaller and humbler. ('Have you conducted this work before? We always take it a little faster.') An enquiry about a complicated transposition ('What should my note be at letter D, please? I'm playing Horn in E flat alto but the composer seems to have written my part in the tenor clef there . . .') soon flusters the impostor. When the conductor goes wrong at rehearsal and the rest of the orchestra (probably playing in any case on automatic pilot), puts him right by *not* following him, our baiter alone will faithfully play *with* the beat, knowing perfectly well he is wrong but forcing the conductor to stop and acknowledge his error. Here an innocent enquiry like 'Excuse me, I couldn't quite follow that bar. When we played it for Mr Giulini last Saturday he beat it in six . . .' may work wonders in speeding the collapse of a pompous party. Downright show-downs, however, do not count as conductor-baiting, and open rows at rehearsal make for bad performances. The distinguished flautist Gareth Morris, for many years principal flute of the Philharmonia, although a man of impeccable manners and old-fashioned courtesy, was much feared by conductors for his extremely polite enquiries. Soon after the end of the war, when Karajan had just been cleared of his BERUFSVERBOT (having been a Nazi party member), the English violinist Peter Gibbs suddenly felt a great resentment of the conductor's imperious manner. He stood up and quietly said, 'I spent five years fighting bastards like you and I've had enough.' He then did the only possible thing and walked out of the Philharmonia rehearsal. Many disagreements arise from the fact that musicians are often under stress and may suffer from CONCERT NERVES.

Conductor solo

See (BAR) FOR NOTHING

Congratulations

An entry for the 1968 Eurovision Song Contest by Martin and Coulter, now frequently played not so much for its musical merit but because the title happens to be apt. Beethoven in 1822 wrote a *Gratulations-Menuett* in E flat, WoO 3, for the anniversary of one of his friends. It is scored for small orchestra and should fit the bill rather better when congratulations are called for in CLASSICAL musical circles.

Contemporary music

Contemporary with whom? The term is usually loosely used when referring to modern CLASSICAL music.

Continuo

See FIGURED BASS

Contra

Abbreviation for the Italian *contrafagotto*, or double-bassoon, pitched one octave lower than the ordinary bassoon.

Contract orchestras

These give their members a salary, negotiated at or above the appropriate MU rates and based on a contract of employment which determines how many hours a player may be required to work in a specified period – day, week or month. If there is no work, the musician still gets his basic wage. If there is more work than fills the permitted hours, he gets what is in effect overtime pay. But this can, conversely, lead to cut-price concerts. Managements, faced with a full wages bill for a period in which they have only one concert engagement, are tempted to offer cheap engagements for a very small fee indeed. There are also freelance orchestras, which engage their players from the general pool of players available, and pay them by the concert or session. These are generally run by a committee of player-administrators – always hotbeds of orchestral politics and intrigue beside which any political party caucus would pale by comparison. The chief difference between contract and freelance orchestras is that the former always complain of being overworked, while the latter complain if under-employed. A typical conversation with a contract musician would be:

Q: *Hello, how's business?*
A: *Absolute murder. Bloody Messiah last night, went on for hours,*

*then a schools concert in the morning under some little squirt
who thinks he's Toscanini. Then a* SITZPROBE, *and now the show
tonight. Shouldn't do it to a dog. How can they expect us to
play properly?*

But ask a London freelance and he or she might reply:

A: *Fantastic! I was* DEPPING *for Fred in the* WIRELESS ORCHESTRA
*every morning last week, had two kids' concerts in the afternoon,
then a quickie commercial session – in and out in less than an
hour – and now I'm doing the* RING *at the* GARDEN *at nights
as well. Except I've got to be up at five for some film sessions.
You've no idea how hard it is to fit in my pupils at the* COLLEGE.
Couldn't be doing better.

Contredanse

Had Mozart and Beethoven not written *contredanses* the word
would now be all but forgotten, like the *cotillion* or the *schottische*.
Several reputable dictionaries say the word is a French adaptation
of the English 'country dance', but this sounds implausible to me.
The first element of the word more likely refers to the French
contre, i.e. 'counter-dancing', as in counter-marching; and dance
notation of the contredanse supports this idea. Besides, the etymological traffic usually went the other way, from French into
English. Also, in the seventeenth and eighteenth centuries people
would more likely have spoken of 'peasant' dancing (cf. *paysanne*),
not 'country' dancing, for the difference between town and
country was far less pronounced than it is now; nor was the
minuet confined to town use. *Contre* from 'country' is as unlikely
as 'country-marching' would be for the Brigade of Guards.

Copyist

We have an ACCOMPANIST, not an 'accompanyist' as formerly
written, but the person who copies music is a copyist, although
the Germans call him a *Kopist*. Many composers copy their own
orchestral PARTS from their SCORES, others give the job to a copyist.
Copyists work in various ways. Some copy 'deaf', i.e. without
mentally 'hearing' what they write – and at least one composer,
Peter Maxwell Davies (b. 1934), confesses to copying out his own
music mechanically, sometimes while listening to other music.
One of the best ways of learning a piece of music is to copy it out:

score to score, score into parts or parts into score. Stravinsky used to do it when he was unable to sleep.

Cor

Standard abbreviation for Cor Anglais, or ENGLISH HORN, which is neither English nor a horn. Another horn that is not a horn is the BASSET HORN.

Cor de chasse

French for a hunting-horn; what the Germans call WALDHORN (literally, 'forest horn', as continental hunts were thought to take place mostly in the woods). Such valveless, crookless instruments were usually pitched either in the keys of D, E flat or F. See also SECURICOR and NATURAL HORN.

Cornet/Cornett

The first is the modern brass instrument, but with double-t denotes the ancient wooden trumpet played with recorder fingering. In Italian *cornetto acustico* is an ear trumpet.

The Corporal

Derisive nickname in some orchestras for the ORCHESTRA MANAGER. See also GEIGER COUNTER.

Cosi

Customary abbreviation of Mozart's *Cosi fan tutte*, and pronounced like the British trades union 'COHSE' likes us to pronounce its foolish acronym. The feminine form *Tutte* (so often misprinted 'tutti') is important. The title means 'Thus Do All Women'; but 'tutti' would be '. . . Men'. It is really quite untranslatable, though many valiant attempts have been made: *Love and Temptation, Tit for Tat, The School for Love, The Bet, One Does like the Next, What's Sauce for the Goose, Women's Wiles and Loves, The Girl from Flanders*(!), *The Two Aunts from Milan*(!!), *The Transvestites*(!!!) and – running out of exclamation marks –

MOZART'S

COSI FAN TUTTE

"THEY ALL DO IT"

with THE CROYDON OPERA ORCHESTRA

Coughers

The concert cougher should be investigated by the psychologists. As soon as he hears the tiniest involuntary cough, the merest clearing of the throat, from somewhere in the auditorium, he, too remembers that he urgently needs to cough. Almost at once the coughing becomes epidemic. It happens especially at concerts for the young. Such coughers reveal that they are bored with the music, or at any rate not fully concentrating on it. For you will seldom hear a cough from the platform; and if there is one, it will be discreetly stifled. Nor is there ever a sneezing-epidemic, even though (or because) sneezing is an involuntary reflex. Have you ever seen a conductor use his handkerchief for anything other than mopping his brow? The concert-goer suffering from a throat ailment should be at home, or at any rate have a hankie ready to act as a mute when necessary. For other concert nuisances, see CHOCOLATE RUSTLERS, and TAPPERS, NODDERS AND TIME-BEATERS.

Counting bars

As explained under SCORE AND PARTS orchestral players are not given a full score to play from: merely their own part extracted from it. Thus when they are RESTING during a performance there is nothing to show them where they are (musically speaking) in

Counting Bars: The trumpeter Glöggl, a brass player who was associated with
Beethoven in Vienna

relation to the other players (except when CUES are supplied or the parts are of the AUBREY WINTER kind). In order to enter again with the right music at the right moment, possibly with an exposed SOLO, they have to count bars. Counting is as important to the musician as to the ballet dancer. The smallest mistake can ruin a performance, or at least lead to a DOMINO. If you watch an orchestra closely you may see lips moving as though in silent prayer, or the occasional, tiny finger-movement (some count units on one hand, tens on the other). Neighbouring colleagues in this manner sometimes indicate REHEARSAL LETTERS to each other as a kind of mutual reassurance. Such signals may be prearranged to save one or the other counting large stretches of rests. Pencilled annotations like 'Wake Fred' are not uncommon; and Fred may then relax, think of other things, sleep (or even listen to the music). Experienced orchestral musicians who know a work well do not need to count but will know almost by instinct where to get ready and where to enter, whether given a CUE or not. In opera performances rests can be very long, and some parts have annotations like 'Time for two pints' or 'A quick one'. And there may be seen from the gallery, especially when the stage is darkened, much distracting coming and going in the pit. There is also much reading. George Bernard Shaw, in his *Music in London* (1889) writes:

> Mr J. A. Smith, the eminent drum player . . . is not the only orchestral player who studies the press (he, I may remark, does so with such diligence that when I compose a symphony for the [Crystal] Palace, or for Herr Richter, I shall not write in the old style, 'the drums count' but simply 'Mr Smith reads the paper'). He does not mean to annoy me, I am sure; but if he only knew how desperately I longed for something to read myself during a tedious movement, he would rightly ascribe my feelings to mere envy.

Shaw in fact got it wrong. No composer or copyist ever wrote 'the drums count', but actual numbers of bars are given, except when they are so great that the TACET sign is employed. It should be added that counting is such an ingrained habit that many orchestral players, faced with any sort of regular rhythmic sound such as that of machinery or the clatter of train wheels, find themselves automatically counting bars (*forty-three*, two, three, four, *forty-four*, two, three, four, etc.). Some can continue counting while dozing off, and one player confessed to doing it on his honeymoon.

The Cowpat School of English Music

Term coined by Elizabeth Lutyens (1906–83) for a very English kind of countrified, countryside and probably folk-song-based, music exemplified by that of vw. An unkind comment but a perceptive one. And yet when the history of twentieth-century music comes to be written, I wonder which composers will be found to have given greater pleasure to more listeners, the English 'cowpat' school or the exceedingly cerebral, central European KNITTING-PATTERN music.

Crit

Musicians' and general theatre and showbusiness slang for a newspaper notice or critique of a performance. The word 'notice' would suffice, but is seldom heard except in conjunction with 'rave'; and the raving is meant to be taken as pleasurable excitement, not madness, rage or anger. See also BROCHURE.

Crook

A detachable piece of tubing used on older brass instruments for changing the key of the entire instrument, and on newer ones to connect parts of the mechanism such as valves. On the bassoon, the CONTRA and the COR the crook is the piece of tubing to which the reed is attached. During a children's concert run by two brothers, the conductor asked the COR player for a demonstration with the words 'Where's the little crook?' To which the player replied, 'He's backstage, counting the takings.'

Crossed hands

A supposed pianistic feat that always impresses the onlooker but is not as difficult as it looks. D. Scarlatti (see CAT'S FUGUE) is supposed to have invented it as a virtuoso effect, but J. S. Bach, Rameau and Couperin used it for genuinely musical reasons. C. P. E. Bach in his autobiography (as told to Charles Burney) said 'In 1731 I composed a Minuet with crossed hands, a natural effect which was at that time looked upon as magic.'

Cross relations

The Americans' name for FALSE RELATIONS.

Crotchet

What the Americans call a 'quarter-note', which they translate from the German *Viertelnote*. The English crotchet is surely to be preferred, as not all bars have four beats.

Crow

The sound and feel of the 'crow' of an oboe, COR or bassoon reed, when placed in the mouth and blown on its own, tells its player much about its quality, whether it is a soft reed or a hard one, for example.

The Crucifixion

When spoken of among singers, this refers not to the events at Golgotha but to the popular composition by Sir John Stainer (1840–1901). He wrote many oratorios, cantatas and songs, most of which were published in his lifetime and enjoyed favour (though he himself modestly dismissed them as mere 'rubbish'). His *Crucifixion* became a great success in English churches and cathedrals because of its simple, devout and deeply-felt qualities and tuneful appeal to congregations. Professional choristers, needless to say, soon tired of it:

A: *What do you think of Stainer's* Crucifixion?
B: *Bloody good idea.*

Stainer was respected also as a conscientious musical scholar, and knighted in 1888, a year after he composed the *Crucifixion*.

Cue

A sign given by the conductor to a player or singer to begin playing or singing; or, in an orchestral or vocal part, a passage printed or written in small notes to help a musician, perhaps while COUNTING BARS, to find (or confirm) his place by indicating to him what others are playing or singing. Printed cues also help when musicians are missing and playing all cues is the order of the day, as in AUBREY WINTER VERSIONS.

Curtain aria

An aria or song in an opera (usually eighteenth century) directed to be sung in front of the closed curtain to enable scene changes to take place behind it. Such arias have little relevance to the plot. The *act tunes, curtain tunes,* and *curtain music* of Purcell and other seventeenth-century English composers filled the same purpose; and so did nineteenth-century *intermezzi* and *entr'actes.* The most famous and most beautiful curtain arias are to be found in Mozart's operas. He also wrote a number of INSERTION ARIAS.

Curtain calls

Thus named even on the concert platform, where no curtain is lowered and raised at the end of a performance. Instead, the conductor and/or soloist keep pretending they are going home after the end of a piece but are repeatedly called back, possibly for an ENCORE. The thing to do under the circumstances is to keep up some pretence by letting a little time elapse between disappearing and reappearing. Everyone *knows* the artist has not in fact got as far as his dressing-room and taken his boots off, but is merely lurking behind the platform-door, wondering how soon he can decently rush on again so as to MILK THE APPLAUSE for the maximum number of curtain-calls – and keep the clapping going until he is finally off the stage. For there are few things more embarrassing for an artist than to depart to the sound of his own footsteps because he has allowed the applause to die on him. In the music boom in London during the 1939–45 war, when theatres were pressed into service to satisfy the unprecedented demand for CLASSICAL music, real curtain calls were possible, as the orchestra played on the stage and the curtain could be raised and lowered. In one concert, at the Scala Theatre, the rising curtain caught the hem of the dress of the woman conductor and, by way of an unscheduled ENCORE, slowly pulled it over her head.

Curtain music/Curtain tune

See CURTAIN ARIA

Cut

As applied to the making of a gramophone record this is both an archaism and a neologism. At first it referred, correctly, to the old process of cutting a wax master, but fell into disuse with the advent of tape recording, which involves not cutting but pressing a master copy. 'He has just cut his first disc' is a phrase generally confined to the pop music industry, the artist more likely being a footballer, boxer, actor or other non-musical entertainer (for today almost everyone can appear as a 'singer' or 'songwriter') and the first disc so cut is likely also to be his last. In a television studio the cry 'Cut!' tells camera crews and others to stop what they are doing. Musicians, on the other hand, may think they are being instructed to 'make a cut', i.e. omit a specified passage in the music. *These* cuts are shown in the PARTS in various ways: usually in soft black pencil (*never* in coloured pencil, ballpoint pen or ink), but best of all by means of blank paper that is cut to the exact shape of the cut and pinned or lightly spot-glued over the passage to be omitted. Wind players who carry CIGARETTE PAPERS as part of their repair equipment sometimes paste a single sheet by its gummed edge to the first and last bars to be cut, and make the required marks on the tissue, not the music. Such beginnings and ends of cuts are often indicated by the word VIDE (Latin for 'Look!') divided so that the first syllable marks the beginning of the omission and the second the point of restart: VI–DE. Careful players may pencil a WARNING SIGN just before a cut, so as not to be taken unawares.

Cycle

A series of concerts devoted to, or containing a sequence of works of, one particular composer, the word translated from the Greek-based German word *Zyklus* being used for the same purpose. The introduction of Wagner Cycles into English musical life coincided with that of the safety bicycle or cycle. Musical cycles are now generally called 'Series' (Beethoven Series, Mahler Series, etc.) except for Wagner's RING, which sticks to the old tradition and remains a Ring Cycle.

Punch, 1898

In the Movement

Athleta: *"I want to see one of those Wagner Cycles people are talking about, and, if I like it, I'll subscribe."*

Daddy Rice

The father of the Black-and-White minstrel movement (1808–60), real name Thomas Dartmouth Rice. He was the first man to 'black up' and do comic negro impersonations on stage, and was famous for the 'Jim Crow' song-and-dance routine which (in spite of an earlier, eighteenth-century, American saying, 'to jump Jim Crow') gave its name to American laws and customs discriminating against negroes. Rice did not confine his satire to blacks: for example, one of his other sketches burlesqued Sarah Bernhardt, as 'Sarah Heartburn'; and he also turned negro spirituals into miniature 'Ethiopian Operas'. See also FATHERS IN MUSIC, FATHER SMITH and other alleged 'fathers' of musical movements.

Danger money

See OBBLIGATO, SITTING UP

Depping

Professional jargon for deputizing. The deputy system was one of the great bugbears of London concert life until Sir Henry Wood (1869–1944) made determined, if not entirely successful, attempts to abolish it. Under the system no conductor could be sure that a key player who attended a rehearsal would also be playing at a concert – and vice versa. But pernicious as it was, it made British orchestral players into the world's best SIGHT-READERS. There is an old story about a trombonist who obtained a more lucrative engagement than the opera performance for which he had been contracted, but was unable to find a deputy. In desperation he took his spare trombone to the stage-door pub and asked one of the drinkers if he wanted to earn a couple of pounds by sitting in the pit. 'Just hold it up, like this – don't blow, but simply look at the fellow next-door to you and move the slide in and out exactly as he does.' The customer took the money and the trombone, sat in the pit and squinted across at his neighbour – who was just as anxiously eyeing him in the same way.

De Sabotage

Nickname for the conductor Victor de Sabata (1892–1967), a man with a fine ear, a prodigious temper, and reputedly a wooden leg. On one occasion he is said to have combined the last two attributes at rehearsal (presumably because his first had been offended) with spectacular results, by hitting a player over the head with his leg.

Desk

The music-stand, but more specifically, in orchestral parlance, a music-stand shared by two string players. 'Six desks of FIRSTS'

Sharing a desk

means twelve players in the first violins, 'three-and-a-half desks of violas', seven players. Wind, brass and percussion players come individually, not in desks, and they hate sharing one.

Diabelli

For an explanation of what musicians mean when they say 'the Diabelli', see below.

Diabolus

Beethoven's nickname for the publisher and composer Anton Diabelli (1781–1858), best known for the two sets of Diabelli Variations he instigated and for which he provided the theme. One set was a big and now seldom heard collection to which almost all his contemporaries (including Schubert, F. X. Mozart, Czerny and the eleven-year-old Liszt) contributed one variation each. The other and more famous one is Beethoven's op. 120, for Beethoven brushed the others aside and, four years later, produced an entire set of his own, as if to show them what *could* be done with a simple SCHUSTERFLECK.

Dickey

A false shirt-front, from cockney rhyming-slang, dickey dirt/shirt. The dickey went out with the advent of non-iron, drip-dry fabrics, which also put paid to the starched shirt and wing-collar (Germans incidentally, call it *Vatermörder*, or 'patricide', which has led to some interesting musical mistranslations). The advantage of the dickey was that it could be tied on over one's day-shirt, causing the occasional bright red check to peep from under the evening dress, and could be cleaned with an india-rubber eraser. One player wore the same dickey for over two years' regular work, using its reverse side for collecting conductors' autographs. There was also the 'Calendar' type, made in Germany, a kind of pad of dickeys glued together at the edges from which soiled ones could be peeled to reveal a clean one underneath. Its bulk, when new, provided excessive stiffness, and cymbal players might find the whole thing popping out at right angles if they raised their arms too high. During and after the 1939–45 war players as well as conductors were sometimes obliged to use paper collars. These brought the risk of button-holes tearing out through a combination of paper-fatigue and sweat.

The Dickie Birds

Nickname for the Glyndebourne Opera Chorus, from the name of Brian Dickie, General Administrator at Glyndebourne from 1981, when he succeeded Moran Caplat.

Dies Irae

'The Day of Wrath': a plainsong tune dating from the thirteenth century or thereabouts which is often quoted in compositions when aweful things are hinted at: in Berlioz's *Symphonie fantastique*, Saint-Saëns's *Danse Macabre*, Liszt's TOTENTANZ and, facetiously, in the 'Obsessions' movement of one of the unaccompanied violin sonatas by Eugene Ysaÿe (1858–1931) dedicated to Jacques Thibaut (1880–1953), who had an obsession with the two works quoted: Bach's E major *Praeludium* and, evidently, the *Dies Irae*. The tune, consisting of long notes, is well suited to being hedged about by all manner of counterpoint (something it shares with MOZART's MOTTO THEME) and may not be immediately noticed by all listeners. 'He quotes the Dies Irae, you know' is always a good observation to make when one wants to impress one's friends.

Digitorium

A nineteenth-century invention designed to strengthen a pianist's fingers.

Discontinuous recording

A recording session at which a piece of music is put on tape in small sections, which are then edited together. The MU discourages the practice, for it may speed up the proceedings and lose the musicians money.

The Dissonance

Mozart's String Quartet in C major, K465, almost universally known by this nickname because of its remarkably 'modern' introduction which, for a bar or two, leaves the innocent ear in doubt as to which century the work belongs to. But, as Haydn does in the 'Representation of Chaos' (*The Creation*), Mozart shows that great composers can make perfect sense of the fiercest dissonances.

Il Distratto

Nickname for Haydn's No. 60 in C major. It is really a kind of suite, and the name belongs to a play, 'The Absentminded Man'. Just before the finale Haydn permits himself a HOFFNUNG-type joke, instructing the violins to de-tune their instruments to a comic SCORDATURA so that the G-STRING becomes an F-string. Then, after the start of the last movement, they screw their pegs back to G, audibly and with much comic effect, while the rest of the orchestra continues regardless. A few years ago a young music-critic who had omitted to do his homework (or to buy a programme) declared in his CRIT that there had been 'some red faces in the violins owing to suspect intonation'.

Divisi

When composers write string DOUBLE-STOPPING they usually do so for good reasons. They not only want each player to make more sound by playing (simultaneously but on different strings) two or more notes with a single bow stroke, but also to change the quality of the corporate sound by the characteristic 'crunching' tone of double-stopping. Unfortunately this can also make for poor intonation and other problems. Players, LEADERS or conductors sometimes therefore countermand the composer's instructions and play them *divisi*, i.e. divided up among two or more players. It is at such moments that the cry 'Divisi!' is heard at rehearsal. The division has then to be arranged and agreed upon, for it can be either by DESK or by player. Composers occasionally write impossible double-stoppings, either through ignorance or forgetfulness. There is a single example of Mozart's writing a passage with two notes to be played simultaneously on one string, which is, of course, an impossibility: perhaps a copying slip or, more likely, a private joke.

Dodecacophony

Nickname for dodecaphonic, or TWELVE-NOTE MUSIC.

Doghouse

Nickname for the double bass. See also BASS, BASS VIOL, BULL FIDDLE, BUM BASS, GRANDMOTHER FIDDLE.

Dog Waltz

Chopin's Waltz op. 64 No. 1 in D flat is supposed to have been inspired by George Sand's dog running round in circles, trying to catch its tail, as dogs will. But Vladimir de Pachmann (1848–1933), the KEYBOARD LION, who at his recitals would play music and tell jokes simultaneously, maintained that it was a different Chopin waltz – or perhaps a different dog? For other clever or cherished pets, see BIMPERL, CATS'S FUGUE, CAT WALTZ, MINA.

Doing a Wigmore

This was until recently the accepted passing-out test of every young soloist. Towards the end of their last year at COLLEGE singers, pianists or string players would say 'XYZ [i.e. my professor] is putting me down for a Wigmore.' The Wigmore Hall in London was for many decades the proper place for a young artist to be noticed; and critics recognized that their attendance at such debuts was considered important. Today the position has changed. Young performers are more likely to advance their career by winning one of the many prizes, sponsorships or competitions. There is such a profusion of good young performers that the Wigmore Hall has been joined by half a dozen other venues, and the chance of a visit (and quotable CRIT) from an important critic is much smaller.

Domino

In orchestral slang to *make a domino* means to play a note or passage on one's own during a silent moment, or else make an obvious false entry. Sir Charles Santley (1834–1922) in his book *Student and Singer* (1892) reveals that in the nineteenth century the word was used by singers as well as instrumentalists: 'I did not notice the bar's rest before the Amen, and performed a solo, which called forth some witty remark from [the conductor Sir Julius] Benedict about the future career of the singer who made the "domino".' Mere wrong notes are not counted as dominoes. In the game of

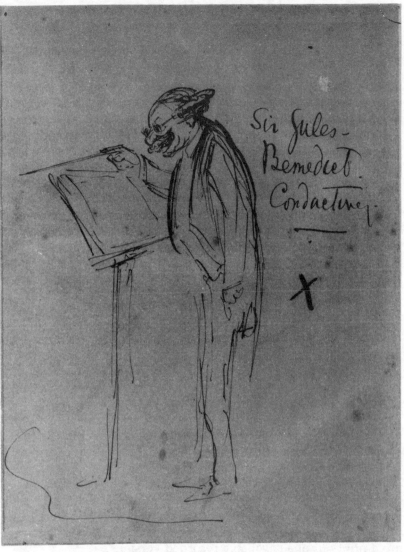

Sir Julius Benedict (1804–85)

dominoes 'making the domino' means to finish first, which may give a clue to the implication of orchestral impatience. A place in the score where dominoes are likely to be made, e.g. a series of isolated chords coming at irregular or tricky intervals (as in Tchaikovsky's *Romeo and Juliet* overture, to name but one) is known as 'Domino Corner'.

Domino thumper

Nineteenth-century slang term for a pianist, common in theatres and music hall (Barrère and Leland's *Dictionary of Slang*, 1889).

Liszt thumping the keyboard in 1886 (from La Vie Parisienne)

The Don

The accepted abbreviation for Mozart's opera *Don Giovanni*, as in 'We're doing the Don at the GARDEN.' Computer programming has produced another name for the same work: *Mozdong*, being the key-word which in at least one computerized catalogue calls up a print-out of all available recorded versions.

Donald Izett

There was once a tradition that Gaetano Donizetti (1797–1848) was of Scottish descent, and that an ancestor by the name of Donald Izett had Italianized his name to Donizetti. See also SOUSA for another fanciful theory.

Donkey music

The derisive nickname for a certain kind of CONTEMPORARY music in which instruments and the human voice alike are expected to perform huge leaps that may span several octaves. These are always chromatic to boot, with their own special cliché-feature, e.g. a topmost squealed A flat is sure to be followed by a growled bottom A natural, or vice versa. It poses no problem for instrumentalists, but the human voice is not designed to do that sort of thing except as an expression of extreme pain or anguish, or in pitchless *sprechgesang*. So when singers perform such leaps the comparison with braying asses is not unapt. But players hate it, too. An early protest came to be remembered as the famous Whitehead Walkout. The noted English (now Australian) cellist James Whitehead in March 1938 made history when, during the first London performance of Webern's (comparatively harmless) String Trio, op. 20, he walked off stage, exclaiming, 'I can't play this thing. It's a nightmare. Not music at all, but mathematics.' (In which he was echoing what Anton Schindler said about Beethoven's op. 133 – see COMPOSING BY NUMBERS.) It was gravely predicted at the time that Whitehead would suffer a fate similar to that of Count Arco, who is now remembered only as the man who kicked Mozart's backside, but Whitehead found considerable renown as a soloist, teacher and conductor in Adelaide, Australia.

The Dots

The printed music. At first only in popular music use but now heard also in CLASSICAL use. Also FLYSHIT for particularly black and fast dots.

Double

Pronounced to rhyme with rouble: the TRIO (i.e. the B element in an ABA form) of certain eighteenth-century compositions. Doubles are often florid variations of the A section, the most notable example being that of the Polonaise in Bach's B minor Suite (BWV 1067).

Double

Verb, pronounced to rhyme with 'bubble'. To play another instrument, usually one in the same instrumental group, i.e. flute, BASS

FLUTE and piccolo; oboe, COR and HECKELPHONE; clarinet, bass clarinet and saxophone, etc. There is usually a doubling-fee laid down by the MU.

Double-handed

Players able to play two instruments: a term mostly used in military bands, whose members are expected, first, to master a wind or brass instrument for use 'on the march' and also a string instrument for indoor entertainment (regardless of any aptitude they may or may not have for it). Clarinettists are generally issued with violins or violas, trombonists with cellos and the lower brass with double-basses. When Queen Elizabeth II gives receptions or dinner parties, and sometimes when she dines with members of her family, a string orchestra from a Guards band plays SELECTIONS in an adjoining room. The Queen thus heeds the MU slogan 'Keep Music Live'. See also AMBULATORY MUSIC.

Double Paradiddle

See PARADIDDLE

Double parts

When orchestral parts are prepared (see SCORE AND PARTS), the copyist may try to save time and paper by putting two parts together – thereby making a kind of subsidiary score. That means players have to read the music from the same stand: something the strings are used to but wind and brass dislike. They get in each other's way and may even drip WATER in each other's lap.

Double-stopping

On string instruments, an effect by which a player with a single bow-stroke simultaneously plays two notes (or more, in which case it should strictly be called multiple-stopping), at least one of the notes usually produced by an open string. The result may *sound* difficult even if it is not (see DIVISI), and one good player often manages to sound like two indifferent ones.

Double-tongueing

See TONGUEING

Dovetailing

Refers to passages divided up between instruments or instrumental sections that alternate, interchange and possibly overlap with each other. They should fit as perfectly as a joint fashioned by a skilled cabinet-maker.

Downbeat

The first and nominally strongest beat in the bar, at which point a conductor's beat (see STICK TECHNIQUE) should move in a downward direction to its lowest point. But in popular, non-musical cliché use it means the opposite, i.e. anything quiet, sombre, reticent or unemphatic. Also, informally, as in 'When's downbeat', the beginning of a performance, or KICK-OFF.

Drag Paradiddle

See PARADIDDLE

The Dream

Depending when heard, this is the abbreviated title of either Elgar's *The Dream of Gerontius* or Britten's opera *A Midsummer Night's Dream*. But it is also the official, though little-used, nickname of Haydn's Quartet no. 40 in F major (in German *Ein Traum*, with the indefinite article and a slightly different connotation).

Dresden Amen

A certain kind of chord progression thought to have been first used by J. G. Naumann (1741–1801) in a composition for the Royal Chapel at Dresden, and since then taught to all students of harmony. It is also known as the Threefold Amen, for naturally its use was not restricted to Dresden. Sir John Stainer, the composer of the famous CRUCIFIXION, composed for St Paul's Cathedral a Sevenfold Amen – an extension of the Dresden – one which is often heard at the close of Church of England services. It also occurs notably and repeatedly in Wagner's *Parsifal*.

Dressing-up allowance

See BANDA

Drum bass

See TROMMELBASS

The Drum Roll

Haydn's No. 103 in E flat, because it starts with a solo roll on the kettle drum. See also THE SURPRISE.

Durchkomponiert

There is no real English equivalent of this German jargon word, apart from the clumsy 'through-composed' – and if you have to resort to words like that you may as well stick to the foreign one. A LIED is *durchkomponiert* when it has a continuous musical strand that fits the words as they develop the story of the song, not a strophic song, which has each verse repeated to more or less the same music. An opera is *durchkomponiert* when all the dialogue is composed, not spoken or set to secco RECITS.

Dynamics

The written or printed indications (or their observance) of how loud or soft music should be – in various gradations between *pianissimo* and *fortissimo*, with other possible variations.

Early music

See CLASSICAL, etc.

ECO

The English Chamber Orchestra took this name in 1960 having previously been the Goldsbrough Orchestra, founded by Arnold Goldsbrough (1892–1964) and Lawrence Leonard (b. 1925).

E flat

The note between D and E natural. But in musical jargon a jocular term for anything that is smaller than expected. A man served a very small portion of meat might dismiss it as 'an E flat steak'; and conductors of shortish stature have been described as 'E flat conductors'. The joke comes from the small, high-pitched E flat clarinet.

Egg timer

Name sometimes given to a piece of music lasting about three and a half to four minutes; from the legend that a certain conductor who could not cook anything except a boiled egg, was able to accomplish that feat only because he timed it by singing Mozart's *Figaro* Overture. If he conducted it at the speed Mozart intended (and marked), his egg would be hard-boiled.

Egk

The real name of this composer (1901–83), who was commissioned to write a work for the notorious 1936 Nazi Olympics (and got a medal for it from Hitler), was the very common German one of Mayer. The story goes that he chose 'Egk' because of the implied acronym it enshrines, 'Ein guter Komponist' (A Good Composer). There is also a Swedish composer, genuinely named Ek (b. 1900) who sounds an altogether more modest sort of man.

Eine kleine

Abbreviated title of Mozart's Serenade in G major, K525, named
by the composer himself *Eine kleine Nachtmusik*, 'A Little Night
Music'. *Eine kleine* therefore simply means 'a little . . .' and
German-speaking musicians who hear their British colleagues call
it that always wonder why they stop short in mid-sentence. It has
been adapted in various jocular ways, from *Eine kleine Beatlemusik*
to Peter Schickele's *Eine kleine Nichtmusik* and Sondheim's *A Little
Night Music*. Take care to pronounce *Nacht* with a *ch* sound as in
the Scottish *loch*, not 'Nacktmusik', otherwise it seriously affects
its meaning ('A Little Nude Music'). Mozart wrote at least one
other *Nachtmusik* (and even a *Nacht Musique*, K388) and Schubert
in 1813 *Eine kleine Trauermusik* (D79) for wind band – 'A Little
Mourning Music', but not a sad piece: it was intended to express
his mock-grief on leaving school.

Eingang

The German word is always used in musical shop-talk, although
it simply means 'entrance' (and can be seen opposite the *Ausgang*
in many public places where German is spoken). But more than
that is implied in music, where it means a small cadenza, a kind of
lead-in that heralds a solo: in Mozart piano concertos, for example,
where the soloist enters; or in a rondo at each return of the main
theme. In some respects an *Eingang* is therefore the opposite of a
fermata, which is a decorated closing-passage. Johann Strauss and
his family developed another kind of *Eingang*: a brief point of rest
consisting of two (or four) bars without any OOM-CHA-CHA or
VIENNESE LIFT and which heralds a new (or re-stated) waltz strain.
The function of this was to give the dancers a little time to gain
or regain their balance and poise themselves for the next waltz,
possibly changing the direction of rotation. *Eingänge* are usually
on a chord of the dominant seventh, the chord of expectancy, for
which see an elementary harmony primer.

Einstein

'Einstein says. . . .' The name is heard whenever people discuss
Mozart or the Italian Madrigal, but mostly when discussing some
finer points of chronology or authenticity in the KOECHEL Mozart
catalogue he revised. He was the great musicologist Alfred

(1880–1952), not his cousin, the great scientist and mathematician Albert, with whom he is often confused and who is sometimes credited with having been a kind of high-powered musical moonlighter ('Name a great physicist who also wrote important works on Mozart and Italian Madrigals . . .' was a question asked on a well-known BBC television quiz). But music must have run in the Einstein family. Albert, the mathematical genius, was also a keen amateur violinist. A much told but probably apocryphal anecdote tells how he was playing chamber music with Heifetz/ Hubermann/ Rubinstein (take your pick) but kept losing his place. 'The trouble with you, Albert,' said Rubinstein, Hubermann or Heifetz, 'you can't *count!*' There is, however, a reliable, first-hand report that Beethoven was unable to keep time while dancing (even before he became deaf). So much for Wagner's APOTHEOSIS OF THE DANCE.

Electric chair music

Nickname given to Richard Strauss's opera *Elektra* (1909) when it was first played. Orchestral players and audience complained it was like 'torture by the electric chair'.

Richard Strauss executing his players in the 'Elektra' chair. Drawing by F. Juettner, 1909

Electric piano

A modern contradiction in terms. See also MOOG.

'The' Elijah

As with THE MESSIAH, music lovers in the North and the Midlands of England prefer to give the prophet a superfluous definite article when referring to Mendelssohn's oratorio.

Music in the Midlands

Intelligent Youth of Country Town: *"Ah say, Bill, 'ull that be t' Elijah goin' oop i' that Big Box?!"*

Elvira Madigan Concerto

A spurious nickname for Mozart's Piano Concerto in C major, K467. The name began to be seen on concert programmes and record sleeves after the appearance of a film called *Elvira Madigan*, whose producer took a fancy to about eight bars of the slow movement of K467, and faded them in and out of the background during the action of the film for no apparent reason. It did not do much for the film but certainly popularized the record – and opened ears to Mozart that might otherwise have remained closed.

Embouchure

From the French *emboucher*, to put in, or to, the mouth; also to discharge by the mouth, as of a river that flows into another or the sea. To the wind player, however, it means either that part of the instrument he puts in, or to, the mouth; or the disposition of his lips producing the sound. But if a man complains he has 'lost his embouchure' it is no use offering to help him find it: all he means is that his lips are tired, or rather 'lip is tired': a curious and false singular convention, for all wind and brass instruments require a pair of lips.

The Emperor

In English-speaking countries Beethoven's fifth Piano Concerto in E flat, op. 73, has always been nicknamed 'The Emperor', probably first by J. B. Cramer (1771–1858). Cramer, himself nicknamed GLORIOUS JOHN, was a good publicist and popularizer of music. But when string quartet players speak of 'The Emperor' they mean Haydn's op. 76 No. 3, whose slow movement is a set of variations on Haydn's Emperor hymn, *Gott erhalte Franz den Kaiser*, later appropriated for the odious *Deutschland über Alles*.

Encore

French for yet, still, again, longer, and many other shades of meaning in colloquial speech. But the one thing it appears not to mean is 'please play it again', or 'please play some more'. For when the French ask for an *encore* they call either BIS! or RÉPÉTEZ! A similar confusion exists in Italian, where the word *ancora* is all but ignored in favour of either *da capo!* or, as in French, *bis!* The English noun *encore* is the piece chosen by the performer(s) as an additional offering. Encore pieces are usually showy and ostentatiously difficult, so as to MILK THE APPLAUSE and increase the number of CURTAIN CALLS. Orchestral players hate them, and mutterings like 'Haven't they got homes to go to?' are soon heard. Notice also, when encores are played, the contrast between the triumphant and grateful smiles on the face of conductor or soloist and the patiently bored looks of the orchestra. Conductors have sometimes to be reminded not to be too generous with their encores or they may run into overtime payments. Albert Coates (1882–1953) once conducted the RLPO in a concert at the Pier Pavilion, Llandudno, with his wife, a singer, as soloist, giving encore after encore. In the end the LEADER told him that if he gave any more he might have to bear the cost of overtime. Coates complied, but was in such a bad temper for the rest of the concert that he deliberately set out to ruin a performance of Beethoven's fifth symphony. 'All right,' he seemed to say, 'if you want to get home we'll see how fast you can play the thing' – and took the work at a tempo so idiotically fast that had the players struggling to keep up with him, and the audience looking at each other in disbelief or walking out. The conductor did not even give the players time to turn the pages between movements, taking each one SEGUE. It was his last appearance with the orchestra. Coates, incidentally, also disgraced himself in the eyes of Elgar in 1919, when he directed a concert in the Queen's Hall at which Elgar was to conduct the first performance of his Cello Concerto. Coates, self-centred and totally oblivious to the importance of the occasion, continued rehearsing other works for an hour after the appointed time at which Elgar should have taken the baton. The resulting performance was a disaster. Needless to say, the orchestra got the blame ('it made a lamentable public exhibition of itself,' wrote Ernest Newman). But the real culprit was 'that brutal, selfish, ill-mannered bounder Coates,' as Lady Elgar noted in her diary.

Encouraging the brass

Traditionally an unwise thing to do; and the old advice to young conductors, 'Never look at the brass – they will play too loudly even if you *don't'* – comes from a famous saying by Richard Strauss.

Engelbert Humperdinck

German composer who wrote children's operas with Wagnerian music but happily un-Wagnerian words, including the much-loved *Hänsel und Gretel*. Humperdinck (1854–1921) lived long enough to be counted a twentieth-century composer, but was fortunate not to be alive when an English pop entertainer appropriated his name.

'England, home and beauty'

The cliché comes from a once well-known song, *The Death of Nelson*, by John Braham and Matthew King, from their opera *The Americans* (1811). The song was one of the greatest hits of the century, much performed and frequently reprinted.

English horn

This is neither English nor remotely shaped like a horn, but the name for the alto oboe, or COR, pitched a fifth lower than the oboe. It could have come about through a misunderstanding of 'cor anglé', i.e. an angled horn, for, like the BASSET HORN, older cors were often angled so as to bring the lower holes and keys nearer to the player's body. That still does not make it into a horn. But there may be something in *cor anglais*, i.e. 'English horn'. The FRENCH HORN was developed in that country but took longer to reach Britain as it had to travel via Bohemia. Thus French wind bands would entrust the *taille* or middle (i.e. filling-in) parts to the horn, whereas other countries, including England, stuck with the reed instruments of the oboe/bassoon family: alto oboes or TENOROONS. It could therefore have come about that the French described the alto oboe as the English 'horn', i.e. 'the instruments the old-fashioned English still use in place of a horn'. That is my theory and I am sticking to it.

Cor anglé

The Enigma

Customary abbreviation for the *Variations on an Original Theme*, op. 36, by Sir Edward Elgar. But he was not the first to write Enigma Variations. Cipriani Potter (1792–1871), a member of the family of English flute-makers, friend of Beethoven and principal of the RAM from 1832, anticipated him by more than 60 years. His are for piano and belong to the in-the-style-of genre: i.e. they imitate composers of his day, including Beethoven and Rossini. The theme is unidentified, merely described as 'A Favourite Irish Air'; and the 'enigma' is presumably that the listener has to guess the models. Potter's 'Enigma' was composed some years after he

The ENIGMA,

Variations and Fantasia,

ON A

Favorite Irish Air.

for the Piano Forte in the Style of Five

EMINENT ARTISTS,

Composed and Dedicated to the

Originals,

BY

CIPRIANI POTTER.

Ent.Sta.Hall. ———— Nº 8. OF AIRS ———— Price 4/-

LONDON,

T. Boosey & Cº 28. Holles Street Oxford Street.

Vienna. Mechetti & Cº

visited Beethoven in Vienna, and published there and in London simultaneously. (In spite of Potter's Italian forename he was of English descent, but the fact that he was nicknamed 'Little Chip'

– he was very short – reveals that he pronounced his name in the Italian way, not the anglicized 'sip-ree-arnie'). It is possible that Elgar came across a copy of Potter's variations and so got the idea for both his title and dedication 'To my friends pictured within', for Potter's 'Enigma', too, is dedicated to the 'Eminent Artists' whose styles he portrays. Elgar provides fewer clues than Potter. The most popular speculation is that Elgar's Theme is a counter-subject to an unstated, unheard tune that 'goes' with it. *Auld lang Syne* and others have been suggested. Such musical games preoccupied the composer, who in an amusing letter to the *Musical Times* (1897) shows that the 5/4 movement from TCHAIK 6 'fits' *God Save the Queen*.

Ensemble

French for 'together'. In musical talk it can refer either to a group of players or the way they play together – or fail to do so. As a conductor complained, 'Gentlemen, the ensemble is not together.'

Entr'acte

See CURTAIN ARIA

Escaping gas

Extraneous sounds made by indifferent flute players and caused by a faulty EMBOUCHURE, i.e. the inability to direct the air-stream neatly across the mouth-hole of the instrument.

Esrum-Hellerup

The new GROVE, that excellent and indispensable musical reference work, suffered a cruel hoax and now contains one spoof entry – the 'Danish composer Dag Hendrik Esrum-Hellerup (1803–91)' complete with a list of his supposed works, accomplishments and a bibliography. There were, of course, immediate requests from American musicologists for further information about this inter-esting musician. See also ZAK.

Punch, 1870

"Wind!"

Brown having unguardedly Confessed to being Musical, his friend Wiffles offers to come and bring Three other Fellows, and Play some beautiful Flute Quartets in his Rooms. Poor Brown says he never Sat for Hours in such a thorough Draught in his Life!

Esterházy/Eszterházy/Esterháza

To clear up a common confusion: the name of the noble Hungarian family, patrons of Haydn and Schubert, is *Esterházy*. The place they came from is *Eszterháza*, sometimes written *Esterház*, meaning 'the House of Esther'. Thus the family name really means something like 'the people from a place called *Esterháza*', just as people from London are called Londoners. The acute accent on some of the a's is obligatory, and is not a stress sign but makes the a sounds into an 'aahh' as in 'charm'; accent-free a's in Hungarian are pronounced 'o', as in 'bottom'. And the stress is on the first syllable, which goes for every other word in that beautiful language.

Eugene One Gin

Nickname for Tchaikovsky's opera *Eugene Onegin* (1831).

Eunuch flute

An ancient instrument consisting of a tube fitted near the top with a vibrating membrane (of a pig's bladder or similar) which distorts the human voice when the 'player' hums into it. It was known to (and illustrated by) Mersenne (1636) and described by Francis Bacon (1561–1626): 'if you sing into the hole of a drum it maketh the singing more sweet'. Eunuch flutes were held like end-blown (i.e. recorder-like) flutes, and fitted with mock finger-holes that were, as such, totally useless – hence the 'eunuch' element in the name. Comb and tissue-paper gives the same effect; and eunuch flutes are still sold as toys called *kazoos*. During the depression in England in the 1920s and 1930s there were kazoo bands, also known as *foo foo bands*, since the instruments cost only a penny or two, and they sometimes also figured in early jazz bands. The French called them *bigophones* or *mirlitons* (which is what Tchaikovsky had in mind in his *Nutcracker* ballet); and in England the name *Tommy Talker* was used by nineteenth- and early twentieth-century BUSKERS. Méhul asks for three *mirlitons* in his *Grande Ouverture burlesque*.

Experimental music

CONTEMPORARY music in which the composer makes experiments at the expense of his audience, and is probably as much in the dark as they are. If cooks, chemists or carpenters experimented thus on those who pay for their services they would be told to go home and continue with their researches until one of them proved successful. See also WORKSHOP.

Extras

Extra, i.e. freelance, players engaged specially to augment an orchestra, either to satisfy specialized demands, e.g. for a HECK-ELPHONE or other instruments not on the normal strength, or to augment or BUMP UP existing sections. The engagement of extras is the job of the ORCHESTRA MANAGER and is done in consultation with the often conflicting advice of an orchestra's treasurer and its conductor: conductors, like generals, like to have big forces under their command, but treasurers must balance their books. Many extras are engaged needlessly. CUES may be played; or a composer's demands (in scores dating from days when labour was cheap) may simply be ignored without loss of effect. Thus, for example, in Berlioz's Hungarian March from *The Damnation of Faust* the extra trumpets called for are nowadays seldom engaged or missed. And in many scores that are in effect extracts from operas or ballets, an instrument listed at the head of the score may not be required at all, e.g. in the score of RIMSKY's *The Flight of the Bumblebee*, where a COR plays a single note in the opening chord but takes no further part in the proceedings, the opening chord being really the final one of the preceding number in the opera. Extras have been known to be engaged for such scores by orchestra managers who stick to the letter of the score or of a conductor's demands. To be booked at full MU rates, plus fares, subsistence and PORTERAGE as applicable, to dress in complete PENGUIN SUIT, merely to play a single, inaudible note, then to collect one's money and go home, is one of the great triumphs of the professional freelance.

'Eyes front!'

See PLATFORM ETIQUETTE

Fag, Faggot

Facetious abbreviation of *fagotto*, Italian for bassoon, which literally means 'a bundle of sticks' and is therefore related to the English faggots of the firelighting kind. But the 'faggot' nickname is based on the German word for the instrument, which is *Fagott*. You will not, however, hear the abbreviation *fag* in the orchestras of America, where a 'fag' is a homosexual.

The Fairy Queen

A masque-opera by Henry Purcell (1659–95) produced in London in 1692. Also Sir John Pritchard's own nickname for the special arrangement of *God Save the Queen* he made for use by the RLPO in the 1950s and 1960s. See also QUEEN IN G.

The Fairy's Kiss

Stravinsky's ballet *Le Baiser de la fée*, based on music by Tchaikovsky, is dedicated to Tchaikovsky, the biggest fairy of them all. See SUGAR PLUM FAIRY.

False relations

When Americans speak of CROSS RELATIONS or Britons of false relations they do not refer to angry uncles or fickle aunts but to a harmonic manifestation by which a note of the same name appears in different parts of the same chord or in close moving parts but modified by a sharp, flat or natural that contradicts its use in another part. If that sounds complicated, consult an elementary harmony primer. Like so many rules of harmony, this one is often broken to good effect by the greatest composers. Purcell in the seventeenth century was especially fond of his false relations – and those who edited his music in the eighteenth and nineteenth centuries often 'corrected' them.

The Farewell

German, *Abschiedssinfonie, -symphonie*. The authentic nickname for Haydn's No. 45 in F sharp minor. The significance of the title is well known from the – equally authentic – anecdote about Haydn's gesture to Prince ESTERHÁZY, which was an early form of musical 'industrial action', and a hint that his players wanted a holiday. But it may have been a Carnival joke, for there is a *Divertissement for the Carnival* by Joseph Eybler (1765–1846) which also ends with a progressive walk-out, leaving two solitary violins, who are instructed to extinguish their candles and walk off, taking their instruments with them. Could this not be a carnival allusion to the Easter office of *Tenebrae*, with its progressive extinguishing of lights?

Farewell recitals

When pianists reach the end of their career they can continue giving solo recitals but may abandon more strenuous concerto appearances, which is what Arthur Rubinstein did, to name only one. Conductors can confine their work to the recording studio, as did Sir Adrian Boult. Stravinsky continued to 'conduct' his own music at recording sessions when he was barely able to mount the rostrum, let alone wave his arms about: and these recordings were chiefly the work of Robert Craft. Famous singers give their public plenty of notice of impending retirement by announcing it in stages : first from opera and then, perhaps a year or two later, from the concert platform. After that comes the lecture recital circuit, and possibly MASTER CLASSES, both giving scope for the telling of many anecdotes interspersed with a few songs. Today's final appearances are broadcast and televised to millions as well as recorded for posterity on gramophone records. But in the past such valedictions took longer. For example, the celebrated nineteenth-century tenor Sims Reeves (1818–1900) spent the last eleven years of his life giving farewell recitals all over the country – and on at least one occasion, owing to indisposition (see STAGE DUST ALLERGY), he got someone else to sing his farewells for him. The tenor John McCormack (1884–1945), in an article headed 'Why I Shall Retire at Fifty', published in 1925, when he was 41, wrote: 'Nine years from now I shall retire from the concert platform, and no power on earth will bring me back except the cause of charity.' His farewell tour took place thirteen years later, culminating at the

Punch, 1870

Brown (enthusiastically): *"Oh—what a remarkably* finished *singer Madame Scriciaulo is!"*
Miss Knipper: *"Yes*, quite *finished, I'm afraid!"*

Royal Albert Hall on 27 November 1938; and he was still merrily broadcasting during the war, as well as singing in charity concerts for the Red Cross.

Fartophone

Orchestral players' derisive nickname for anything thought to make a noise appropriate to the first element in the word, whether such a noise is produced intentionally or not. But see also LE PÉTOMANE for a once celebrated musician who gained fame from making such noises on purpose, and without an instrument.

Fathers in music

Fathers abound in music, though it is generally not known who invents these facile oversimplifications. The title 'The Father of the Symphony' is traditionally applied to Joseph ('Papa') Haydn, and there is, of course, some truth in it; but the term was probably coined at a time when less was known of Haydn's symphonic precursors. J. H. Roman (1694–1758) has been called 'The Father of Swedish Music'; and Giovanni Gabrieli (c. 1553–1612) 'The Father of Orchestration'. Clementi's tombstone in Westminster Abbey claims he was 'The Father of the Pianoforte'. See also THE BEETHOVEN OF THE FLUTE and its cross-references and DADDY RICE.

Father Smith

Neither a priest nor one of the 'fathers' above but Bernhard Schmidt (ca. 1630–1708), the senior member of the family of English organ-builders of German origin. He came to England in 1660 to help repair the damage many church organs had suffered under Cromwell and should really be 'Uncle Smith', for he worked not in collaboration with his sons, but his nephews. Some of his instruments survive more or less intact, and are magnificent; some only in much modified form, having suffered alteration at the hands of later builders.

Feminine endings

Also 'feminine cadence': a form of musical phrase-ending analogous with the feminine rhyme in poetry in which the rhyming word comes not on the last syllable but an earlier one. In music this means that the stressed part of a cadence occurs on a weak beat of the bar, usually the penultimate one, or even the penultimate bar. Many performances betray a misunderstanding of feminine cadences and give too much stress on the final beat or bar, simply because it happens to be the last one of a piece or movement. Nearly all waltzes by the WALTZ KING, for example, have feminine endings on the penultimate bar, as though they had been written not in three-four but six-eight time, ending '*pom*-pom-pom/pom', never 'pom-pom-pom/*pom*'. The word 'feminine' is also often applied to the second subject of a movement in sonata form, which is almost always of a gentler nature than the first. 'This is a hangover', says Michael Kennedy in the informative *Concise Oxford Dictionary of Music*, 'from the age when women were regarded as the weaker sex.'

Feuersnot

One-act opera by Richard Strauss (see RICHARD II), op. 50. It means something like 'fire-emergency', the two elements being *Feuer(s)* + *Not* – and not, as many English music critics and their typesetters seem to think, *Feuer* + *Snot*. The word should rhyme approximately with 'goat', not 'got'.

Fiasco

The Italian word for a bottle, or flask. But since the middle of the nineteenth century and probably earlier, a word in common use for a breakdown, failure or other noticeable disaster in a musical or theatrical performance. It has been adopted also by the French, and into German as *Fiasko* (as well as literally translated as *Flasche(n)* in German slang); and the Italians themselves use the word both for a flask and an artistic disaster. The origin is unknown. Could there perhaps be some connection between a fiasco and a colloquial 'washout'? When orchestral musicians have nothing better to do, or are collectively killing time, as on trains, coaches, planes or in airport lounges, they like to exchange reminiscences about memorable fiascoes. These usually begin with 'Do you remember the time . . .' (e.g. 'when Boult beat four instead of two in *Forest Murmurs* and the violas finished halfway through and so they all simply went back to the beginning and played their WOODLES all over again?') Such tales invariably acquire additional embellishments in the retelling.

Fiddle

Few violinists refer to their instruments as 'my violin' but, informally, 'my fiddle', even if it is the costliest, rarest STRAD. But see also BASS FIDDLE.

Fiddler on the hoof

This would do as a translation of the Austro-German word *Stehgeiger*, literally, 'stand-up-fiddler', i.e. a LEADER who doubles as conductor and directs an orchestra at the same time as playing the occasional passage on his fiddle. The most famous *Stehgeiger* were, of course, the Johann Strausses, father and son. But many an orchestra leader has recently copied Willy Boskovsky's

Fiddler on the Hoof. Strauss conducts from the violin. Silhouette by Otto Boehler

discovery that conducting is easier than playing the fiddle, especially when the tunes are as much in the players' repertoire (almost in their blood) as the Viennese music he specialized in. Fiddle-conductors stand up in front of an orchestra, play the bits that are hard to conduct and nominally wave their bow about when the hard-to-play passages come up. The original printed score of Strauss's Overture to *Die Fledermaus* contains a famous printed annotation in the first violin part: 'If there are no decent fiddles available this passage is to be played by a solo flute.' Sometimes *Stehgeiger* play from a SHORT SCORE, sometimes from a CUED violin part (or 'Violin Conductor') or even a PIANO CONDUCTOR. Musical history has shown that, for some reason, LEADERS do not often become conductors, which is strange as they know more about string technique than conductors. But some of them have naturally progressed from stand-up fiddling to full-time conducting.

Figured bass

(Italian *continuo*, German *Generalbass/Bezifferter Bass*) A kind of musical shorthand in which the bass line of (mostly) eighteenth-century music has certain figures that indicate the harmonies above it. A skilled keyboard player was (is) expected to turn this bass line into a two-handed keyboard accompaniment. The greater his skill the more complete and melodic will be the part he creates. In seventeenth- and eighteenth-century music the continuo line may be reinforced by single-line bass instruments such as the cello, bassoon, double bass or bass-lute, whether stipulated by the composer or not. In England the term *thorough-bass* was often preferred to the above. See also TRIO SONATA.

Fingering charts

Diagrammatic representations of wind instruments to show the student which holes would be opened or closed to play certain notes, or produce certain trills. They show the finger positions of each hand, sometimes reinforcing these with numbers given to each finger (although such numbers suffer from lack of standardization: No. 1 is sometimes the thumb and sometimes the first finger). Others give names to fingers, some of them quaint and curious – from 'Pointing Finger' for the index finger to 'Ear Finger' (old German *Ohrfinglein*) for the little finger (called 'Pinkie' in modern American or old English); and from 'Ring Finger' or 'Gold Finger' for the fourth to 'Lewd Finger' (*digitus lascivius*) for the middle finger. See also TABLATURE.

Fingering the parts

Players who are said to have 'fingered their PARTS' have written into them their own (or their teachers') best way of solving certain

117

technical problems – determining which finger is used for which note; for there is nearly always a choice, especially on the piano. Some of these fingerings are highly personal and may not suit others; though in the orchestral string sections fingering unanimity is important and insisted upon. Professional pianists who attend the recitals of their rivals try to sit on the KEYBOARD SIDE so as to observe their fingerings. The Liverpool pianist and teacher Gordon Green (d. 1981) told me about a KEYBOARD LION (whose name he did not at the time recall) who would never reveal the secret of the way he fingered the great leaps to top D sharp in Liszt's *La Campanella* – until his TUNER divulged it. Before any recital in which the piece figured, the pianist instructed him to re-tune the entire top octave of the instrument (notes not required for any of the other pieces he played) to D sharp so that whatever note he hit, it came out as the right note. See also THE BOWING OF PARTS.

The Fire Symphony

Haydn's No. 59 in A major.

First chair

See HOT SEAT, PRINCIPAL

First-time bar/Second-time bar

Space-saving devices used in the copying and printing of music. For example in CLASSICAL symphonies the exposition (which occupies about half of the first movement and presents most of the thematic material) is – or should be – always repeated. To save writing or printing the same material twice, standard repeat signs are used. But the second time round, at or near the turning-back point, the music usually changes direction as it enters the development section (which, as its name implies, 'develops' previously heard material), and this kind of musical 'road junction' is known as the second-time bar. The *first-time bar*, if there is one, leads to the repeat. The term may denote one, several, or a whole group of bars. In Mendelssohn's 'Italian', for example, the repeats are seldom made. When they are, and the first-time bar material is played, members of the audience may hear music they had never heard before. The same goes for some Beethoven symphonies. For a tale of an orchestral FIASCO by the Vienna

Philharmonic because of a mixed observance of first- and second-time bars, see YES/NO. Urgent cries of 'Yes!', 'No!' or 'Second-time bar!' giving last moment instructions to players, may be heard during rehearsal – or, in the event of a performance disaster, whispered through clenched teeth ON THE NIGHT.

Five and five. . .

. . . makes ten. The favourite gesture of many singers. Jules Massenet (1842–1912) wrote in his *Recollections*: 'We had a famous tenor of the time, Signor Fanselli. He had a superb voice but a mannerism of spreading out his arms wide open in front of him, with his fingers opened out. In spite of the fact that an obsessive fondness for this method of expression is almost inevitably displeasing, many other artists I have known employ it to express their feelings – or at least they think they do when, as a matter of fact, they feel absolutely nothing. His open hands won for this remarkable tenor the nickname *"Cinque e cinque fanno dieci!"* (Five and Five make Ten).'

The Five Frankfurters

As good a collective name as any for the Frankfurt School of English composers: five men who went to study in that city under the famous teacher Iwan Knorr (1853–1916). They were Cyril Scott (1879–1970), H. Balfour Gardiner (1877–1950), Roger Quilter (1877–1953), Norman O'Neill (1875–1934), and Percy Grainger (1882–1961). They were known as 'The Frankfurt Five', 'The Frankfurt Group' and 'The Frankfurt Gang'. Grainger's nickname among them was 'Perks'. He revealed that the one thing that united them was a unanimous hatred of Beethoven. Unlike him, (and Beethoven), the remaining four are still posthumously having to fight for the recognition they all felt they deserved. For other schools of composers, see under THE FIVE/LES CINQ, THE SECOND VIENNESE SCHOOL, THE MANCHESTER SCHOOL, LES SIX, and perhaps even the GIANT HAMBURGERS.

The Five/Les Cinq

The name was coined almost by accident by the Russian writer Stasov, who was closely associated with Balakirev, Borodin, Cui, Mussorgsky and Rimsky-Korsakov – 'The Five'. Writing in 1867, he called them *moguchaya kuchka*, 'the mighty handful', and the name stuck. In the West the French title *Les Cinq* is more often used than the English or Russian ones. Unlike LES SIX who were not very sociable in the way one would expect cronies or colleagues to be, the famous Five almost lived in each others' pockets, always collaborating on this or that piece, writing a movement each for a joint project, or orchestrating/completing some work one of the others had failed to finish through laziness, forgetfulness or death. Another thing they had in common was that they were all amateurs and (in a strictly non-English sort of way) gentlemen: not amateurish in their outlook or accomplishments, to be sure, but in the nineteenth-century sense of the word. They had no need to earn money from music, with the possible exception of Mussorgsky, who needed all the cash he could get his hands on to keep himself in a permanent alcoholic haze. Rimsky was a naval officer, and incidentally wrote part of his first symphony on board ship while stationed off Gravesend, Kent. Cui was really General Cui of the Imperial Russian Army, his *forte* being the ancient science of military fortifications. Borodin was a medical doctor as well as a professor of chemistry, and gained his doctorate for a dissertation on *The Analogy of Arsenical with Phosphoric Acid*. Balakirev studied mathematics at the University of Kazan, but managed all the same to become a pianist of great virtuosity as well as a prolific composer; and being small, fat and jolly, with a round face, button nose and white beard, could have doubled as a garden-gnome. Mussorgsky was probably the greatest genius of the Five, a military officer and almost a professional drunkard. His portrait, done by Repin in the year the composer died, shows him in the pitiful and final state of alcoholic and mental dissolution. Although all Five were strong Russian nationalists (and Mussorgsky was always ranting about alleged Jewish influences on Russian music, of which there were, in fact, almost none), they were Czarists through and through and would not remotely have approved of the Communist revolution. Soviet claims to the contrary are political fabrications. See also THE FIVE FRANKFURTERS, above, and the GIANT HAMBURGERS.

Fixer

An essential middle-man in the freelance orchestral world of the GIG. He is invariably a freelance himself and prides himself on his many contacts and comprehensive address book. Every freelance has the makings of being a fixer, if only because he is sometimes obliged to 'fix' a deputy for himself in case of accident, sickness – or a better gig turning up. It is probably fair to say that the best fixers are not usually the best players: for one thing, they spend more time on the telephone than practising scales. But they are always prosperous and seldom out of work. Their income from fixing-fees (usually a percentage of the total costs of the group he fixes for a promoter) is usually modest. But fixers always fix each other, and as all players love a fixer for the work *he* is able to put in *their* way, they in turn will put as much as possible in his. Behind every successful fixer is an efficient, message-taking wife, who keeps pencil and paper as well as his engagement and address books constantly by the telephone. Telephone answering machines are no substitute. Fixers know the quality, experience and specialities of the musicians they fix; and will advise conductors and promoters on the SEATING of string players and relative capabilities of PRINCIPALS, SUB-PRINCIPALS and RANK-AND-FILE players.

Flam

'A lie or sham story: also, a single stroke on a drum', says Grose's *Dictionary of the Vulgar Tongue* (1796) – but not entirely accurately as far as the musical definition is concerned. *Rees's Encyclopaedia* (1817) conforms more to the modern drummer's flam: 'a beat made by two sticks striking almost at the same time on the head' (i.e. of the drum!) 'but so as to be heard separately.' See also PARADIDDLE.

Flash

Nickname given to Sir Malcolm Sargent (1895–1967), never 'Flash Harry', as sometimes asserted, although the allusion to the flashy fictional character was probably intended. If that is so it was, however, unjust, as Sargent was not a swaggerer, but a man of impeccable manners. But of course he liked showing off, or he would not have felt the need to become a conductor. For example, when he once laid down the law to a London orchestra about the nature of the VIENNESE LIFT in a Strauss waltz, and a player tentatively questioned it, he brushed him aside with the brusque statement, 'I was dancing a waltz only last night with the Queen Mother', as though this somehow gave him direct access to the soul of Johann Strauss. 'Flash Harry' generated a whole series of nicknames for other conductors, among them *Flash Haggis* for (later Sir) Alexander Gibson; and *Flash Harriet* for John Hollingsworth (1916–1963), of whom Beecham wickedly said, 'Some conductors are born . . . [meaningful pause] . . . and some are Hollingsworth.'

Flat trumpet

The seventeenth-century English nickname for the slide trumpet. Purcell called it 'flatt' because unlike NATURAL brass instruments which produce only the notes of the harmonic series, it could play the flattened third note of the scale and therefore in minor keys. Flat trumpets were really a kind of small SHAGBUT. Purcell used them to wonderful effect in some of his funeral music.

Flautist/Flutist

The English prefer the anglicized Italian-based term (from *flauto*), whereas the Americans have adopted the German-based *flutist* (from *Flötist*). Only the Irish still use the once common old English word, *fluter* (as in *Phil the Fluter's Ball*): 'Here at Mr Debusty's, I saw in a gold frame a picture of a Fluter playing on his Flute – which for a good while I took for painting, but at last observed it a piece of Tapstry . . .' (Pepys, *Diary*, 21 June 1666).

Flautist's Chin

See under CELLIST'S NIPPLE

Flexatone

Modern music movements are littered with discarded instruments, supposed instrumental revolutions and would-be world-shaking innovations: e.g. the AEROPHOR, GRAPHIC SCORES, MUSIQUE CONCRÈTE, QUARTER-TONES, etc. The flexatone was a piece of flexible metal with a handle, a kind of house-trained musical saw, and had a tone not unlike one. On either side was mounted a wooden ball. When the instrument was shaken it made a sort of wailing noise, the pitch being altered as the player varied manual pressure on the flexible metal and as the ball struck it in various places. Schoenberg asked for a flexatone in his *Variations for*

Orchestra, op. 31 (1926) but now seldom gets one, as most specimens were thrown away when their short-lived popularity with jazz musicians lapsed (together with the GOOFUS, HOT FOUNTAIN PEN, KAZOO and other light-music novelties). I suppose Schoenberg thought he was being daringly proletarian when he invited one into his *Variations*. Since then the flexatone has been called for by Honegger, in his *Antigone* (1927), Khachaturian, in his piano concerto of 1946, and in works by Henze and Penderecki. VIBES generally make a perfectly acceptable alternative, especially when the music is somewhat indeterminate anyway. Even German musicians – who are not on the whole given to taking what they call heavy music lightly – joke about the flexaton (they drop the final e), calling it a *Drohleier*, or 'Threatening Lyre', from the fist-shaking motions the player has to make when using it. The joke loses in the telling, as it requires translation: *drohen* = to threaten; *drehen* = to turn; *Drehleier* = hurdygurdy (literally, 'turning-lyre'), hence the German pun, *Drohleier* = threatening lyre.

The Flute

The usual professional abbreviation for Mozart's opera *Die Zauberflöte* or 'Magic Flute'.

Flute/recorder

Confusions occasionally occur, as seventeenth- and eighteenth-century composers often wrote 'flute' or 'common flute' when they meant 'recorder', but specified the 'German flute' for the transverse instrument. In seventeenth-century England the recorder was the more common instrument, but was overtaken and finally ousted by the transverse in the eighteenth century. The Germans called the latter *Querflöte* or 'transverse flute' (sometimes jocularly mistranslated 'queer flute'). But there is nothing specifically German about it, except that they and the French were perhaps quicker in discarding the end-blown recorder. When Handel specified 'small flute' or 'flauto piccolo', as he does in *Acis and Galatea*, he meant the sopranino recorder, not the modern, transverse piccolo.

Flutter-tongueing

An effect first(?) used in their scores by Mahler and R. Strauss and often demanded by other composers since. It means playing a wind or brass instrument while interrupting the flow of air into the EMBOUCHURE or mouthpiece by pronouncing the letter R – either with the tip of the tongue, or by gargling the uvula, like a French R.

Flyshit

Very florid passages which, with a preponderance of semiquavers, demisemiquavers, hemidemisemiquavers (see QUARTER NOTES) and probably even 'blacker' notes, give an effect of speckled blackness on the page. Playing very fast notes high up on the doublebass or cello would be called 'Flyshit IN THE SNOW'.

Fog horn

Facetious description of a certain kind of BOILED (contralto) VOICE as exemplified by that of Dame Clara Butt who, according to a remark attributed to Sir Thomas Beecham, 'could on a clear day be heard across the English Channel'. In Britten's *Peter Grimes* the tuba player is required to imitate a foghorn, and has to make his way out of the pit to produce his mournful blast OFFSTAGE.

Foo foo bands

See EUNUCH FLUTE

Foot-tapper

A piece of music with an insistent beat which 'will make their feet tap' – though not so insistent as pop.

Formalism

One of the Soviet '-isms' which, as Prokofiev confirmed, is applied in music to compositions not simple enough for commissars to understand at first hearing.

(Bar) for nothing

When a conductor wants to prepare the players for the tempo he has in mind at the start of a movement (or its restart if it has come to a stop) he may give a prearranged number of beats, or bar(s) 'for nothing'. They are, of course, silent beats, when nobody plays, and are known also as 'conductor's solo'. This device may be used when a piece of music starts in the middle or at the end of a bar, and the conductor decides to 'beat the whole bar', i.e. from its beginning. Such movements of the baton act as PREPARATORY BEATS and help to establish the tempo right away, although they pose the risk of a DOMINO from a player who has not marked his PART with the necessary reminder ('3 beats for nothing', or 'Full bar'). However, it is a point of false pride on the part of some conductors to go 'straight in', for they feel that the practice of silently setting the tempo could be construed as a lack of technique or courage; or that it smacks of the jazz and dance-band count-in ('a-one, a-two, a-one-two-three-four') or the preliminary drum-beats in some light music. During the last war the famous Central Band of the Royal Air Force (which normally played ON THE MARCH) occasionally re-formed itself as an ordinary symphony orchestra – which was not difficult, with such distinguished conscripted Aircraftsmen/musicians in it as Norman Del Mar, Dennis and Leonard Brain, Gareth Morris and the entire Griller String Quartet. However, the RAF bandmaster was unfamiliar with the work under rehearsal, Beethoven's Violin Concerto. Indeed, he failed to notice in his score the opening bar, in which the solo kettle-drum plays the reiterated D crotchets, which took him by surprise. He stopped conducting, impatiently rapped his baton on the desk, and called to the timpanist, 'I don't need *you* to give me the tempo, thank you very much!'

Fortepiano

Not to be confused with the *pianoforte*, though neither now has any literal meaning. The difference arose for the sheer convenience of distinguishing the two instruments. Fortepiano was the earlier name for the HAMMERKLAVIER, whose action predates that of the modern pianoforte, or GRAND. But *fortepiano* should not be used for a square piano, an old English misnomer.

The Forty-Eight

The almost universal name for Bach's *Das wohltemperierte Klavier*, written to demonstrate equal TEMPERAMENT in tuning keyboard instruments. The Forty-Eight are really two sets of twenty-four, dating from 1722 and 1744 respectively, now known as Book I and Book II.

Foursome

Percy Grainger's BLUE-EYED ENGLISH word for a quartet. The term is reminiscent of the German term *Vierstück* (literally 'piece for four') used in Hitler's time, when Germans were urged to use 'Blue-eyed German' in place of the internationally accepted musical terms. See HAMMERKLAVIER.

French horn

Misnomer/solecism for the orchestral valve horn, which is now almost always a *German* horn (though perhaps made in Britain, America, Japan, Taiwan or almost anywhere). Nor is the traditional 'French' horn necessarily made in that country. But the old, piston-valved horn has been all but superseded by the rotary-valve instrument of bigger bore. The revolution took place before and during the last war, and was completed soon afterwards, for the big-bore instrument, variously nicknamed WOOFING-MACHINE, circular trombone or SECURICOR (because of its greater 'safety' from cracked notes) almost completely swept the board. But with the advent of authentic performance many horn players are reverting to the older instruments – the 'French' horn and even the NATURAL instruments such as the COR DE CHASSE and WALDHORN.

The Frog

Haydn's Quartet No. 41 in D major, so nicknamed because of the leaping main theme of the last movement. The same work is also known as 'The House on Fire' or 'The Squabble in Vienna', both for reasons now no longer known.

Front line

A jazz term not used by symphonic musicians, who use words like front DESK or BACK DESK.

Fugue

A composition in which the main theme, or 'subject', enters by successive turns. These are paradoxically called 'answers'. If subject and answer are identical (i.e. at the same pitch) it is called a Real Answer – though merely repeating a question can hardly be described as an 'answer' at all – and if transposed ('Fugue at the Fourth', etc.) a Tonal Answer. See also STRETTO, but best of all, see a good book on Musical Form.

Für Elise

The supposed dedication of what is (after the MOONLIGHT SONATA) Beethoven's most popular piano piece. It is based on a misreading. Closer examination of the AUTOGRAPH revealed that Beethoven, who had notoriously untidy handwriting, put *'Für Therese am 27. April zur Erinnerung and L. v. Bthvn'* ('For Therese on the 27th April in remembrance of L. v. Bthvn'). Therese Malfatti owned the manuscript. So we should really now start calling the piece 'Für Therese'. It might help in the pronunciation, for the now standard anglicized name is an approximation of 'Führer Lees', whereas the Germans say the name something like the French 'Elysée'.

Furniture music

A kind of early MINIMAL MUSIC devised with facetious intent on 8 March 1920 by the eccentric genius Erik Satie (1866–1925), for an art exhibition held at the *Galéries Barbazanges*. He had been asked to provide background music but, like most composers, was probably loth to have his work treated in such a manner. So he composed a work he called *musique d'ameublement*, music to be ignored, or at any rate (like modern MUZAK or WALLPAPER MUSIC) hardly noticed, a short fragment played over and over again by an ensemble of three clarinets, trombone and piano. It is said that those who came to see the pictures listened attentively, knowing that the famous Satie had written the music. This made the composer furious and he ran round the room shouting, *'Parlez!*

parlez!'. Satie also composed a work called *Vexations*. This consisted of two different harmonizations of an eighteen note theme, to be played 840 times continuously. It is occasionally revived by musicians eager to publicize themselves (or a good cause) by a MUSITHON and to attract the attention of the news media. It also inspired the well-known American musical joker John Cage to engage in some of his eccentric activities.

Futurism

A political-musical movement launched in 1909 with a manifesto (what else?) by some Italian painters and musicians who called themselves *musicisti futuristi*, doubtless with reference to the German *Zukunftsmusik* (MUSIC OF THE FUTURE) movement of the nineteenth century. It prophetically proposed combining the performance of music with other arts (now called 'happenings' and 'mixed-media events'). New and special instruments, e.g. Russolo's *Russolophone* and 'noise-intoners' (or *intonarumori*) were to be introduced. The initiators were one Marinetti, a dramatist, poet and aspiring musician, and men called Balla, Boccioni, Casavola, Fiorda and the aptly-named Silvio Mix, who experimented in electronic music and actually foreshadowed elements of another now dead musical duck, MUSIQUE CONCRÈTE, but died at the age of twenty-seven before he could do very much except write and talk about it at great length. In fact, the movement consisted of less music than words, theories and hot air: the New GROVE lists more than forty books and other writings about Futurism. It soon fizzled out, as do, did and will other trendy fads thought up by musical nutters and self-publicists. But as always happens, it left behind here and there a small residue of influence that may still be detected. The entries under FLEXATONE and MUSIQUE CONCRÈTE point to several other lost causes.

Gala Concert

A concert with higher ticket prices than usual; like a 'Celebrity Concert' without a celebrity.

Galway

Anglo-Irish-American slang for 'an ear-to-ear, narrow chin beard, as worn by stage Irishmen' (Wentworth and Flexner's *Dictionary of American Slang*), presumably one that does not interfere with playing the flute and may even help to protect the wearer from 'Flautist's Chin' (see under CELLIST'S NIPPLE).

The Garden

None but the rawest novice would say 'We're performing Mozart's *Don Giovanni* at the Royal Opera House, Covent Garden'. The proper jargon abbreviation is 'We're doing the Don at the Garden.' The building has not always enjoyed this lofty status. During the eighteenth and nineteenth centuries much of the entertainment was more like MUSIC-HALL. Johann Strauss II wrote a set of Waltzes called *Memories of Covent Garden* (op. 329) in which the tunes he quotes give some indication of the memories he had of the place: *The Mousetrap Man*, *The Daring Young Man on the Flying Trapeze*, *Champagne Charlie*, and *Home, Sweet Home*. Haydn wrote an Overture *'Coventgarden'* while he was in England in 1791 or a little later, but it is unfortunately lost (though it may have resurfaced as the Overture to J. P. Salomon's Opera *Windsor Castle*). Which recalls the fact that Johann Strauss also wrote a delightful waltz called *Windsorklänge*, popularly known in orchestral circles as 'Windsor Clangers'. It means 'Windsor Echoes' but does not quote English tunes.

Gear change

See BREAK

Geiger Counter

Jocular name among some orchestral players (who are exposed to many foreign languages during the course of their work) for the official usually known as the CONCERT MANAGER or ORCHESTRA MANAGER (or THE CORPORAL) whose duties include making sure that all musicians are present. *Geiger* = German for a fiddler.

Gemshorn

Gems(e) is German for a *chamois* (the quadruped, not the wash leather); and a *Gemshorn* is a wind instrument made from the animal's horn; also the name of an organ-stop sounding nothing like the instrument. The *Gemshorn* (sometimes incorrectly Gamshorn) is in effect a woodwind instrument made of natural horn (but see NATURAL HORN in a different context) with finger-holes and a mouthpiece of the recorder type at the wider end. It therefore looks odd, as though it were held upside-down, for one expects wind instruments to get wider towards the end, not narrower. The word is pronounced with a hard *g* (not unlike 'games horn') and has no connection with gems or precious stones.

Gérard Numbers

Usually abbreviated to G (followed by a number), from Yves Gérard (b. 1932), whose *Thematic Catalogue of the Works of Luigi Boccherini* (London, 1969) is that composer's 'KOECHEL'.

German band

A small woodwind and brass band of itinerant musicians. These were a common sight on the streets of England before and up to the First World War. Such BUSKING bands were not always German, although the original ones were, and arrived in large numbers, just as many young British musicians and music students now go abroad to work or busk. References to German bands abound in late nineteenth- and early twentieth-century liter-

ature, magazines and the press – most of them derisive or derogatory: 'When German bands/With music stands/Played Wagner
imperfectly' (*Princess Ida*: Gilbert and Sullivan). However, they
often provided the only form of organized music the poor would
hear; and they had other uses. For example, Liverpool Corporation
used 'oom-pah bands' as municipal pied pipers to help enforce
the 1870 Education Act. They would be engaged to travel round
the city and play on street-corners; and as soon as the truant
children emerged from their houses they would be collected by
the school inspectors.

German Sixth

This is no more German than the NEAPOLITAN SIXTH comes from
Naples. It is 'the chord of the augmented sixth, one having a major
third and a doubly-augmented fourth or perfect fifth in addition
to the augmented sixth above the flattened submediant.' Hence
the need for a snappy nickname.

Getting one's feet under the table

British army expression adopted by travelling orchestral musicians. It means being invited for hospitality by local music-lovers.

The Ghost Trio

This nickname for Beethoven's Piano Trio in D major, op. 70, has
never become popular outside German-speaking countries, where
it is the standard name for the work. But it is in any case a
mistranslation from the German *Geistertrio*. *Geister* may be either
spirits or ghosts: in this case they are spirits – if the story is true
that Beethoven was inspired to write it by his reading of *Macbeth*.
He was fond of Shakespeare, and had the *Complete Works* in Esch-
enburg's translation; and also asked his friend Therese Malfatti
(see FÜR ELISE) to lend him her volumes of the Schlegel version.
Beethoven also knew *King Lear*, but in what was known as the
'Viennese version', in which Lear survives and triumphs over his
children and enemies.

The Giant Hamburgers

If we are to put composers into 'schools' like whales, e.g. THE
FIVE, THE FIVE FRANKFURTERS or LES SIX, we may as well call the

members of the Hamburg School, best-known of whom are Johann Mattheson (1681–1764) and Georg Philipp Telemann (1681–1767), the Giant Hamburgers. Telemann (who would have pronounced his name like 'tail-a-man', not 'telly-man' as now common in English) was actually born in Magdeburg but spent more than half a century in Hamburg, where he died at the age of 86 having composed so many works that he not only failed to recognize the earlier ones, but savagely criticized some of them, thinking they had been written by another. Mattheson began life as an operatic boy soprano (non-castrato), was a pupil of the great Praetorius, and is important in musical history also for having written what would now be called musicological books.

Gig

Originally jazz jargon for an engagement, usually a one-night stand. The *Melody Maker*, a light-music paper, used the word in inverted commas in 1926, but Louis Armstrong, in *Satchmo, My Life in New Orleans* (1958) suggests it was in ordinary use in his youth during the early years of the twentieth century. Like so many jazz terms (including the word *jazz* itself) it is thought to have sexual overtones, in this case a *gig* being anything from an uninhibited party to a wild orgy. Whatever its origin, *gig* is not a contraction of 'engagement', as sometimes asserted.

Girl tenor

The female answer to the boy soprano, or perhaps even the castrato or CAPON. In the early part of the twentieth century a young woman appeared on Columbia Records singing music by Balfe and Wallace under the name of 'Miss Ruby Helder, the Girl Tenor'. She sounds more like a very low MEZZO than a male tenor. See also HELDENTENOR.

The Girl with the Lines of a Horse

Like CLEAR THE SALOON, a facetious mistranslation: Debussy's *La Fille aux cheveux de lin* (from *Piano Preludes*, 1910).

Glass harmonica

Glass objects can make musical sound, from a pleasing tinkle when gently struck to a nasty and ominous crunching and cracking when broken. In Harold G. Davidson's *Auto Accident* (New Music Publications), for example, both effects are used – 'two glass plates, each resting on a wash bowl or crock, with a hammer or mallet in readiness to break them in measure [i.e. bar] four, these glass plates to be smashed with a hammer. . . . In the next measure, the bowls containing the broken glass are to be emptied on a hard surface, table or floor . . .' – illustrating with unpleasantly realistic pseudo-music what everyone knows may happen in an accident. When the rim of a wine-glass is gently rubbed with a dampened finger, a high-pitched and curiously irritating noise may be produced. The size of the glass and/or the amount of water it contains determine the pitch of the note. This discovery, probably going back to Pythagoras, seems to have been put to more or less musical use since the time of the ancients. Gluck is known to have played a concerto on twenty-six glasses in London in 1746, if a report in the *General Advertiser* is to be believed (surely he had better uses for his considerable talents?). Benjamin Franklin invented a *Glassychord* around 1760 which he called the *Armonica* – not to be confused with the 'Harmonica' or MOUTH ORGAN. Mozart during the last months of his life found time to write a delightful quintet (K617) for glass harmonica, flute, oboe, viola, and cello, for Marianne Kirchgässner, a blind virtuoso. In recent years the German Bruno Hoffmann developed a remarkable dexterity on static water-tuned glasses, and recorded this as well as other works. Franklin's *Glassychord* had the glasses mounted concentrically on a pedal-driven, revolving spindle (rather like a treadle sewing-machine), the rims kept wet by their revolving in water. Gluck's glasses were probably merely struck with rods, like chimes. The extremely high and irritating sound produced by rim-rubbed glasses, combined with the constant stimulation of the fingertips, was said to have a bad effect on the players, who all went mad. Did Donizetti know about this? Could it be the reason why the original OBBLIGATO instrument in the MAD SCENE of his *Lucia di Lammermoor* was a glass harmonica, not a flute? But then again, the ancient Greeks maintained that the sound of an insistent flute, too, posed a threat to sanity. For another kind of glass musical instrument, see BOTTLE ORGAN.

Gliss(ando)

This sounds like an Italian word but isn't. It is Italianized bastard French, from *glissant*, the gerund and present participle of *glisser*, to slide. The musical term describes (or demands) a sliding effect involving two or more notes, but is not the same as PORTAMENTO. There are true *glissandos*, such as can be produced on a string instrument or trombone, or false ones that are no more than smooth chromatic scales, or even, as with a glissando on piano or organ, a rapid scale of C major played with the thumb (or thumb and forefinger combined) which can be very painful: see under CELLIST'S NIPPLE. That eccentric and original composer and pianist Percy Grainger always wrapped a handkerchief round his thumb to protect it. But unlike other pianists, who keep their hankies in their pocket, he attached it to his clothing with a rubber band, so that it would spring back out of sight after use. Many composers, even very famous ones, show that they do not know what is possible in *glissandos*. Berlioz, for example, asks for a downward gliss (covering an octave G – G) from the flutes and oboes in his *Symphonie fantastique* but fails to say how it could be done: it is impossible on those instruments. The German conductor Hans von Knappertsbusch (1888–1965) described the long gliss on the solo fiddle in Strauss's *Till Eulenspiegels lustige Streiche* as a 'zip-fastener solo'.

Glock

This has now reverted to its original meaning – the abbreviation of the unwieldy German word *Glockenspiel*. But between 1959 and 1973 it could have referred to Sir William Glock (b.1908), who was Controller of Music at the BBC; or a famous French clown (not to be confused with 'Grock', who was another).

Glorious John

Vaughan Williams's name for JB. But Barbirolli was not the first musician to carry it. VW probably got the idea from the nickname of an earlier JB, the German-born London composer, pianist, publisher and publicizer of music, Johann Baptist Cramer (1771–1858), who became something of an idol of the English. He was one of the founders of the (later Royal) Philharmonic Society, was declared by Beethoven to be the finest pianist of his time, and is said to have been responsible for nicknaming Mozart's K551 The 'JUPITER'.

The Gluepot

Sir Henry Wood's nickname for the public bar *The George* in Mortimer Street, near BBC Broadcasting House in London and just behind the former Queen's Hall. TIMBER would often wait in vain while some of his players refreshed themselves. The tradition has been preserved by many BBC broadcasters and producers. See also ROOM NINETY-NINE.

Gobstick

Jazz musicians' word, now rather dated, for the clarinet. Never used in symphony orchestras.

God-is-an-Englishman music

COWPAT music with a strong patriotic or imperial flavour, like Elgar's and Walton's coronation marches. Its characteristics are STRIDING BASSES and BIG TUNES.

The Goldberg

Short name for Bach's great set of Variations for Harpsichord, the fourth book of the KLAVIERÜBUNG. J. G. Goldberg was J. S. Bach's pupil and court musician to an insomniac nobleman. Bach wrote the variations for Goldberg to play to his sleepless master (or perhaps eventually to send him to sleep, as they are gloriously long). There is more gold to the story than the name, for Bach's reward was a golden goblet filled with one hundred *louis d'or*. Contrary to an occasionally expressed belief, Goldberg was not Jewish: German Jews were not allowed to have surnames until the end of the eighteenth century.

Golden Syrup

Orchestral players' name for Lehár's 'Gold and Silver' waltz, op. 79. Its appearance in programmes brings a little silver to the orchestral flautists, who may qualify for a DOUBLING fee because Lehár asks for two piccolos in the introduction of the waltz.

The Good-humoured Quaker

See LA PASSIONE

Goofus

Instrument fashionable in 1920s and 1930s, like the FLEXATONE and musical saw but, unlike these, never used outside jazz. It was – unnecessarily – made to look like a saxophone, with a couple of dozen finger points, each controlling its own single-beating reed and could thus play more than one note simultaneously. It was sometimes played with a rubber tube leading to the player's mouth (see AEROPHOR) and laid flat on a table; a kind of imitation saxophone for keyboard players. A modern version is sold under the trade name 'Melodica'.

Grand

Always thus shortened in professional jargon, never 'grand piano', which betrays the amateur. But the player will probably also specify further: Bechstein, Steinway, concert, six-foot, etc., though seldom BOUDOIR. Did ladies really keep their small grands in their bedrooms? See also MINIPIANO.

Grandmother fiddle

'The double bass, it is intriguing to note, was always called "a grandmother fiddle" in Sussex [church bands] – an unexpected change of sex in an instrument usually known by such obstinately masculine names as "bull fiddle" and the "dog house"', 'says Spike Hughes in his book *Glyndebourne*. See also BULL FIDDLE, DOGHOUSE, HORSE'S LEG, SNORKEL.

Grand opera

Never used by true opera lovers. To them it is all *opera*; qualification is called for: Italian opera, comic opera, SINGSPIEL, operetta, etc.

Graphic scores

Scores written, drawn, scratched, doodled or scribbled in some random manner by modern CONTEMPORARY composers of the avant garde or EXPERIMENTAL kind who lack the skill or patience to write conventional scores. For a more reasoned and less dismissive analysis of such short-lived fads, see Hugo Cole's *Sounds and Signs: Aspects of Musical Notation*.

Grecian-urn conductor

A conductor whose right hand movements are mirrored by the movements of his left – i.e. one who is deficient in STICK TECHNIQUE and does not know what can be done with the hand not holding the baton. *Sotto voce* suggestions may be heard from the orchestra, such as 'Put it in your pocket!'

Greek titles

Classical Greek has been all but abolished in education but seems to flourish among AVANT GARDE, CONTEMPORARY or EXPERIMENTAL composers, who like to use it for the titles of their works, usually followed by a Roman numeral: *Amitosis I, Phagadena II, Petechia III, Kyphosis IV, Collyrium V, Presbyopia VI, Halitosis VII*, etc. They do this not for the meaning of the words but the sound they make.*

* The examples I have quoted sound authentic enough, but I have made them up, to avoid hurting any composer's feelings. They are all names of distressing complaints and are taken from the *Concise Oxford Medical Dictionary*.

Green Room

Also Soloist's Room, Artists' Room, Conductor's Room, etc. It is seldom painted green, which some superstitious artists consider an unlucky colour. The origin of the name is theatrical: 'I do know London pretty well, and the Side-Box, Sir; and behind the Scenes, ay, and the Green-Room, and all the Girls and Women-Actresses there' (Colley Cibber: *Love Makes Man*, 1701). It has been suggested that it is a corruption of 'scene room' but that is unlikely. In concert halls where orchestras play the Green Room is usually reserved for the conductor but may be shared by the LEADER and guest soloists. The orchestra uses the BANDROOM.

Groan box

The accordion, or squeeze box, or BOX OF TEETH.

The Grosse Fugue

The customary 'English' title and adaptation of the unauthorized German nickname (*Grosse Fuge*) of the original last movement of Beethoven's String Quartet, op. 130: *grosse* = German for 'big' (though not necessarily 'great'). The fugue was later given its own opus number (133) and replaced by a different last movement for op. 130. The term, sounding uncomfortably like 'Grocer Fugue' (and sometimes thus misprinted) is absurdly macaronic. But 'Great Fugue' would not do either, and 'Big Fugue' even less. In any case, Beethoven specified neither size nor greatness, calling it simply *Fuga*; and he heads the Allegro which precedes it *Overtura*. Hans Keller has suggested 'Grand Fugue', which is better but still not absolutely right: many other Beethoven pieces deserve to be described as 'grand'.

'Grove says. . .'

Like 'QUANTZ says . . .' this is a frequent opening in support of a musical assertion of opinion. Sir George Grove (1820–1900) was one of the great examples of many-sided British genius: a civil engineer, Bible scholar, linguist, lexicographer, writer on music, biographer of Beethoven, Mendelssohn, Schubert, prolific letter-writer and amateur(!) musician. And, of course, compiler of the great musical dictionary that bears his name. It is not his only surviving monument: he also worked on the famous Britannia Tubular Bridge over the Menai Straits in Wales. *Grove's Dictionary* has run into several editions, the latest one called *The New Grove*, published in 1980.

Grunt Iron

American nickname for the tuba.

G-String

The fourth and lowest string of the violin, on which players can make a particularly S(C)HMAL(T)ZY sound if they are so inclined, and can play, among other things, Wilhelmj's arrangement of the AIR ON THE G-STRING. Some find the name comic, as it reminds them of the garment of minimal cover worn by dancers and others to draw attention to their pubic region. The proper spelling of that is, however, 'Gee String', for the word comes from an ancient American Indian word for a rudimentary loin string worn by Indian boys and men.

The Guildhall

Not the old civic building in London but the Guildhall School of Music in the City of London.

The Guitar Bo-ing-ggg

Jocular name for a cliché used by ACOUSTIC guitarists. It takes the form of an exaggerated VIBRATO on isolated high notes that form a point of rest. It may be combined with RUBATO, not according to musical context but technical considerations; employed perhaps in the way some singers hold on to a high note merely because they happen to make a good sound on it.

Gymnopédie

Title given by the French composer (of Scottish descent) Erik Satie (1866–1925) to three of his piano compositions. The Greek word means 'Naked Boys', a fact that can in no way be deduced from the music. Nor should one make scandalous inferences about Satie's sexual habits. Although he was not married there is nothing to suggest that he was not like other men: he simply kept his private life private – much to the disappointment of biographers and television programme makers. 'Naked Boys' is here the concept of a naked Greek statue seen from three different angles; hence the three *Gymnopédies*, which are really three subtle variations of the same musical idea. They have achieved their deserved popularity since 1975, when Satie's music became free from copyright and many commercial arrangements were published.

Hairpins

These come in two kinds, hairpin-up and hairpin-down, and in many sizes, the normal informal name for signs indicating that the music should get louder or softer. Carelessly hand-written, hairpins may be confused with accents, which are indicated by means of a sign like a very small, obtuse-angled hairpin-down. Schubert, for example, often wrote his accents so big in his MSS that they were often printed as hairpins-down. The most notable example is the last bar of his UNFINISHED where he asked for a sustained *fortissimo* chord reinforced by an initial accent, but the printers made it *fortissimo/diminuendo*. The mistake makes this great symphonic torso fade into the distance and thus lends force to the romantic misconception that he abandoned the work because his strength was failing. Hairpins were the secret of much of Beecham's renowned phrasing: every bar of his SCORES AND PARTS was littered with them, in red or blue, and his hand movements merely confirmed what the players saw in their music.

Hallé

Carl Halle (1819–95) a conductor and pianist from Hagen in Westphalia, adopted the acute accent after he left Germany (first for France and then England) so as to remind non-Germans that the last letter of his name (or that of the town of Halle) is not mute. In 1849 he came to Manchester and in due course took over an existing amateur orchestra which he re-formed and augmented with musicians he invited over from Germany. Many of these stayed in England to found musical dynasties. The orchestra was known as 'Mr Hallé's Band' and he himself eventually became Sir Charles Hallé. He was a pioneering conductor in many ways, one of which has been insufficiently chronicled: Hallé used to perform piano concertos, even one by his contemporary, Johannes Brahms, directing the orchestra from the keyboard, albeit with the help of the LEADER.

Hammerklavier

The AUTOGRAPH of Beethoven's Piano Sonata, op. 106 contains the words *Grosse Sonate für das Hammerklavier*. The last word could be taken for an eccentric tautology: for after all, *every* piano has hammers; and by the time the sonata was written in 1817–18, the harpsichord (in which the strings are plucked by plectra) was considered obsolete, and the usual names for what we call the piano were *Pianoforte*, *Fortepiano* or *Klavier* (alternative spellings, *Clavier*, *Clavir*, *Klavir*, etc.). So why did Beethoven use *Hammerklavier* and state the obvious, equally applicable to *all* his piano sonatas? The answer may be found in Beethoven's Conversation Books of the period. Certain passages reveal that he and his nephew Karl repeatedly discussed the work of a German teacher, lexicographer and eccentric, Joachim Heinrich Campe, who proposed (as Hitler was to do later) 'the Germanisation of foreign terms foisted upon our language'. Karl, then a university student, was much taken with Campe's ideas, and for a time Beethoven tried to employ such 'newly-made words and expressions', including *Klangstück* for a sonata and the idiotic *Schmetterrohr* ('Blasting Tube') for a trumpet; and he also occasionally remembered to write German expression-marks into his scores instead of the customary Italian ones. However, the facetious tone of several of Beethoven's letters on the subject suggests that he was not taking it very seriously. At the time of the printing of the 'Hammerklavier' he writes to his publisher Steiner (whom he addresses as 'Dearest Herr Lieutenant General!'): 'Coincidence has decreed that I have stumbled upon the following dedication: Sonata for the Pianoforte or Hammerklavier . . .' and soon afterwards (23 January 1817) Beethoven follows it with another one. 'To the High-born Lieutenant General von Steiner, personally: To Whom It May Concern: We have hereby resolved and concluded, following our own Researches and in due Consideration of Counsel's Advice, that henceforth all the Titles of our works shall bear the word "Hammerklavier" instead of "Pianoforte" . . . to be Understood, Observed and Agreed, Once and for All Time . . .' etc. The letter is signed 'Generalissimus'. Schumann, Wagner and Strauss had a similar Germanic bees in their bonnets; and 'PERKS' Grainger propounded his BLUE-EYED ENGLISH without success.

Handel

Do not make puns on his name. They have all been made before: 'Hot Handel', 'Mishandled', 'Handel to his Name', etc. are best left to newspaper journalists, who use punning as a substitute for thinking. The Germans however, have an extra source of feeble jokes on Handel. For in that language it retains the Umlaut dots on the a (which he himself dropped when he came to England), and *Händel* is homophonous with *Hendel* (Austrian: *Hendl*), meaning 'little hen', or (when served at table) 'spring chicken'. Fried in breadcrumbs it is known as the Austrian delicacy *Backhendl* (*Backen* = 'baking/frying'). Haydn is supposed to have said, while

Punch, 1898

He: *"Awfully jolly concert, wasn't it? Awfully jolly Thing by that Fellow—what's his Name?—something like Doorknob."* She: *"Doorknob! Whom do you mean! I only know of Beethoven, Mozart, Wagner, Handel—"* He: *"That's it! Handel. I knew it was something you caught hold of!"*

eating this, 'Here am I, Haydn, simultaneously enjoying both Bach *and* Händel.' (It was probably funnier the way he said it.) An earlier near-namesake of Händel/Handel, Jakob Handl (1550–91), punningly translated his own name into at least three pseudonyms. He Frenchified it to Jacob le Coq, Latinized it to Iacobus Gallus, and also used the German dialect word *Hähnel*, meaning 'little cock'. And as he was a Slav, some think that his original name was in fact Jacob Petelin (Slavonic for 'cockerel') which he translated into German. He was a very fine composer, so it hardly matters whether the Handl preceded le Coq, or vice versa.

Handel's Largo

An absurd but well-established name, even less authentic or logical than ALBINONI'S ADAGIO, BOCCHERINI'S MINUET and PACHELBEL'S CANON and a veritable nest of misconceptions. Handel wrote hundreds of movements marked *largo*, a word which in Italian may mean many things – wide, broad, roomy, ample, generous, liberal, abundant, open-handed, etc. – but does *not* mean 'slow'. Handel's so-called Largo comes from his opera *Serse* and is not a love song but one addressed to a plane-tree. The proper title, taken from the opening words, is *Ombra mai fu*. It is not marked *largo* but *larghetto*, and its sustained, long notes would in eighteenth-century performance have been broken up with all manner of ornaments and decorations.

Hand rest

See BOEHM'S CRUTCH

Handshakes

An important element of PLATFORM ETIQUETTE. At the end of a performance the conductor shakes hands with the soloist as well as the LEADER, although the latter may not have played a single note on his own. The same routine may be followed even *before* the concert, perhaps in order to keep up some kind of pretence (familiar from television chat shows) that the protagonists have only just met for the first time. Handshakes may be offered also to others, especially front DESK players. Only in exceptional circumstances does a conductor make his way through the orchestra to shake hands with wind or brass; those congratulations are normally achieved by beckoning the musicians to rise and take an individual bow. Hot and sweaty post-performance handshakes – sometimes even augmented by hugs and kisses – are borne with courage and resignation because they help to MILK THE APPLAUSE: such rituals take time and, as the people in the audience watch, they naturally continue the applause whereas, without the hand-shaking (which may be taken to extraordinary lengths) they might long have stopped clapping and gone home. The practice has been imported from the continent, where players shake hands with each other even when they arrive at rehearsal in the morning and, for all I know, when they return from the pub after lunch.

Harmonica

Old-fashioned genteel name for mouth organ. Even Larry Adler, that great exponent of the instrument who helped to make the instrument musically respectable, has abandoned it and is now happy to call himself 'mouth organist' instead of a 'harmonica virtuoso'. The polite name came via translation from the German *Mundharmonika* and the Italian *Armonica a bocca*. The more down-to-earth name avoids further confusion with the GLASS HARMONICA, a muddle perpetuated in a gramophone record of Saint-Saëns's *Carnaval des animaux*. The record producer must have seen the word *Armonica* in the score (by which the composer meant the eerie, liquid-sounding glass harmonica for the *Aquarium* movement) and engaged Tommy Reilly to play the part on the mouth-organ.

The Harp

Beethoven's String Quartet in E flat, op. 74, has certain PIZZ arpeggio passages in the first movement, sounding not at all like harp strings being plucked. But nevertheless the quartet has carried the nickname 'The Harp' for as long as anyone can remember: a bad one at that, as it might lead audiences to expect four harps to appear on the platform.

Harpic-Cord

A hybrid instrument devised for APRIL FOOLS CONCERTS (i.e. HOFFNUNG-type concerts). It consists of the top half of a euphonium fitted to a 'lavatory' (i.e. 'toilet') bowl, which acts as a sound resonator and BELL. Also registered under the name of LOOPHONIUM.

The author playing the Harpic-cord
(or Loophonium)
(Photo courtesy of TV Times)

Haydn's last words

Not his dying speech but the work known in English as *Our Saviour's Seven Last Words on the Cross*, of which Haydn made several versions. Each 'word' is represented by a solemn movement of great beauty and intensity. During the last war the Griller String Quartet, which consisted of four serving members of the RAF (see CONDUCTOR SOLO), was ordered to provide background music for a cocktail party given by their commanding officer. At a loss for suitable salon music, but confident that no one ever *listens* to party music, they took their copies of Haydn's *Last Words*, which they were about to perform at a National Gallery Concert in London, and quietly rehearsed the work – with all the stopping, discussing and repeating they would have done in a private rehearsal. See also FURNITURE MUSIC, MUZAK.

Haydn's Serenade

The second movement, *Andante cantabile*, of Haydn's String Quartet in F major, op. 3 No. 5, an enchanting tune familiar through its use for many years as a signature tune *Music in Miniature* on the BBC. Although the title 'Serenade' is spurious it suits the music, with its PIZZ accompaniment to the singing violin tune. It is now suggested in the new GROVE that the composer is not Haydn but one Hofstetter. A man able to write music like that deserves to be better known – but he does not even rate an entry in GROVE itself.

Head voice

See BREAK, CAPONS, COCK ALTO

The Heavenly Long

Schumann's name (*Die himmlische Länge*) for Schubert's C major (D944), also known as 'The Great' – not only for its greatness but also to distinguish it from his LITTLE C MAJOR, D589. Orchestral musicians on the whole deplore having to play TAPEWORMS, however heavenly, so the nickname is never heard in BANDROOMS.

Heckelphone

It sounds like some sort of loudhailer for use at elections but is in fact a bass oboe – and anyone who thought that there already *was* such an instrument, called the bassoon, should consult a good book about wind instruments, e.g. one by Anthony Baines. The Heckelphone is so named after the German instrument-maker Wilhelm Heckel (1865–1909) whose firm in Biebrich is best known for its bassoons but had a habit of trying to immortalize the family name in its other products. Its founder was Johann Adam Heckel (1812–77) who at Wagner's request made the *Heckelclarina* for the shepherd's pipe in *Tristan und Isolde*, as well as the *Heckelphonklarinette*. There are parts for the Heckelphone in works by Delius, notably the first *Dance Rhapsody* (but called 'bass oboe' in the score) as well as music by Richard Strauss (see also AEROPHOR). The Heckels also made a *Piccolo Heckelphone*, with which they very nearly re-invented the oboe.

'He doesn't get in the way'

Orchestral players' high praise for a conductor; as is also 'He lets us play.'

Heldentenor

Nearly all operatic heroes are tenors, but *Heldentenor* denotes a kind of big voice required for Wagnerian opera. Not many tenors are big in stature, however, and producers devise all kinds of ruses, from built-up shoes to the careful placing of ill-disguised wooden boxes, to bring a small tenor up to the size of his PRIMA DONNA. But see also TENORINO.

Henry V

A member of the organ-building Willis family, not a king (except perhaps in his own estimation). See FATHER SMITH.

Herbie

James Galway's alleged nickname for Herbert von Karajan ('so I said to him "look 'ere, Herbie", I said').

Hibernicon

An 'Irish Helicon', which sounds like an Irish joke but was a real instrument invented and patented (1823) by the Rev. Joseph R. Cotter, vicar of Castlemagner, Co. Cork: a giant bass-horn of which an enraptured critic said when he heard it at the York Festival of 1835 'like Goliath, [it] towered heavenwards . . . such is the power of this Hibernicon that the trumpets at the walls of Jericho, nay the last trump itself, would be as child's play to it'. It went out of use soon afterwards.

Highbrow

'Highbrow' and 'lowbrow', when used to describe music, usually told one more about the speaker than the music. For other almost meaningless terms, see under CLASSICAL and LONGHAIRED.

Hire fees

This subject takes us into the murkier waters of the music business. At the top, and reasonably respectable, end are the music publishers who issue new works only in score (probably a tiny and all-but-illegible POCKET SCORE). If anyone likes the music well enough to organize a performance he has to *hire* the PARTS, whereas in former years he would have been able to buy them. The reason for this is twofold: money and money. To *print* the material necessary for the performance of, say, a new opera, oratorio or symphony, would be prohibitively expensive, as only half a dozen sets might be sold. Also, when a single handwritten set is hired out for each event, the number of performances can be both checked and controlled, and the performing-fees demanded from the appropriate collecting agency. A less reputable hire system is operated in orchestras. For his normal work, the orchestral player is expected to provide his stock-in-trade: a flautist must own a flute and piccolo, and oboists specializing in playing the COR also buy their own. In return for a considerable outlay all they can expect is an occasional DOUBLING-FEE or OBBLIGATO. But ask a flautist to play the BASS FLUTE, an oboist the HECKELPHONE or a bassoonist the TENOROON, and – even if they own such instruments – they will demand a hire fee. It is a harmless racket designed to screw a little extra money out of concert organizers. But the most inveterate hirers are found among the percussionists, and the exhibitionistic demands made by many avant garde and CONTEMPORARY composers only compound their often slightly shady dealings. All kinds of strange noises are asked for in the pursuit of uglier and yet uglier noises: drainpipes struck with a toffee hammer, suspended cymbals bowed with fiddle-bows, corrugated cardboard rubbed with chopsticks – and many other more or less silly effects. Even if percussionists own such utensils, or can easily borrow one (such as an old fiddle-bow) from a colleague, they invariably charge both a hire fee and PORTERAGE. I was once charged £15 hire fee (plus doubling-fee and porterage) for a bird-call six inches long. Some London percussionists have gone so far as to form their own hire companies so that they can hire the instruments to themselves, charge themselves fees, and pass these on to their employers. One national symphony orchestra, while existing precariously on Arts Council and local authority grants, gave to one of its players an interest-free loan of several thousand pounds so that he could buy a CONTRA. When after many years' minute salary deductions the instrument finally became his, the orchestra paid him a hefty hire fee each time he used it, plus porterage – although of course it never left his place of work except when he performed outside engagements on it.

Hit

Samuel Pepys used the noun in the sense of commercial good luck, a coup, or a stroke of financial fortune: 'An opportunity . . . which might have been such a hit, as will never come again' (*Diary*, 1666); and indeed many popular musical 'hits' owe their success more to commercial acumen than intrinsic quality; for what is briefly and transitorily approved of by millions is sure to have been commercially stimulated and possess little merit. (Is not the taste of the masses almost invariably bad taste?) As a description of a successful and popular piece of music, the word *hit* dates from the first decade of the present century, when 'Broadway hits' began to be advertised. Since TIN PAN ALLEY 'Musicals' owe their existence to immigrant musicians who went to America and adapted the Viennese operetta, I suggest they may also have brought with them the word *hit*. The German word for *hit* is *schlagen* (*Schlag* = a stroke or a blow); *Schlager* is the equivalent of the English musical hit. *Schlagen* has a colloquial synonym, *hauen*; and the old German word for a popular song has been *Hauer* since at least the sixteenth century: a collection of *Gassenhauer*, or 'street hits' was published in Strasbourg in 1562.

Hob

Hob numbers often appear in conjunction with works by Joseph Haydn, an abbreviation of *Hoboken Catalogue*. See KOECHEL.

Hoffnung concert

It is always unwise in music to claim a totally original invention, but it can be safely stated that the German-born British cartoonist and humorist Gerard Hoffnung (1925–59) did not invent the 'funny concert'. There were such concerts in Liverpool from 1952, when a group of players of the (later Royal) Liverpool Philharmonic Orchestra gave the first of a quarter-century-long series of annual APRIL FOOLS CONCERTS. Hoffnung was recommended to them as 'a cartoonist who does a funny lecture with a tuba which he can't play'; and therefore invited to take part in the fifth AFC. In the following year he gave his first 'Hoffnung Music Festival' in London, largely with material previously heard at Liverpool, and with the active participation of players from the North. It should also be put on record that when first approached to take part in the April Fools Concert (to play the tuba solo in *Tubby the Tuba*) he replied that he took his tuba playing – which was then at a very early stage – very seriously and could he instead try his hand at the vw Tuba Concerto? He was persuaded to play *Tubby the Tuba* (narrated by Thomas Hemsley) and doubtless never looked at the VW again. From that day onwards until his untimely death (and indeed for some years after it) he was heavily promoted, with the support of publishers and record companies, as a Funny Musician.

'Hohoje! Hohoje! Halloho'

The much repeated opening words of Wagner's *Der fliegende Holländer*, the composer's own. They are an excellent example of this otherwise great man's over-rated literary powers. When his libretti are not laughable, like the ho-ho example above, they are overblown and sound absurd even in German.

The Holy Family

In London freelance circles during the 1950s and 1960s, the nickname for an elite group of woodwind players who, it was claimed by the less fortunate, cornered all the most lucrative engagements, mostly SESSIONS. Various more or less scurrilous or blasphemous titles were bandied about; and the distinguished oboist Leon Goossens (b.1897), who in the later stages of his long career preferred the broadcasting studios to the concert platform, was known as 'The Holy Ghost' – 'You never see him, just hear him over the air.' See also ROYAL FAMILY, WAX CONDUCTOR.

The Home Straight

This horse-racing term is applied by orchestral musicians to that final part of a work which begins to move inexorably to the end, a point where the music may gain in speed, movement and volume, and always a welcome one as a TAPEWORM reaches its coda – the Italian word for a tail. (See also CABALETTA for another horsey comparison). In a FUGUE the home straight is usually heralded by a *stretto* (Italian for close, together, tight) when the fugue subject seems to appear neck-and-neck with its answers.

Honky-tonk piano

Said facetiously of an out-of-tune piano. Real honky-tonk instruments, however, are specially detuned and sometimes have wire fitted over the hammer felts so as to make them jangle all the more.

Horlicks

'Who was conducting?' – 'Oh, old Horlicks.' Occasional nickname for Sir Adrian Boult (1889–1983), known for his reserve, and performances that were by some critics (unjustly) considered bland in comparison with those of extraverts like Sargent or Beecham. It was Beecham who supposedly once said, 'There was Adrian – positively *reeking* of Horlicks.' Sir Adrian could, however, be quite fierce at rehearsal, though always gentlemanly.

Horn

For the musician this is the normal way of referring to the instrument the layman often misnames the 'FRENCH' HORN (which please see, and its various cross-references). Nationality is mentioned in musicians' talk only when it is germane to the context. In jazz parlance 'horn' means the trumpet or – latterly – perhaps any wind or brass instrument.

Horn harmonies

The kind of basic harmonies characteristic of horns (and to some extent trumpets) which take into account the limited range of notes available on a 'NATURAL' brass instrument. Horn harmonies are based on the common chord (i.e. as exemplified by bugle calls). Thus *Three Blind Mice* expressed in horn harmonies would begin:

Because the horn was traditionally associated with hunting (indeed was first used for the chase and only later tamed for the concert-room) the representation of horn harmonies in classical music became a kind of musical shorthand, always invoked when the hunt was to be suggested. And because hunting on the continent of Europe often took place in woods and forests, the horn also acquired sylvan associations; and I can think of no CLASSICAL instrumental work about woods that does not make use of the horn and, usually, its characteristic harmonies. On the other hand, the simplicity of horn harmonies makes them an attractive cliché for inferior composers. While Beethoven and his friends were preparing for the first performance of the Ninth in 1824, they found time to ridicule a new work by one Stockhausen. 'His Mass is pitiful rubbish. All the themes go like this' one of them writes down for Beethoven, adding a music example like the one shown above.

The Horn Signal

Haydn's No. 31 in D, also known in German-speaking countries as *Auf dem Anstand* ('In the Hide'), which would suggest more a shooting than hunting significance.

Horse's leg

Nickname for the bassoon, current among Sussex church bandsmen in the nineteenth century according to Spike Hughes's book *Glyndebourne*. See also FAG, GRANDMOTHER FIDDLE, SNORKEL.

Horst Wessel Song

Germany's second national anthem from 1933 to 1945. It was invariably played after *Deutschland über Alles* (originally known as the EMPEROR hymn). The song (a characteristic example of the German folk-tune turned into an odious marching-song) commemorates a thug called Horst Wessel, killed in a drunken pimps' dispute in around 1933, and cynically turned into a martyr by Hitler's propagandists. The tune had in fact been stolen from a love-song by Peter Cornelius (1824–74), the composer of *The Barber of Bagdad*, which goes to the words 'If you love me . . .'. It is noteworthy that whenever a demonstrator or rioter now meets his death, the political folk-song strummers manufacture an appropriate commemorative ballad.

Hosenrolle

Literally 'trousers role' in German; what the French and Italians call a *travesti* (transvestite) part, from the past participle of *travestir* (Italian *travestire*), to disguise. The parts of Cherubino, in Mozart's *Le Nozze di Figaro*, and Oktavian, in Richard Strauss's *Der Rosenkavalier*, are trouser roles. Nowadays, used as we are to nudity (and worse) on the stage, we forget that such roles, like those of principal 'boys' in English pantomime, were chiefly designed to give male members of the audience the erotic thrill of seeing girls' legs; and the sight of on-stage undressing and cross-dressing (for *travesti* roles usually involve girl-dressed-as-boy-pretending-to-be-a-girl situations) would only heighten that excitement.

Hot Fountain Pen

Like the FLEXATONE, GOOFUS, and other lost causes and shortlived vogues, the Hot Fountain Pen enjoyed a brief fashion in jazz of the 1920s and 1930s: a kind of rudimentary, miniature clarinet.

Hot seat

The section PRINCIPAL'S position, or what in American orchestras is called the First Chair. A player temporarily SITTING UP may say, 'I'm in the hot seat tonight.' It originally meant the electric chair used for executions.

House on Fire

See THE FROG

'How D'you do' Quartet

Haydn's op. 33 No. 5, so called in Britain because the opening figure fits the rhythm of those words.

Hugo and Les Misérables

During the late 1940s and early 1950s, a nickname for the Liverpool Philharmonic, then under the conductorship of Hugo Rignold and going through a turbulent period of its history, both musically and in 'industrial' relations.

The Hunt

Mozart's Quartet in B flat, K458, whose first movement is in the characteristic tempo of the HUNTING FINALE, its opening theme based on HORN HARMONIES.

Hunting Finale

Classical last movements in the characteristic six-eight time associated with the hunt, whether the music contains HORN HARMONIES or not. Mozart was fond of hunting finales, especially in his horn and piano concertos; and in the first movement of K458, above.

Hurdygurdy/barrel organ/street piano

A subject for endless confusion, even among the musical. The *hurdygurdy* is a stringed instrument bowed by a rosined wooden wheel instead of a bow, the kind of CIRCULAR BOW string players often wish they had. Playing the hurdygurdy requires a great deal of skill. The *barrel organ* needs little practice, and is played by turning a cranked handle. This pumps air into a wind chest which transmits it to organ pipes, at the same time turning a barrel whose pins open and close the PALLETS that give voice to the pipes. Some barrel organs, however, have reeds like the harmonium. The *street piano* works on the same principle, except that the pins activate piano-type hammers that strike strings (hence its characteristic, jangling HONKY-TONK sound). The confusion arose because street musicians used them all, beginning with the hurdygurdy in the seventeenth century but moving on to the other instruments as mechanical advances relieved them of the need to acquire playing-skills. But the general public, seeing that all three kinds of instrument were turned by a handle, kept the old name.

'I know what I like'

When music-lovers say this, as they often do, they are quoting Zuleika Dobson, in Sir Max Beerbohm's novel (1911) of that name: 'I don't,' she added, 'know anything about music, really. But I know what I like.' It means, of course, that they like what they know.

The Imperial

Haydn's no. 53 in D.

Impromptu

The musical equivalent of a carefully prepared spur-of-the-moment remark; in other words an oxymoronic title. The word means 'improvised' in French, and should therefore strictly be applied to a work thus created, not one that is written down. But the naming of musical works follows no rules. Rossini's *Petite Messe solennelle* is neither *petite* nor *solennelle;* there are long-winded *Bagatelles, Overtures* that open nothing, freestanding *Intermezzi,* and *Entr'actes* that have no acts on either side of them.

Incipit

The Latin word for 'here beginneth', but in musical shop-talk the opening bar or bars of a work or movement, e.g. in a THEMATIC CATALOGUE. Musicians pronounce the word like the English 'insipid', but classicists prefer 'inkipit', for the word has non-musical academic uses as well. Mozart kept a thematic catalogue of his own (later) works, in which he noted down their dates and incipits, which gave the idea to KOECHEL.

Indeterminacy

Much CONTEMPORARY music sounds as though the notes had been chosen at random but, as in SERIAL MUSIC, the very opposite is true: in KNITTING-PATTERN music, for example, each note may be strictly predetermined by mathematical considerations. But composers make composition even easier for themselves by turning the whole process over to ALEATORIC chance.

The Inextinguishable

The usual English translation of the title of Carl Nielsen's Fourth called in Danish *Det Uudslukkelige* and in German *Das Unauslösch-liche*. For once the English language is inadequate. The significance of the title lies in the neuter gender (German *das*), which makes it 'the abstract concept of the inextinguishable'. If it were in the feminine *die*, which the English translation implies, it would suggest a work so flammable that its fire cannot be put out.

Insertion aria

Composers of the past were less possessive or mutually exclusive about their work than those of today, and critics less obsessed by stylistic differences and pseudo-psychological minutiae. Thus if an opera by, say, Gluck was being performed in Vienna it was considered perfectly natural for, say, Mozart to compose an aria for it, and vice versa: perhaps to suit local conditions; to pander to currently fashionable taste; to satisfy the whims or special capabilities of certain singers; or merely to suit the production in hand by making time for special scene-changes (see CURTAIN ARIA) etc. That is precisely what Mozart did, to Gluck, Paesiello and one or two other composers; and it goes without saying that in some instances he was inserting pure gold into dross. Yet his contemporaries saw nothing strange about the practice, and presumably failed to notice the joins.

Inside player

See SEATING

Instrument surgery/clinic

Musicians, like politicians, have appropriated the names of medical stations for their own purposes: MPs hold 'surgeries', musicians 'clinics'. An instrument clinic is a kind of musical dolls' hospital, where musicians, especially young ones, can have their instruments examined and perhaps be shown how to look after them and keep them in good order.

Interval signals

On the radio, a kind of noise transmitted so as to avoid silence and thus reassure listeners that they are still tuned to their favourite station. But in concert halls, an interval signal may summon the audience back to their seats. In some halls this is tuned to the standard A, so that musicians can check their instruments as they return to the platform – and probably then get a different one from the first oboe.

(Playing/singing) In the cracks

I.e. between the piano keys – a facetious way of describing out-of-tune sounds. See also QUARTER-TONES.

(Playing) (up) In the snow

Said by string-players when they have to play at the top of the fingerboard, among deposits of white rosin dust (especially double bass players, who are less used to the dizzier heights).

Iron horn

Jazz nickname for the trumpet; also SQUEEZE HORN. When Beethoven went through a phase of preferring German words to foreign-based ones (see HAMMERKLAVIER) he called it the 'blasting-tube'.

ISM

The initials stand for the Incorporated Society of Musicians, a kind of upmarket MU. It was founded in 1882 by two Lancashire men who stated as their object the formation of a 'union of the musical profession in a representative body; the provision of opportunities for the discussion of matters connected with the culture and practice of the art; the improvement of musical education; the organization of musicians in a manner similar to that in which other learned professions were organized; and the obtaining of legal recognition by means of the registration of qualified teachers of music as a distinctive body'. In other words, the ISM is a true crafts guild, for it will be noticed that nowhere in the above paragraph is money mentioned.

Jähns

See KOECHEL

J.B.

Abbreviated nickname for Sir John Barbirolli. His players did not, however, pronounce it 'jay bee' but 'j'b' – the pronunciation being somewhere between 'jub' and 'job', the vowel almost soundless. Busoni, in a letter he wrote to his wife in 1919 during a concert tour in Britain, reports meeting George Bernard Shaw, whom he calls 'G. B. S.' He explains to her, 'In England it is a sign of the greatest popularity to be spoken of by your initials.' See also GLORIOUS JOHN.

Jena Symphony

A spurious 'Beethoven' symphony. See under BEETHOVEN'S TENTH.

Jingling Johnny

It is perhaps not surprising that there are many delightfully-named instruments in the percussion box, since noise-making instruments are often rooted in folklore. 'Jingling Johnny' is a hobson-jobson mistranslation of some Turkish word (see also NAKERS), descriptive of its sound. It consists of a long pole festooned with a number of small bells. The top is usually in the shape of a Turkish crescent and of gleaming brass, decorated with horses' tails. Occasionally the shape is that of a big brass lyre, and miniature cymbals (as on the tambourine) are mounted in addition to the bells. The German word for the jingling Johnny is *Schellenbaum* ('jingle-tree'); the French, who apparently deny the Turkish connection, call it *Pavillon Chinois* ('Chinese hat' – not, as sometimes seen, 'Chinese Pavilion'). Another English name for the instrument is 'Turkish Crescent'. Berlioz includes one in his *Symphonie funèbre et triomphale*, (1840); and it figures in some late eighteenth- and early nineteenth-century military and TURKISH MUSIC. This ceremonial object was enthusiastically revived by the Nazis and the Hitler Bodyguard Band had a huge and magnificently awful one. Australian sheep-shearers derisively call a 'Jingling Johnny' one who still shears sheep by hand, presumably making a jingling sound as he does so.

Joachim

Joseph Joachim (1831–1907) is now chiefly known as the violinist who composed the cadenzas for Beethoven's Violin Concerto and

Joachim conjuring up the spirit of Beethoven. Drawing by Franz Stassen

all but composed those in Brahms's. Thus when someone says, 'She doesn't do the Joachim' it can be taken that the player under discussion does not play the customary cadenza in Beethoven or Brahms. Joachim was himself a composer of considerable gifts and wrote a large number of important works, not merely display pieces for himself to shine in, like so many other instrumental virtuosi. Joachim was for many years considered the foremost

159

violinist, though the few recordings that survive are of too poor a quality to give one much idea of his powers. He was of Jewish birth, and the Nazis tried to 'blame' him for the preponderance of Jewish violinists. See also VIBRATO.

The Joachim of the Horn

Nickname given to Franz Strauss (1822–1905), who was for nearly half a century the principal horn player of the Munich Court Opera Orchestra; and father of Richard Strauss, whose wonderful horn parts he inspired much as Joachim influenced Brahms's violin writing. See also THE BEETHOVEN OF THE FLUTE, THE LIBERACE OF THE ORGAN and other equally silly comparisons.

John Brown finish

A loud and rousing ending to a piece of music, sure to inspire enthusiastic and prolonged applause. Such works are likely to be placed either at the end of the concert or to conclude the first half. The way a work ends may strongly influence its inclusion or omission in or from a programme. For example, statistics show that Brahms's third symphony, the only one that ends quietly, is played less often than the other three, with their exciting John Brown – or at any rate John Brahms – endings.

The Joke

Haydn's Quartet No. 30 in C major. The 'joke' is that he begins the first movement in the way one might have expected him to end it. Jokes that have to be announced (see MUSICAL JOKE) are usually less comic than those, like many of Haydn's, that take one by surprise.

The Joker of the Orchestra

Old-established nickname for the bassoon, but an unjust one. For every comic passage such as the tune in *The Sorcerer's Apprentice* by Dukas, there are dozens of lyrical or sad ones, especially those in the tearful tenor or even alto register of the instrument. Mozart was well aware of this, and in many of his works for wind instruments the bassoon is given passages (or entire variations) in the minor key, in a way that almost constitutes a Mozart fingerprint.

The Jupiter

Mozart's No. 41 in C major, K551. The name is said to have been coined by the first GLORIOUS JOHN, J. B. Cramer (1771–1858), and appeared on English concert programmes as early as 1819. The Germans have always preferred the more cumbersome name, *Sinfonie mit der Schlussfuge* ('Symphony with the Final Fugue') so as to distinguish it from the other seven or so C major symphonies

opera ... ~en compared to the four or five great works of its distinguished composer.

MOZART'S *celebrated Symphony*, THE JUPITER, *newly adapted for the Piano-Forte, with Accompaniments for a Flute, Violin, and Violoncello, ad libitum, by* MUZIO CLEMENTI. *No. 6. Published by Clementi and Co., Cheapside.*

This splendid symphony derives the name of *Jupiter*, now first publicly given to it upon any thing like an authority, from a very distinguished orchestral performer, who, unpremeditatedly, in conversation remarked, that such a title would well denote its majestic grandeur. We record this little anecdote for the purpose of saving Mozart from any future charge of vanity that might be advanced, should it ever be supposed that he himself gave so high-sounding an appellation to one of his own works.

Mr. Clementi has arranged for the piano-forte, with *ad libitum* accompaniments, many of the best symphonies of Haydn and Mozart, with that judgment and scrupulous care by which all his publications are so distinctly marked. It is evident that he has not calculated any of them for inferior performers; and, indeed, we do not see how such compositions can, with the slightest propriety or effect, be adapted to the powers of those who have not a considerable practical knowledge of music, and the physical advantage of a commanding hand.

The present symphony is the sixth of Cianchettini and Sperati's edition of Mozart's Symphonies in score, and is the most popular of them all, except, perhaps, that in E flat. It consists of an allegro, an andante, a minuet, trio, and finale, each of which is remarkable for some pre-eminent and striking beauty. The finale, a fugue with four subjects, is alone enough to immortalize its author. We have examined carefully this adaptation, with the score before us; and, admitting that it is, necessarily, rather difficult of execution, are, nevertheless, surprised to find so many obstacles to its general performance removed, while so much is preserved of the original fifteen parts, and so very little sacrificed in order to bring it within the compass of two hands. The accompaniments added to this arrangement, though not absolutely necessary to it, improve it much, and render it a very interesting quartett.

THREE AIRS *from* HAYDN'S CREATION, *arranged for the Piano-Forte, with a Flute Accompaniment, by* JOSEPH PINN... ~lement~d Co.

Mozart wrote. The name is inaccurate: for although the last movement begins fugally and employs wonderful contrapuntal skills, it
is not a fugue in the accepted sense. In the first volume (1823) of
the English musical magazine *The Harmonicon* a piano arrangement
of the symphony, made and published by Muzio Clementi, is
reviewed. The writer, probably William Ayrton, says 'This
splendid symphony derives the name of *Jupiter*, now first publicly
given to it upon anything like an authority, from a very distinguished orchestral performer, who, unpremeditatedly, in conversation remarked, that such a title would well denote its majestic
grandeur. We record this little anecdote for the purpose of saving
Mozart from any future charge of vanity that might be advanced,
should it ever be supposed that he himself gave so high-sounding
an appellation to one of his own works.'

Kamikaze conductors

Applied to young conductors who fail to observe normal courtesies while rehearsing but feel they will impress the players by imitating the antics of TOSCANONO. This inevitably leads to loss of co-operation at rehearsal and indifferent performances; and the aspirant is seldom invited again.

Kanewas

Schubert's nickname among his friends. The word comes from his pronunciation of 'Kann er was?' ('Can he do anything?' – i.e. 'is he clever?') which he used to ask of his friends when meeting strangers. See also SCHWAMMERL.

Kanoon

A mysterious instrument apparently invented by the editors of the big *Oxford English Dictionary* (1931 edition): 'A species of dulcimer, harp or sackbut, having fifty to sixty strings.' A stringed sackbut, i.e. trombone, is an interesting idea. I looked in vain for the word 'Harpoon', in the hope of finding a bassoon with ninety strings and seven pedals . . . .

Kapellmeister

German for 'bandmaster', but now derogatory of a conductor thought to be a mere TIME-BEATER: what Mozart in a pianistic context described as a MECHANICUS.

Kazoo

See EUNUCH FLUTE

Kegelstatt Trio

In his list of works Mozart simply calls it 'a Trio for Piano, Clarinet and Viola,' meaning the one in E flat, K498, written for Anton

STADLER. The name, which is the German word for a bowling-alley, is derived from an unsupported anecdote that Mozart 'composed the piece while playing skittles' – an unlikely tale, although many passages in his letters confirm his interest in the game. The correct spelling is as above, not 'Kegelstadt', which would be a town.

Kéler Béla

Austro-Hungarian composer (1820–82) of light music, and successor to Joseph Lanner, whose orchestra he took over in 1855 after the latter's death. English concert programmes usually refer to him as 'Béla', a name he shared with that other Hungarian composer Bartók Béla before his fame was established. Béla is their forename, as the name-order is reversed in Hungarian. For English purposes they should be billed as Béla Kéler and Béla Bartók, respectively. Béla Kéler's name should be pronounced and stressed like 'fail a sailor'. He composed some of the Hungarian Dances later attributed to Brahms.

Ker-doink

Onomatopoeic term for imprecise ATTACK in chording, especially in a PIANO DUET or two-piano partnerships.

Key

Two sorts figure in musicians' talk. One concerns the system of tonality on which Western music is based (as in 'What key is it in?') for an explanation of which see a standard dictionary of music. The other is mechanical, and serves to cover the note-holes of wind instruments (in effect, a kind of artificial finger-tip), in places fingers are perhaps unable to reach. Keys may be *open-standing*, that is, the fingers press on them or their extension-levers to close them; or *closed*: press-to-open keys. Both are spring-loaded and designed to return to their normal position, the springs delicately balanced and an occasional source of trouble. Every wind player therefore carries rubber bands for use as emergency springs; and CIGARETTE PAPERS in case a key sticks because of WATER.

Keyboard Knights

German, *Klavier-Ritter*: J. S. Bach's name for composers unable to write music without the help of a keyboard instrument. See ABSOLUTE PITCH.

Keyboard Lion

Pianists of the older school, who often wore leonine hairstyles, like Liszt, Rubinstein, Pachmann, Paderewski, and many others. But Germans called these lionized LONGHAIRED MUSICIANS *Klavier-tiger* – 'Piano Tigers'.

The keyboard side

The more desirable seats of a concert room. Many concert-goers like to see the pianist's fingers; and professional colleagues may wish to study his FINGERINGS.

The keyhole

No connection with the KEYS of a wind instrument, but the keyhole or lock on the piano lid, which plays a role in music only because the beginner pianist is told to line it up with his navel. 'Note : Middle C is at left of lock', explains the *Lawrence Wright Piano Tutor*. Hence facetious remarks like 'Keyhole must be in the wrong place' about a pianist who plays a lot of wrong notes.

Kick-off

Informal name for the starting-time of a performance, as in 'What time's kick-off?' See also DOWNBEAT.

Kinked trumpet

One which has the BELL of the instrument pointing heavenwards instead of straight at those musicians who have the misfortune of sitting in front of it. It has been established that trumpets are the primary cause of premature deafness that afflicts many orchestral players. Pop musicians fare even worse.

Kist (-fu)-o Whistles

Scottish nickname for the organ. *Kist* = chest.

Kitsch

German slang word for something considered artistically worth-less, in bad taste, sentimental and ingratiating, but possessed of a certain charm that makes it temporarily rather fashionable. The Kitsch of yesteryear is often acclaimed as 'folk art', 'charmingly primitive' or 'natural expression' by succeeding generations.

Klavarskribo

A strange and eccentric system of pianoforte notation devised in 1931 by a Dutch musician called Pot, who founded the Klavar-skribo Institute to publicize and promote it. I don't know whether the Dutch had football pools then, but if they did, Pot must have scooped the jackpot. For by 1950 he had issued at his own expense some 10,000 works of the piano repertoire, printed in the notation. Every browser in second-hand music shops knows by the amount of unsold Klavarskribo music he encounters that no one seems to want it; and I have yet to meet a pianist who can read the system. Standard notation, with all its faults, is the best system for writing music yet devised, and is not as difficult to master as may at first appear to the beginner. Yet repeated attempts have been made to replace it with other methods. Arnold Schoenberg (1874–1951) suggested a system he considered more suitable for his DODECAPHONIC music, presumably one designed to express the musico-Marxist theory that all twelve notes of the scale are equal (which, like men, they patently are not). It has come to nothing. For, as Percy Scholes said in his *Oxford Companion to Music*: 'The enormous amount of capital locked up in the world's stock of printed music, and the conservatism of musicians . . . are two formidable obstacles in the way of adoption even of the simpler reforms.'

Klaviertiger

See KEYBOARD LION

Klavierübung

German for 'keyboard practice', used by J. S. Bach for a group of works, including six partitas, the Italian Concerto and the GOLDBERG Variations. Some say the term was invented by Johann Kuhnau (1660–1722); but it can be applied to any keyboard exercises, of whatever date or style. See CLAVIER.

Kna

Nickname of the conductor Hans von Knappertsbusch (1888–1965). See YES/NO.

Knee-trembler

Suggestive nickname for a knee-lever which on some small organs and harmoniums is used to bring into play various changes of register, stops, tremolos, etc.

Knitting-pattern music

TWELVE-NOTE or SERIAL music; also COMPOSING-BY-NUMBERS, DODECACOPHONY.

K(oechel)

Ludwig von Köchel (1800–77) was an Austrian nobleman, botanist, mineralogist, pedagogue and musical amateur, who used his skills in classification to compile the first thorough THEMATIC CATALOGUE of Mozart's works, although Mozart himself had set the scene for such an undertaking by compiling a thematic list of his own works composed between 1784 and 1791. Köchel's catalogue was first published in 1862, and his name has ever since been associated with the composer. The initial K (or K. V. for the German *Köchelverzeichnis*) followed by a number, denotes the chronological order of Mozart's works. There have been several revisions; and that by EINSTEIN is sometimes referred to as K. E. Others who followed Köchel's brilliant example, and have been rewarded by having their names immortalized when their respective composers' works are discussed, are Schmieder (Bach), Kinsky (Beethoven), Gérard (Boccherini), Cauchie (Couperin), Hoboken (Haydn), Wotquenne

(Gluck, Galuppi, C. P. E. Bach, Rossi, etc.), Deutsch (Schubert), and Jähns (Weber). The accepted English spelling is Koechel.

Konzertmeister

The German word for an orchestra LEADER, translated by the Americans as 'Concert Master', which is more suggestive of a whip-cracking ringmaster than a *primus inter pares* violinist. In American usage it is the conductor who 'leads' an orchestra.

Kortholt

An old instrument related to the bassoon family whose long sounding-length is obtained from a short piece of wood by means of bores that double back on themselves – in a manner used to some extent on the bassoon itself. The word is an ancient corruption of the German words *kurzes Holz*, ('short wood'), and should be pronounced approximately to rhyme with 'bought colt', not like the town of Northolt in Middlesex. Kortholts (the anglicized plural is accepted, though the old English equivalent 'curtal' is surely to be preferred) are now played again after centuries of neglect.

The Kreutzer

Beethoven's Sonata op. 47 in A major for violin and piano is so called because of its dedication to Rodolphe Kreutzer (1766–1831), who was not aware of Beethoven's dedicatory intentions and never played the work, at any rate in public. It was originally written for the English half-negro violinist and composer George Bridgetower (1779–1860), and inscribed *Sonata mulattica composta per il mulatto Brischdauer, gran pazzo* e compositore mulattico*. The inscription was good humoured, not a racial insult, for the two men were good friends, at least until they fell out over a girl and Beethoven withdrew the dedication. Bridgetower lived for most of his life in England, where he enjoyed the patronage of the Prince of Wales (later George IV). He was, so to speak, a grand-pupil of Mozart, having had composition lessons from Mozart's pupil, Thomas Attwood. He took the degree of Bachelor of Music at Cambridge and appeared as soloist with the Royal Philharmonic Society. Bridgetower died at Peckham, near London. There is also a string quartet by Leoš Janáček (1854–1958) with the confusing title 'The Kreutzer Sonata', but its name is derived from a story by Leo Tolstoy, itself in turn based on the Beethoven sonata.

* *gran pazzo* = big idiot.

Labyrinth

A composition, usually eighteenth-century or earlier, with frequent and wide-ranging modulations. The progression from one key to another is governed by certain rules of harmony, the application or breaking of which makes for interest and originality. A composer writing a successful labyrinth engages in a kind of musical escapology: he daringly poses problems for himself, but like Houdini, makes sure he knows his way out before he even starts tying himself in knots. The authenticity of Bach's *Kleines harmonisches Labyrinth* (BWV 591) has recently been declared doubtful, but whoever wrote it knew his way through the keys. Johann Caspar Ferdinand Fischer (c.1670–1746) wrote a set of Preludes and Fugues in all keys (some twenty years before Bach's FORTY-EIGHT) called *Ariadne musica*, after the classical conqueror of a labyrinth, although his are not labyrinths in the strict sense.

The Lark

Haydn's Quartet in D, op. 64, No. 5, so called because of the soaring nature of its glorious opening tune – which could equally describe THE SUNRISE.

The last trumpet

The passage in the Latin mass about the last trump, *Tuba mirum spargens sonum*, has given rise to all manner of confusions. It has been scored with an OBBLIGATO for almost every brass instrument – except the tuba. Mozart's *Requiem* has a trombone solo, and in his arrangement of Handel's *Messiah* he gives the trumpet part to a horn, for the art of high CLARINO playing had by then died out. Handel himself adds further confusion: the bass singer ends his recitative with the words 'at the last trumpet' and up stands the *first* trumpet to play his OBBLIGATO.

Late playing

Perceptive concert-goers notice that orchestras do not play *with* the conductor's beat but *after* it. That is to say, sounds which are meant to coincide with the downbeat appear only to materialize as the STICK once again returns to the topmost point of its travel. The observation is correct, although the natural time-lag between sight and sound, especially in a large hall, may make the delay appear worse than it is. But some orchestras do play very late, responding sluggishly to the conductor's beat. The Vienna Philharmonic is notorious for it, and the Berlin Phil was worse, having developed the habit under Furtwängler, with his notoriously slow, unclear downbeat. When he conducted at La Scala, Milan, a member of the orchestra called out from the back 'Coraggio, maestro!' It was Karajan who brought the orchestra back to a more sensible practice. Most London orchestras play slightly late. The Hallé played with a time-lag under Barbirolli because he liked it that way. A slight vagueness, even a CIRCULAR BEAT, means that the players tend to wait for each other (none wishing to be first, or make a DOMINO); and the small degree of uncertainty involved in a later ATTACK produces a better sound. Much atmospheric music, like that of Delius and the French impressionists, is ruined by too clear a beat which brings an instant, hard-edged response. Conductors who want their players to play *with* the beat say they like to 'lean on the sound'; and it can indeed be disconcerting for a conductor when nothing happens as his stick reaches its lowest point: like treading on a step which isn't there. The sound, in fact, usually materializes on the 'flick', which is the tiny movement of the baton as it reaches its lowest point and embarks on its upward or sideways travel, as explained under STICK TECHNIQUE. Two more points should be made. One is that the conductor's movements are intended to indicate what he wants his players to do; so it would be useless to expect them to do it precisely at the same time: as John Thornley has neatly pointed out, 'No one starts rushing out of a building on the *f* of the word *fire!*' The other point is that the problem is not as great as it may appear to the spectator. Orchestral musicians seem to play late more naturally than on time. Only pianists never seem to get used to it. Whether they are playing a concerto or an orchestral piano part, they nearly always come in too early, producing the well-known KER-DOINK effect. Members of the audience who feel worried by the phenomenon might try closing their eyes simply to enjoy the music.

Conductors – at any rate good ones – are there for practical reasons, not to look graceful. People who want to watch pretty movements performed in time to music should go to the ballet.

Laudon Symphony

Properly *Loudon*: Haydn's No.69 in C, the name sanctioned by the composer. It refers to a Field Marshal.

Laughing-song

A common nineteenth-century operatic cliché, ranking in inevitability (at any rate in comic opera) with the SOLDIER'S CHORUS and the drinking-song. Operatic TAPEWORMS that are long and turgid (however beautiful) are sometimes sarcastically described as being 'Like *Parsifal* but without the *Laughing-Song*'.

Leader

The orchestra leader's job is full of anomalies and anachronisms. It is a throwback to the nineteenth century and earlier, when the best player of a group of fiddles would as a matter of course take charge of the proceedings, his bow a useful implement for beating time when required. When Beethoven's Ninth was first performed in 1824, the direction was shared by the principal first violinist, Schuppanzigh, the choir-trainer Umlauf, and Kreutzer at the piano – with the stone-deaf Beethoven beating time as well. During the next few decades there was a power-struggle between the pianist-director and the leader, which the leader lost. The pianist left his keyboard (as orchestras got better he had less need to fill in missing parts on his SPINETTL) and told the leader of the violins to sit down and keep playing his fiddle. (This coincided approximately with the introduction of the baton.) The deposed leader was allowed to keep his title, now honorific, by way of compensation. Only in dance-orchestras of the Johann Strauss type, which used no keyboard, did the leader retain the double function of playing and conducting. The Germans awarded the symphonic leader the courtesy title 'CONCERT MASTER' and his dance music colleague that of 'Stehgeiger', literally 'stand-up fiddler' (see FIDDLER ON THE HOOF) – fortunately resisting any temptation to translate 'Leader' literally into 'Führer'. The French, incidentally got it right: they call him *chef d'attaque* (see ATTACK), which perfectly defines his function as leading first violinist, *primus inter pares*. The leader usually has his name printed on the programme, wears white tie and tails when the rest of the orchestra are dressed in black tie and dinner jackets, and makes a separate entrance, just before the conductor. (Only in Britain: orchestras touring abroad have occasionally followed this practice and several unfortunate leaders found themselves walking on to the sound of their own footsteps, mistaken for a latecomer.) In fact the leader does not 'lead' like, say, a dancer: if he played everything a quaver in front of his colleagues he would be a poor leader. But any first violin solos there may be in the score will be taken by him, although these are rare compared with wind solos, and he is seldom heard playing on his own. The leader is, however, in charge of the string BOWINGS. Here he may override the opinions of the other string section PRINCIPALS, for he is in effect the principal string player. He also acts as an important liaison-man between management and conductor, on the one hand, and his orchestral colleagues, on the other. He usually has the privilege of sharing the conductor's GREEN ROOM (unless the latter is so exalted that he insists on complete privacy). If the conductor falls ill or drops dead, the leader is expected to take up his baton, although statistics show that it is usually not violinists but wind-players who harbour conducting ambitions and secretly carry a conductor's baton in their knapsack; and who are therefore likely to have had far more practice at conducting an orchestra. The leader/conductor substitution is, however, a sensible and natural one: for the leader, as one of the fiddle-players, is more expendable than one of the wind or brass. If the second bassoonist fails to turn up, a minor panic develops, and the ORCHESTRA MANAGER frantically telephones for a replacement. Should the leader suddenly be prevented from playing, the manager merely says, 'Move up one, lads, Jack won't be coming tonight'; and the REPET takes the leader's place. The orchestra will sound no different. But it should be stated that a leader's qualities are important in the longer term and a good leader is essential for a good orchestra. The leader should not be confused with a dance band leader (whose direction is usually nominal and confined to a few snaps of the finger); nor should English writers follow the American practice of describing the work of a conductor in a leader's terms: 'Mr Muti led the orchestra in a performance of the fifth symphony.'

Leaning on the sound

A phenomenon known only to a conductor. As he beats time, so he expects the music to sound in a certain time-relationship with the beat – see LATE PLAYING. When he beats a fortissimo chord in the wrong place (see DOMINO) and nobody plays, he has no sound to lean on; and conductors have under such circumstances been known to fall off the rostrum.

Left-handed musicians

The normal way of playing is right-handed. That is, wind instruments are held with the right hand below the left: flutes, bassoons and horns are held to the right of the player's body, and trombonists work their slide with the right hand. String instruments are bowed with the right hand and fingered with the left. Harpists rest their instrument on the right shoulder, so that the bass notes are played with the left hand, as on the piano (except Irish folk harpers, who do it back-to-front). But the evidence of old paintings and drawings suggests that musicians of the past had the choice of playing ambidextrously. On most instruments it make no difference, since there were few if any KEYS, and those there were could be fitted with SWALLOW TAILS. Only when mechanical keywork began to be fitted did right-hand standardization take place. There have been, and still are, some notable left-handed players of the violin and viola. The entertainer Vic Oliver played the fiddle back-to-front, and so did Charlie Chaplin. Harpo Marx played the harp the wrong way round, resting the instrument on the left shoulder. Left-handed players are usually those who 'picked up' their elementary technique without tuition and were unable to change when told about it. But it should be mentioned that the CBSO has had a left-handed viola player since the early 1950s – a courageous young lady who, after suffering a serious accident, taught herself to play the viola the other way round. Strange as it may seem, there are a few left-handed professional conductors. For them no excuses can be made, since conducting is an art that requires many qualities but no great manual dexterity. Left-handed conductors are surprisingly difficult to follow, as all their directional side-beats go the wrong way. Left-handed string players, too, tend to be a nuisance in orchestras, because the sharp end of the bow is a constant threat to the eyes of colleagues; except in a string quartet, where the ideal second violin would be a left-handed one, because both fiddles are able to project their sound towards the audience. See also NAKERS.

Le Midi

Haydn's No.7 in C, part of a set that includes *Le Matin, Le Midi* and *Le Soir*. Also the title of a popular piece by John Field (1782–1837) in an orchestration by Sir Hamilton Harty (1879–1941), known as *Rondo: Le Midi*. See also MORNING, NOON AND NIGHT IN VIENNA.

Les Six

Although writing music is essentially solitary work, many composers seem to be gregarious by nature, willing to form themselves into groups and schools. However, the term *Les Six* was coined in 1920, almost perversely, by a French critic, Henri Collet. The group was a very loosely connected band of Satie disciples: Auric, Durey, Honegger, Milhaud, Poulenc and Tailleferre – the last-named being the token woman. All their music has in common is a certain unmistakable Frenchness. See also THE FIVE, THE FIVE FRANKFURTERS, THE GIANT HAMBURGERS.

The Liberace of the Flute

Publicist's nickname for James Galway. Various more or less silly sobriquets of this type will be found elsewhere in this book.

The Liberace of the Organ

Ditto for Carlo Curley; both named after the tinselled piano entertainer.

Licorice stick

American nickname for the clarinet. Also AGONY PIPE, BLACK-STICK, GOBSTICK, WOP STICK.

Lied

The German word for 'song'. But there is more to it than that. Lieder (which is the plural form) are in English usage considered to be songs belonging to, arising from, or leading up to, the

German romantic movement of the late eighteenth, the whole of the nineteenth, and part of the twentieth centuries. They thus include Mozart (only just), Beethoven, Schubert, Schumann, Brahms, Wolf, R. Strauss and Mahler. The real father and largely unsung creator of the romantic *Lied* was, however, one Johann Loewe (1796–1869). Yet the *Lieder* of the SECOND VIENNESE SCHOOL, e.g. Schoenberg's, are usually referred to as merely 'songs'. It all shows how silly it can be to use foreign words unnecessarily in English. The Germans, after all, have no choice: to them all songs of all periods, from medieval *Minnelieder* to non-melodic, anti-romantic DONKEY MUSIC squeals, are *Lieder*. So why do we not simply call them 'songs', qualifying further when necessary? For to be consistent one should refer to an Italian song as a *canto*, a Hungarian one as a *tál*, and a Norwegian one as a *sang*. The French, curiously enough, are more wide-ranging in the naming of their songs: they do not have merely CHANSONS but also BRUNETTES and BERGERETTES, etc., and since there is no English equivalent for these, the use of such foreign words is not only acceptable but desirable in the interest of clarity.

Ligature

The metal clamp with which clarinettists fix the reed to the mouthpiece of their instrument. The word comes from the Latin word *ligare*, to bind; and clarinet players did until quite recently *bind* the reed on with twine, a practice still followed by some Austrian players.

Lightning conductor

One who takes everything he conducts at an unusually fast speed; in other words, a SPEED MERCHANT.

'Like Parsifal but without the Laughing-song'

See LAUGHING-SONG

Lipping

A verb made from a noun, used almost exclusively by musicians. It means the action of a wind or brass player as he adjusts his

EMBOUCHURE so as to change the nature of a note, usually to make it sharper or flatter. Hence also 'lipping up' and 'lipping down'.

Lip-salve

Lips are important to wind and brass players. Some rely on the well-known skin-hardening properties of alcohol, others resort to lip-salve. It should not be mistaken for lipstick.

Liquorice stick

See LICORICE STICK. As it is an American nickname for the clarinet it should have its American spelling.

L'istesso

When a conductor says at rehearsal, 'We'll go from the l'istesso . . . ' he means a place in the SCORE AND PARTS marked *l'istesso tempo*, i.e. 'at the same speed'. However, as *l'istesso* means 'the same' in Italian it could preface any other instruction. The score of Schoenberg's *Variations for Orchestra*, op. 31, contains the interesting polyglot tempo marking *'L'istesso tempo aber etwas langsamer'* – 'the same speed but a little slower'. Schumann, in one of his piano pieces, writes *'So rasch wie möglich'* ('As quick as possible'), and a few pages later, *'Noch rascher'* ('Still faster').

The Liszt of the Violin

Paganini. See BEETHOVEN OF THE FLUTE.

The Little A Major

This diminutive, without further qualification, is generally applied to the earlier and smaller of Mozart's two piano concertos in that key, so as to distinguish it (K414) from K488. Such a distinction is, however, not made in the case of his three A major symphonies – K114, K134 and K201. As the two earlier ones are seldom played, 'Mozart's A major' is generally taken to refer to the last one – which is also the first of his greatest symphonies. But true Mozartians would specify the KOECHEL number anyway. Identifications such as 'Mozart's piano concerto No.14' are a misleading solecism, as these numberings were made before it had been established that the earliest piano concertos were in fact only arrangements by the young Mozart of other men's music.

Little-box-you-push-him-he-cry-out-little-box-you-pull-him-he-cry-out

Pidgin for an accordion, concertina or squeeze-box. See also BIG BOX.

The Little C Major

The smaller of Schubert's symphonies in C major, D598, so as to distinguish it from The Great C Major, also known as THE HEAVENLY LONG. It must, however, be pointed out that in the AUTOGRAPH the composer entitles this symphony *Grosse Sinfonie*, but that was before he started on the really big one.

LMP

The London Mozart Players, founded in 1949 by Harry Blech (b.1910) for the performance of chiefly eighteenth-century music.

Lollipops

Short pieces of music of charm and grace that make no great demand on the listener. The term was coined by Sir Thomas Beecham when he included them in his concerts or used them as ENCORES.

The London Bach

Mozart's name for J. S. Bach's youngest son, Johann Christian Bach (1735–82), who had the good sense to take up residence in London for the latter, most fruitful and successful, part of his life. He was a close friend of the painter Gainsborough, who made at least one fine portrait of him. Other members of the huge Bach clan also had geographical distinguishing names. J. S. Bach's sixteenth child and ninth son, Johann Christoph Friedrich (1732–95), was known as the *Bückeburg Bach*; and Johann Sebastian's brother, Johann Jakob (1682–1722), as the *Swedish Bach*, for he was an oboist in the Swedish army and court musician at

Stockholm. J. S. Bach's third son, Carl Phillipp Emanuel was for a time known as the *Hamburg Bach,* for he succeeded Telemann in that city as church music director. See THE GIANT HAMBURGERS

The London Symphony

There is one by Haydn (No.104 in D major) and one by vw, both titles official. But the situation is confused by the fact that there are no fewer than twelve London symphonies by Haydn, including THE SURPRISE, THE MIRACLE, THE MILITARY, THE CLOCK and the DRUM ROLL – some of which have further confusing names.

Longhaired musicians

This used to be the standard insult thrown at CLASSICAL musicians by the young and ignorant. They thought that everyone engaged in that kind of music cultivated the hairstyle associated with the KEYBOARD LIONS of old. But the advent of the Beatles changed all that. Within a year or so, their hair was being not only aped but exaggerated by the unmusical young – and later the musical and not so young; and even a few well-known conductors were seen sporting tresses far longer than Liszt, Schumann, Paderewski or the young Brahms ever had. Orchestral players, on the other hand, usually try to look as un-musicianly as possible, hoping to be taken for bank managers or civil servants. If they are busy they are as likely as anyone else to put off going to the barber's, so that their hair by turns will be either too long or too short. On going for an overdue haircut at a barber's shop in the West End of London, I was greeted with the supercilious remark, 'Put a fiddle in your hand, sir, and you might be taken for a musician.' Beethoven had to be reminded to have a haircut before the first performance of his Ninth; and among the praises heard afterwards was 'a compliment to the Master who cut your hair'. Musicians are, in truth, as careless, or as vain, about their hair as anyone else. They hate going bald just as much; and engage in the same subterfuges. Several well-known conductors wear (or wore) wigs or hairpieces that deceive no one. One was so worried by his incipient bald pate that he was observed combing his hair with one hand while conducting the Eroica with the other. Other distinguished conductors feel they must keep their hair, especially a distinguished coif, at a constant length (like any politician proud of his image) which must mean frequent visits to (or more likely from) their barber – for which the ordinary hard-working musician would have neither the time nor the money. Toupées have been known to go embarrassingly awry during exertions occasioned by an energetic performance. Sir Malcolm Sargent used to resort to a little hair-dye, allowing only his temples to go slightly grey towards the end of his life. Pierre Monteux (1876–1964) let his luxuriant, bushy moustache turn naturally white, but dyed his head hair a blatant jet black. One colleague asked him in feigned innocence, 'Maestro, why is it that your hair is still black, whereas your moustache has gone white?' Monteux replied with a twinkle, 'Becoz ze 'air on my 'ead 'az not 'ad ze same experiences.' On another occasion, asked about his *joie de vivre*, he answered with a shrug of his shoulders – and a pun on the French title of Rimsky-Korsakov's opera – *Le Coq d'or*.

Long-service medal

A gold medal (probably now made of some lesser metal gilded) awarded to players with twenty years' or more service to the HALLÉ. Ever since Hans Richter (1843–1916) started a pension scheme, the Hallé has had a fine reputation for looking after the well-being of its older members. I recall seeing Sir John Barbirolli, when there was some confusion over the allocation of hotel rooms in some foreign hotel, fussing to see that they were comfortable before he accepted a room for himself. Hallé string principals nearing the end of their career, instead of being pensioned off, may be tactfully offered a job on or near the BACK DESKS, where their experience is as useful as at the front of the section. So far as I know, no other orchestra awards a long-service medal; but several give their veterans the Order of the Boot.

Loo-John

Not some kind of Anglo-American lavatory but the common corruption of *lujon*, an instrument developed in America, probably by French-speaking creole jazz musicians. It is a percussion instrument, a big wooden box fitted with tuned wooden resonators inside it, and is played with soft marimba sticks. For other oddly named jazz instruments see FLEXATONE, GOOFUS, HOT FOUNTAIN PEN, etc.

Loophonium

See HARPIC-CORD

The loud bassoon

An instance of poetic-musical licence. The instrument Coleridge might have heard in 1798, when he wrote *The Ancient Mariner*, ('The Wedding-Guest here beat his breast/For he heard the loud bassoon') would have made a gentle, buzzing noise, not the firm, strong tone of the modern alleged JOKER OF THE ORCHESTRA. The eighteenth-century bassoon was played with a softer, broader reed than the modern one. 'Loud' was probably the best one-syllable adjective Coleridge could think of: all others evoking that instrument seem to be polysyllables. The poet Samuel Taylor Coleridge should not be confused with the composer Samuel Coleridge-Taylor.

LPO

The London Philharmonic Orchestra, founded by Sir Thomas Beecham in 1932. He also started the RPO, in 1946.

LRAM

See ARCM

LSO

The London Symphony Orchestra, founded in 1904 as a breakaway body from the Queen's Hall Orchestra because of Sir Henry Wood's ban on DEPPING. Its first conductor was Hans Richter.

Luftpause

For some reason musicians seem to prefer this German term to the English 'breathing-space'. It is a source of possible confusion; for the German word *pause* means that there is a period of silence; whereas the English PAUSE means a prolonging of sound, not of silence. A *Luftpause* is usually indicated by a comma placed above and after the note that precedes the breathing-space.

Luigi Jaja

John Amis's inspired nickname for the Italian political activist and composer Luigi Nono (b.1924). He wrote quartets, quintets, sextets, octets, and works for thirteen and more instruments, but apparently no Nono nonet.

Lustspiel

German word for 'comedy': literally 'lust play'. But it is the German *Lust*, which means a general kind of joy and jolly well-being, not the English carnal variety, although both words come from the same source.

Lyre

A small, lyre-shaped brass clip, fixed to a bandsman's instrument or strapped to his arm, for holding his PART. See also AMBULATORY MUSIC.

McTell, William

Included here for the curiosity of his name, which sounds like a Scottish version of the Swiss folk hero immortalized in a French opera by the Italian Rossini. In fact he was a black American blues singer, born at the end of the nineteenth century and died around 1962.

Mad Scene

There are a few examples of *Mad Songs* dating from the seventeenth and eighteenth centuries, including at least one by Henry Purcell. But it was in the nineteenth century that the *Mad Scene* became an operatic cliché. This dictated that a cruelly jilted heroine should lose her reason while singing a florid aria. The effect was considered to be enhanced if there could be an OBBLIGATO instrument as well. Bellini wrote a *Mad Scene* in *I Puritani*, Ambroise Thomas in *Hamlet*, and Donizetti several: in *Linda di Chamounix*, *Anna Bolena* and the most famous of all, in *Lucia di Lammermoor*. Gilbert and Sullivan deliciously parodied it in *Ruddigore*: 'Mad Margaret, a poor crazed creature whose brain has been turned by Sir Despard Murgatroyd's heartless conduct', but who (unlike the heroines she is modelled on) becomes a District Visitor and discovers a recipe for recovering her sanity: whenever madness threatens, she repeats the word 'Basingstoke'. (Today, thanks to what the town-planners have done to that once attractive town, the word would be likely to induce a relapse.)

Maestro

Italian for master, teacher, foreman, etc. In music it is the standard abbreviation of *maestro di cappella*. Foreign conductors working in Britain expect to be addressed as maestro; but equally, British orchestral players find it difficult to utter the word. Conductors may, however, be slightly offended when addressed informally: 'I say, Mister Toscanini, what's my note three bars after letter

C?' But the title can also be used as an insult; as when some inexperienced, young and possibly bumptious conductor is pointedly addressed as 'Maestro!' The Italians, incidentally, have a large choice of such insults: *maestruccio*: a wretched little teacher; *maestrone*: a fat one; *maestrucolo*: a paltry one; *maestruzzo*: a humble teacher – or conductor; *maestrino*, a little one. See also KAPELLMEISTER.

The Manchester School

Name given, without irony and in imitation of the SECOND VIENNESE SCHOOL, to a group of young composers who studied at the then Royal Manchester College of Music during the 1960s and decided to rebel against their composition teacher, whom they considered insufficiently CONTEMPORARY. As usual, most of them later grew into useful and on the whole law-abiding citizens.

The Mannheim Crescendo/Rocket/Rush/Sigh/Steamroller

Terms relating to the famous eighteenth-century German orchestra of Mannheim, in the province of Baden-Württemberg, its manner of playing, and the style of the music composed for it by various composers like Stamitz, Holzbauer, Richter and Filtz. It is no exaggeration to say that had it not been for the enlightened musical policies of the Electors of Mannheim, Austro-German orchestral music, its style and practice, would not be as we know it. Even the relative strengths of woodwind, brass and strings were established largely through Mannheim custom from the 1720s onwards. Many of the Mannheimers' favourite effects became typical eighteenth-century clichés and were recognized and derided – even by Mozart's father Leopold (who had a large repertoire of musical clichés himself). In a letter to Wolfgang (11 December 1777) he writes of 'the mannerism-ridden Mannheim *goût'*. The *Mannheim Rocket* is an impetuously rising Arpeggio figure in equal note values, as exemplified by the opening bar of the last movement of Mozart's No. 40 in G minor, K550. The *Mannheim Sigh* is a typical eighteenth-century sighing Appoggiatura, but was by Mannheimers used in quick movements as well as slow ones, where such sighs were common currency in *all* eighteenth-century music. The *Mannheim Rush* and *Steamroller* are figurative descriptions of what is more succinctly called the *Mannheim Crescendo*, an effect resulting from the excellent technique and discipline for which the Mannheim players were famous throughout Europe. They had, in fact, borrowed it from Italy, where the crescendo had long been an important operatic effect; and the Italians later reimported it and called it the ROSSINI CRESCENDO. (It should be added, however, that the translation of *Walze* ('Roller') as 'Steamroller' is anachronistic by about 100 years; and that *Walze*, a roller, and *Walzer*, a waltz, are different and unrelated words). The *Mannheim Crescendo* is closely associated with the TROMMELBASS, another orchestral device that lasted almost the whole eighteenth century and well into the nineteenth.

March King

See SOUSA

Maria Theresia

Haydn's No. 48 in C major, named after the Austrian empress.

Master

The finished, edited, mixed and balanced tape from which gramophone records are made.

Master class

An uneasy translation from the German *Meisterklasse*. In the continental teaching-system, which is largely based on class tuition, this simply means a class for the most advanced students, just as advanced craftsmen would together work on their masterpiece. In such master classes students not only learn from each others' mistakes but also become accustomed to performing before the severest critics they are ever likely to encounter – each other. But in Britain and America, and thanks to television, master classes have been made into a spectator sport, in which the emphasis is on the master, not his pupils. They are present not so much for what they can learn but as accessories to help a world-famous player or singer expound his ideas, usually with plenty of 'how-to-do-it' illustrations, reminiscences and anecdotes ('. . . as Fauré said to me . . .').

MD

See MUSICAL DIRECTOR

Mechanicus

Mozart's harsh description of Muzio Clementi (1752–1832) in a letter to Leopold Mozart (12 January 1782): 'Clementi plays well, so far as execution with the right hand goes. His greatest strength lies in his passages in thirds. Apart from this he has not a Kreutzer's worth of taste or feeling – in short, he is simply a mechanicus.' Nevertheless Mozart borrowed the fugal theme in the *Magic Flute* overture from a piano sonata by Clementi.

Megaphone

Literally, 'big sound', from the Greek *mega* and *phone*: in music a kind of giant ear-trumpet in reverse, one of which was used for Walton's entertainment *Façade*, first performed in 1922 privately, and publicly a year later.

Menu

Jocular term for the programme, as in 'What's on the menu tonight?'

Mercury

Haydn's No.43 in E flat.

Messiah/The Messiah

Which should it be: *with* or *without* the definite article? Some say there should be no article, as Handel himself entitled it 'Messiah'. However, when he referred to the oratorio in German he called it *Der Messias*: and he was hardly an authority on correct English usage. In the North of England, where the oratorio established its true home, THE *Messiah* prevails. Besides, Lancastrians and Yorkshiremen know all about t'definite article, when to hint at it and when to drop it altogether. But then they also sometimes refer to Mendelssohn's best-known oratorio as '*THE Elijah*' See also THE YORKSHIRE MESSIAH, and the picture on p. 102.

Punch, 1895

Undesigned Coincidence

Curate (to Parish Choir, practising the Anthem): *"Now we'll begin again at the 'Hallelujah,' and please linger longer on the 'Lu'!"*

The Met

In operatic circles, short for the Metropolitan Opera House, New York. Elsewhere it means either the London Metropolitan Police or the Meteorological Office.

Mezzo

The customary abbreviation of *mezzo-soprano*, a female voice of middling range, neither as low as a (possibly BOILED) contralto nor as high as a soprano. In opera mezzos are seldom heroines but are given roles like nurses, matrons, mothers or mother-figures and serving-women of the older kind: the role of a serving-wench is more likely to be given to a SOUBRETTE.

Middle eight

The pop musician's name for *any* middle section of a piece, whether it consists of eight bars or not. The most common length for musical phrases is four bars, or a multiple thereof: one of the things that makes the British National Anthem so distinctive is that it consists of two phrases making fourteen bars: one of six bars and one of eight.

Mighty Handful

See THE FIVE

The Military Symphony

Haydn's No.100 in G. It could equally well have been called 'The Turkish', because of Haydn's extraordinary use of TURKISH MUSIC in the slow movement. Although the title is authentic, and was used at the first performance of the work, on 31 March 1794 in Hanover Square, London, the 'military' connotation was something of a puzzle for musicologists. But during the early 1950s I bought an English barrel organ contemporary with Haydn which played a version of the last movement of the symphony, the tune entitled on the programme label 'General Cathcart'. It transpires that the symphony's appearance coincided with the victorious return to London of Lieut. Gen. Sir William Cathcart after settling some minor local difficulty abroad.

Milking the applause

An art practised both by conductors and soloists who, when taking CURTAIN CALLS, carefully judge their temporary departure from the platform and re-entry so as to prolong the applause as much as possible. Invitations from a conductor to selected orchestral players (who may or may not have had prominent solos) to take individual bows always help to revive tired palms, as the audience then has someone new to applaud. When the artist mistimes his re-entry, the applause may die on him, and he is obliged to walk off in silence. Such occasions are relished by others; and ill-mannered orchestral players have been known to echo the departing footsteps by surreptitiously synchronizing their own tramping feet on the platform floor (while seated) with those of the conductor or soloist. At choral concerts extra applause is always guaranteed, as members of the choir customarily applaud until they themselves are motioned to stand – when the volume of applause may drop alarmingly. Choirs have instructions to keep clapping, or start again at the slightest sign of flagging audience enthusiasm. Some musicians have started to copy the practice seen at communist political rallies of clapping back, in other words, applauding the audience for applauding them so enthusiastically.

Mina

Elgar's last dog. Not to be confused with Wagner's first wife, who was Minna. Both words, incidentally, are related to an Old High German word meaning 'a beloved object, darling or favourite'; and also gave us 'minion' – which brings us back to Wagner's wife though not Elgar's dog. Wagner abandoned Minna for Cosima, but Elgar and Mina remained faithful to each other until his death; and his last published orchestral work was written for the cairn terrier and named after her: 'a haunting, halting, wistful morsel of nostalgic charm', Michael Kennedy calls it in his *Portrait of Elgar*. See also BIMPERL, who had a more carefree, uncomplicated but perhaps equally loving relationship with her master, Mozart.

Miniature score

See POCKET SCORE

Minimal music

Name given both by critics and its composers (*composers?*) to the aural equivalent of the equally briefly fashionable 'op art' fad of the 1960s. Minimal music involves the endless repetition of a simple musical figure or melody (more in the nature of a jingle). The good thing about minimal music is that it requires minimal talents from both composer and performer. What little skill it calls for lie in *not* playing together: two or more players start out in unison but gradually get out of phase with each other, thus creating an endless number of shifting sound patterns. A computer could do it better. The ultimate effect is one of mind-numbing monotony, reminiscent of narcotics-induced African and pop drumming. Minimal music is an American invention although it was for a time promoted in Britain by the composer and Marxist self-publicist Cornelius Cardew (1936–81), albeit with crypto-dialectical deviationism towards his own particular minimal-talent invention, SCRATCH music. It also harks back to, and was probably inspired by, some of Satie's jocular extravagances in the realm of *musique d'ameublement*, or FURNITURE MUSIC.

Minipiano

Introduced in 1932 by the English firm of W. G. Eavestaff, but based on a Swedish type of miniature piano. It was 'made to harmonise with every type of decoration and can be had stream-lined and cellulosed to suit the ultra-modern flat'. The Minipiano was only 2 ft 9 ins high, beating Steinway's rival *Pianino* by a foot. Contrary to the claims of a motor-car company, it was Mr Eavestaff who started the modern craze for the *mini*-prefix: from the mini-skirt to the minicab and mini-everything-else. And long before Austin/Morris (later to resurface under a variety of names and at present trading as 'BL') launched the car known as the Mini, the English composer of light music, Geoffrey Hartley, was writing a series of at least eighteen 'Minicantatas'. These are small cantatas designed for amateur performance, modelled on various CLASSICAL composers but with texts taken from some very unclass-ical limericks.

Minute Waltz

Chopin's op.64 No. 1 is so called because it is supposed to take a minute to perform. If the nickname is authentic then either Chopin's metronome was wrong or his watch had stopped; for to make any sort of musical sense of this (in any case rather silly) little piece it has to last about 90 seconds, and even then sounds rushed. Perhaps a phonetic mistake, and the name should be pronounced as 'my newt waltz' because of its brevity?

The Miracle

Haydn's No.96 in D. Although the title is not Haydn's and the facts as traditionally related are wrong, it *is* based on an actual occurrence. As has been established by H. C. Robbins Landon, it was not during this symphony that a chandelier fell from the ceiling but during (or possibly before the start of) No.102 in B flat (one of the LONDON symphonies). A contemporary eye-witness account quoted by Landon suggests that eighteenth-century concert-goers behaved more like modern pop fans: 'When Haydn appeared in the orchestra and seated himself at the Pianoforte, to

conduct a symphony personally, the curious audience in the parterre left their seats and pressed forward . . . with a view to seeing
Haydn better at close range. The seats in the middle of the parterre
were therefore empty, and no sooner were they empty, but a great
chandelier plunged down, smashed, and threw the numerous
company into great confusion. . . . Those who had pressed
forwards realized the danger which they had so luckily escaped
. . . shouting loudly, "miracle! miracle!" Haydn himself was much
moved, and thanked merciful Providence that he . . . could . . .
be the reason . . . by which at least thirty lives were saved. Only
a few of the audience received minor bruises.' But – then as now
– much depended on which paper one read. The *Morning Chronicle*
of 3 February 1795 was more restrained in its account: 'The last
movement was encored; and notwithstanding an interruption by
the accidental fall of one of the chandeliers, it was performed with
no less effect.' Perhaps we should content ourselves by reflecting
that *every* Haydn symphony of that period is a miracle.

Mirliton

See EUNUCH FLUTE

Mitschnitt

German jargon word sometimes heard in English musical talk. It
describes the process of making a gramophone record from a live
concert, whether this is broadcast or not. The word means literally
'with-cut', i.e. 'a record "cut" at the same time'.

MM

Abbreviation of 'Maelzel's Metronome', and followed by a number
which (unless otherwise stated) signifies how many crotchets may
be counted per minute. Similar calibrations appear on the metronome itself.

Modernsky

Schoenberg's derisive nickname for Stravinsky, and pronounced
in the German/Russian manner, with the stress on the second
syllable, as in Stra*vin*sky. It occurs in a German doggerel diatribe
Schoenberg wrote against Stravinsky, whom he hated almost as

much as he abhorred his music, especially his neo-baroque excursions into imitation Bach, Pergolesi and Mozart:

Vielseitigkeit

Ja, wer tommerlt denn da?
   Das ist der kleine Modernsky!
Hat sich einen Bubizopf schneiden lassen:
   Sieht ganz gut aus:
Wie echt falsches Haar!
   Wie eine Perücke!
Ganz (wie sich ihn
   der kleine Modernsky vorstellt)
Ganz der Papa Bach!

Versatility

Well, diddums, who's tumming here?
   Yes, it's little Modernsky!
and with a new pigtail* hairstyle, too!
   Suits him quite well;
Just like genuine imitation hair!
   Just like a wig!
Just like (at least that's
   what little Modernsky thinks)
Just like Papa Bach!

* *Bubizopf* is an untranslatable German pun, a play on *Bubikopf*, the close-cropped little-boy hairstyle favoured by women in the 1920s and 30s and on ZOPF, a pigtail as well as a musical style.

Monkey tempo

See 'WHERE'S THE FIRE?'

Monteverdi's Flying Circus

Nickname given at Glyndebourne to Monteverdi's opera *Il ritorno d'Ulisse in patria* (1640), in a production noted for its many aerial effects, which had singers flying across the stage on wires.

Moog

Robert A. Moog (b.1934) is an American physicist and electrician who in collaboration with a composer, H. A. Deutsch, designed the synthesizer that bears his name. Moog later synthesized and transformed much CLASSICAL music, including that of Bach and Debussy, in a most imaginative fashion and in collaboration with Walter Carlos (who himself later underwent a transformation into Wendy Carlos, without apparent loss of originality or inventiveness). The Moog (pronounced in the English manner, not to rhyme with 'vogue') is now so common that its sound, in the hands of ordinary people, has become little more than a commonplace cliché. Almost every radio and television jingle, commercial, pop song and signature tune, every space-invader and electronic cash register can now produce moog-like, radiophonic noises.

Moonlighting

'Tell me,' said a lady to the LEADER of a well-known English symphony orchestra at a reception given after a concert, 'what do you people do during the day?' If the musician is not rehearsing in the orchestra he may be practising, teaching, playing chamber music or taking part in SESSIONS. But many musicians are unemployed, or at least underemployed, spending much of their time RESTING. While waiting for the FIXER to telephone with an offer of a GIG, many develop secondary careers. These not only help them stave off poverty but act as an insurance against retirement; in the case of wind and brass players against premature loss of TEETH. Some work as arrangers, music-copyists or in musical journalism, others go outside music. The RLPO at one time had one or two players moonlighting as insurance agents. Some find that they are able to turn a hobby such as photography or woodwork to good account. A noted harpsichordist/conductor is also a knowledgeable (and prosperous) antique-dealer. Another musician owns a flourishing portrait studio, some run printing-shops (producing their own as well as colleagues' BROCHURES and concert programmes); a well-known viola player restores antique clocks; and a bassoonist takes horrifying risks with bandsaw, lathe and router to produce beautiful reproduction music-stands. Makers of replica baroque instruments generally start their career as players, for what is the use making an instrument if you are unable to try it?

The Moonlight Sonata

Name said to have been given to Beethoven's *Sonata quasi una fantasia* op.27, No.2 by H. F. L. Rellstab (1799–1860). He was a famous German poet and (fruitlessly) suggested to the composer various libretti to make into operas, including *Antigone, Orestes,* and *Attila the Hun.* According to tradition he also told Beethoven that op.27 No.2 reminded him of moonlight glinting on the waters of Lake Lucerne. Hence *Mondscheinsonate.* Several German editions bear what their publishers think is an exact English translation: 'The Moonshine'. Which is what the whole story probably is.

Morning, Noon and Night in Vienna

An overture to an opera of that name by Franz von Suppé (1819–95). Like many of his 200-odd stage works, the opera is as neglected as its overture is hackneyed; which is sad. It would be interesting to see a production of Suppé's *Lohengelb, oder Die Jung-frau von Dragant*, whose very title, a pun on *Lohengrin,* promises a comic Wagner send-up. Suppé (like HALLÉ) added an accent to the e to avoid confusion (in his case with the German word for 'soup'). His full name was itself almost satirical: Francesco Ezechiele Ermengildo Cavaliere Suppe Demelli. In spite of all that he was a Dalmatian of Belgian descent. See also LE MIDI.

Moses

Shortened title used at the GARDEN for Schoenberg's opera *Moses and Aron* (not to be confused with Rossini's *Mose in Egitto,* which is generally given the abbreviated French title, *Moïse.* Only the first two acts of Schoenberg's opera were staged at Covent Garden in 1956, the third being incomplete. There were difficulties over the casting of the 'Four Naked Virgins' for the sacrificial scene in Act 2, the Dance Round the Golden Calf – the virginity perhaps posing greater problems than the nakedness, which was by then nothing unusual on the British stage. *Moses* also became known as the 'Chuck Steak Opera', as the stage manager was obliged to make a daily trip to the meat market for cheap chuck-steak, to be used in simulation of the human flesh Schoenberg directs to have thrown around on stage at the sacrifice.

Mottled arrangements

Transcriptions made by Felix Mottl (1856-1911), who specialized in adding ADDITIONAL ACCOMPANIMENTS to works like Bach's *St Matthew Passion* and Handel's *MESSIAH.* Mottl was assistant conductor to Richter at Bayreuth and conducted Wagner CYCLES at the GARDEN in 1898 and 1890. He died after collapsing during Wagner's *Tristan und Isolde*.

Mourning symphony

Trauersinfonie in German: Haydn's No.44 in E minor.

Mouth organ

See HARMONICA

Mozart Guarneri

Not a fiddle formerly owned by Mozart (see under STRAD for some of the strange namings of rare violins) but a Brazilian composer (b.1907), a kind of latter-day Villa-Lobos who makes use of Brazilian folk-elements in his music. How did his parents *know* when they christened him that he was going to be a composer?

Mozart's Motto Theme

A four-note theme (C–D–F–E) which Mozart used in many of his works – in the first as well as his last symphony, for example – and which seems to have preoccupied him all his life. However, he never mentioned it, let alone gave it the name by which it is now known. It is in fact an ancient plain-chant motif and also appears in the works of other composers. Spotting examples of it in works – from Haydn to Bloch – is a common sport among musicians: 'He quotes Mozart's motto theme, you know . . . . '

MU

Short for the (British) Musicians' Union, one of the longest established trade unions, with some 35,000 to 40,000 members. It operates a strict but benevolent closed shop, i.e. one must be in the MU to play in a professional orchestra, although keyboard players sometimes get away without it on the pretext that they are soloists, even when they only tinkle an inaudible CONTINUO and professionals may help out or BUMP UP amateur orchestras. Soloists, chamber music players, teachers and conductors have no need to belong to a union, though they are usually members of the ISM.

Professional singers in chamber and cathedral choirs (boy trebles excepted) and opera houses are generally members of the actors' union, Equity. While union officials in newspapers and the printing-industry are known as Fathers (now also Mothers) of the Chapel, the unionized performers (even those in cathedral choirs – what a chance missed!) call their conveners 'shop stewards', as in factories. The MU was formed in 1921 by amalgamation between the National Orchestral Union of Professional Musicians, founded as a genuine craft guild in 1891, and the Amalgamated Musicians' Union, formed in 1893. Both admitted as members only those who could prove some proficiency in music. The MU, on the other hand, now admits anyone, whether full-time professional, part-time amateur or musical illiterate (like many a pop group entertainer) who is able to persuade an existing member to propose him. He does not even need to possess an instrument, let alone know how to play it. The MU does much advisory work with public bodies, controls the amount of recorded music permitted to be broadcast, supports young musicians from its extensive funds, and runs a free instrument insurance scheme for its members. Those who fail to opt out of paying the political levy are automatic members of the Labour Party; and even if they do opt out their vote is still used for deciding Labour Party policy, under the block vote system.

Muck

Karl Muck (1859–1940), the German conductor, never seems to have had much success in English-speaking countries ('How do you do? My name is Muck') and unlike the brilliant young Austrian conductor Christof Prick, who now conducts as Christof Perick, he evidently did not believe in changing his name for English audiences. Muck did, however, conduct at Covent Garden for one season, in 1906, and with the Boston Symphony Orchestra during the First World War, when he was interned in the USA.

Mummy-daddy

A drum roll (usually on the side-drum) is made up from a series of double beats – Left-Left/Right-Right/LL/RR/LL/RR etc., i.e. left and right sticks in double alternation. To practise rolls the player starts at a very slow speed, learning to the words, 'mummy-daddy'. See also PARADIDDLE.

Murphy's Law (Sod's law)

In its orchestral application exemplified by the truism, 'If a KEY or valve sticks it will do so during a solo rather than a TUTTI'. The orchestral management's version is something like, 'If a horn player splits a note it will be during the last few seconds of the final take and the re-take will mean paying overtime.' See TACTICAL ERRORS.

Musardine

An old name for a female promenader who is a prostitute. Promenade Concerts were invented in France by Philippe Musard (1793–1859), and were not at first symphony concerts in the modern sense but light-music entertainments with elements of the later music-hall. He took his Promenade Concerts to London, and these were the first PROMS, so called because they provided space for members of the audience to stroll about in. In the earliest proms the music was merely an accompaniment to the strolling. Such places therefore became favourite places for prostitutes to look for customers. No respectable woman would be seen in the promenade of a theatre or music-hall; and the very word 'promenader' became a euphemism for a 'tart' in nineteenth-century slang. At today's Promenade Concerts the promenaders are expected to stand but not to sit, and discouraged from promenading during the music.

The music

Musicians never refer to 'sheet music', which betrays the non-musician or the journalist who wants to make the distinction between music that is heard and the written or printed. The musician simply speaks of 'the music' ('I've left my music at home') but will generally be more specific, revealing whether he means a SCORE or a PART.

Musical Director

The term is only now beginning to be used again for principal conducting posts in symphony orchestras, following the gradual demise of small light orchestras. The Musical Director, or MD for short, was usually the chief musician of a seaside, theatre, music or circus band, though not necessarily always the conductor. He could have been a directing pianist, or piano conductor, or a violin conductor.

A Musical Joke

English mistranslation of Mozart's *Ein musikalischer Spass*, K522. *Spass* in German means 'fun' rather than 'joke'. 'Musical Joke' is therefore misleading, for it makes the listener expect comic turns on the lines of HOFFNUNG. The piece is only mildly satirical, making fun more of third-rate contemporary composers than bad players. In some (non-contemporary) German editions the piece is called 'The Village Musicians' Sextet ' or 'Alpine Yokels' music', which is also misleading. The bad-composer satire is evident from the beginning. He starts one idea after another, and each one peters out because he does not know what to do with it. His themes are plodding and foursquare. The Minuet sounds like a thousand others of the period. Only the TRIO contains a jape that qualifies for the description of 'joke', when the two horns play outrageously wrong notes; but if these 'wrong' ACCIDENTALS in the horn parts are omitted, the Trio sounds just like one of the lesser works by Leopold Mozart. The Adagio satirizes the baroque fiddle player who piles decorations upon ornaments and ornaments upon decorations. This now should – but is unlikely to – strike home at our present-day authentic over-embellishers as sharply as it would have done in Mozart's day. The Finale gallops away merrily without going anywhere in particular, attempting a fugal passage that comes a cropper at the first fence. The similes are intentional, for this movement, in a jazzed-up version by the unspeakable Waldo de los Rios, has become popular as the very pedestrian signature tune for an equestrian television programme. The last three bars of *Ein musikalischer Spass* are polytonal, in five keys; and again Mozart's joke is lost on our ears, accustomed as they are to worse clashes than the simultaneous sounding of E flat, F major, G major, A major and B flat with which Mozart attempts to shock his audience. All very harmless, you may say. But there is the curious matter of the work's chronology. *Ein musikalischer Spass* is dated in Mozart's own hand 14 June 1787. It was the first work he wrote after getting the news of Leopold Mozart's death. Is this the work of a grief-stricken young man whose father, to whom he owes so much, died only a few days earlier? Or is it perhaps a filial black joke, a kind of catharsis by which Mozart subconsciously celebrates his new freedom from Leopold's over-solicitous meddling, his constant, well-meant but tiresome, advice and criticism? Perhaps even an unwitting act of revenge for the way Leopold had dragged the sickly Wolfgang and his sister round Europe like circus exhibits? Compare almost any one of Leopold Mozart's works with the *Musikalischer Spass* and you cannot fail to notice that his musical shortcomings are very much those which Wolfgang sends up in K522: the superfluity of feeble ideas that come to nothing; tunes leading nowhere, just as in K522; the self-consciously thumping rusticity; and those plodding basses (always the first sign of a bad eighteenth-century composer) so characteristic of Leopold Mozart. Some of the florid excesses of the over-ornamented Adagio can indeed be traced to Chapter XI of Leopold's *Violin Tutor*, with which he was grappling when Wolfgang was conceived. Wolfgang was constantly making critical and often scathing comments on the compositions of some of his contemporaries: 'miserable note-scribblers', he called the Stamitz family, whose music was brimming with inspiration compared with Leopold's. And although not a word of criticism of his father's work has come down to us, he cannot but have been aware of the contrast between his own gifts and those of his father, of the mediocre talent he outstripped almost as soon as he could walk. In *Ein musikalischer Spass* Mozart perhaps for the first and last time answers his father back.

Musical rebus

Rebus = Latin for 'of things': 'An enigmatical representation of a name, word or phrase by figures, pictures, arrangements of letters, etc., which suggest the syllables of which it is made up.' The dictionary definition might have added also 'notes'. For the making of words and puzzles from a combination of pictures and music was once a popular nursery game. See B/B FLAT.

Music hall/Music-hall

In American English music hall means a hall where music is to be heard. But in Britain the term is irretrievably associated with places of popular entertainment and the style of music heard there. A hyphen usually makes things clear.

Punch, 1898

"Fond of Music! Why, when I'm in Town I go to a Music-hall every night!"

Music of the future

A once popular catch-phrase based on the German ZUKUNFTSMUSIK, which was much discussed, derided, argued about and quarrelled over, and whose most hated proponent was Wagner, although others, including Berlioz, at various times incurred the anger of traditionalists. See also FUTURISM.

Conductor at rehearsal for Tannhäuser: "Gentlemen, would you please be so kind as to play your notes."
Orchestral musicians: "Not till next week. It's the Music of the Future isn't it?"
Cartoon in Charivari, *1861*

Musique concrète

The MUSIC OF THE FUTURE of the 1950s and 1960s. Where is it now? Where indeed are MINIMAL MUSIC, QUADRAPHONY, QUARTER-TONES, and SERIAL music? See also MOOG.

Musique d'ameublement

See FURNITURE MUSIC

Musithon

After a runner in A.D. 490 covered the distance between places called Marathon and Athens the word was long used for a race of 26 miles 385 yards. Journalists and publicists have adopted the *-thon* ending as though it were a legitimate Greek suffix: *talkathon, telethon, sexathon,* etc., and, of course, *musithon.* Satie's *Vexations,* described under the heading FURNITURE MUSIC, were an early kind of 'musithon'.

Muzak

A manufactured trade name (well, they couldn't call it *music,* could they?) registered in 1938 by Rediffusion Ltd to describe background music of a neutral and unobtrusive sort, often specially composed for the purpose (by 'muzacians'?) 'We needed a catchy name, and the best-known trade name at the time was Kodak . . . so we just combined Kodak and music and got Muzak,' said a member of the firm (quoted in the *New York Times* in 1974). Muzak is 'piped', i.e. distributed by loudspeakers, throughout buildings such as supermarkets, buses, trains, factories, restaurants and even some American concert halls and churches. It is said by those who sell it to give hearers a subliminal sense of well-being. Muzak continued unchecked while grace was being said before a dinner given in America in honour of the RPO, competed with the conductor's speech after it; and was switched off only with great difficulty during the concert itself. No one knew how to silence it, and few were even aware of its presence until reminded of it. But Muzak was comparatively harmless. Commercial radio stations now make much noisier junk music available twenty-four hours of the day; and shops, restaurants and other places to which the public is admitted use it to assault their customers' ears. Traders can also make up their own, pirated, Muzak-type wallpaper music on cassette, and the chances are that it will be loud. The excuse is usually that 'the customer likes it'; but in truth the more likely reason is to entertain the staff. Anyone who cares about music, or, in a restaurant, likes to talk over a meal, should make a point of always asking for to be switched off, or at least lowered to the level of unobtrusiveness that was the mark of the now lamented Muzak. It is also worth remembering that a licence is required from the Performing Right Society for providing recorded music to the public. Offenders should therefore always be reported.

'My friends laughed when I sat down to play' . . .

Musicians' catch-phrase, used in a variety of sardonic ways. It refers to a formerly well known advertisement for a method by which, it was claimed, one could learn to play the piano in three weeks.

N

Nakers

Small drums played with two sticks or the palms of the hand. They were brought to England from Persia in the middle ages, variously called *nakers*, *nakeres*, or *nakeren*, from Persian/Arabic *naqqara*. The instruments, and the way they were hung from the loins, gave to the language the word 'nackers' (not 'knackers') meaning the testicles; also 'feeling nackered' for extreme tiredness – which is what ancient nakers players may well have experienced after over-energetic bouts of inguinal drumming. The French call them *nacaires*, and they, too, use the word with sexual connotations. The larger of the two nakers was always hung from the left, conforming with the normal left=low/right=high disposition of musical instruments; except, curiously enough, in the British Army, whose mounted kettledrummers have always hung the lower drum on the right, the higher on the left side of the horse. In German orchestras the lower TIMPS are on the right. The word should rhyme with 'crackers', not 'acres' as nervous BBC usage sometimes has it.

Playing the nakers. After the Luttrell Psalter, fourteenth century (British Library)

Natural horn

A brass instrument without valves. This does not imply that valve horns are in any way unnatural, or that the word carries suggestions of a 'natural son' or bastard, although some say it is a so-

and-so to play. 'Natural' refers to the Harmonic Series (for which see a musical dictionary).

Neapolitan Sixth

Short name for 'the first inversion of the major triad built upon the flattened second degree of the scale', so called because it was favoured by Neapolitan composers like Cimarosa, Paesiello, Pergolesi, A. Scarlatti and others. The chord will be instantly familiar to anyone who knows the sort of music these composers wrote. But, of course, its use was not confined to them. Beethoven was fond of it, for example in his HAMMERKLAVIER. The Germans call the Neapolitan Sixth *Leittonwechselklang*. See also GERMAN SIXTH.

Nearer, my God, to Thee

The popular hymn (words by Sarah Adams, tune by Dr Dykes) which the band of the sinking *Titanic* is said to have played 'as the water rose to their chests', in order 'to calm the nerves of the passengers'. A likely story. This hymn, with its traditional suggestion of imminent death, would not have soothed people hoping for rescue but only added to their fears. Nor has anyone related what the band's cello, double-bass or piano sounded like while immersed in water. What *is* substantiated, however, is that when the Musicians' Company held a dinner about a week after the disaster, homage was paid to the eight drowned bandsmen with a performance of the slow movement of Schubert's *Death and the Maiden* Quartet.

Negative markings

Most verbal instructions in orchestral PARTS tell players what to *do*. But some composers also write what they should *not* do, notably conductor-composers like Strauss and Mahler, whose practical experience with orchestras enabled them to foretell where musicians would be likely to hurry, drag, play too loudly or remain unheard. Mahler was almost neurotic about it, and his SCORES are like boarding-house notice-boards – stopping short only at 'Gentlemen Lift the Seat'.

Nigger quartet

See AMERICAN QUARTET

No Applause

'Owing to the Nature of this Work, it is requested that there be No Applause' used to be a standard announcement in oratorio programmes, and may still occasionally be seen. It was sometimes absurdly amended to 'No Applause at the Interval, but Patrons may show their Appreciation at the End of a Performance' – thus respecting the nature of the work, except at the end. Works accorded this treatment included Bach's *St Matthew Passion*, Handel's *Messiah*, Mendelssohn's *Elijah*, his *Hymn of Praise* and other joyful noises made unto the Lord. Massed hand-clapping is not the most pleasant sound to follow great music, especially when it ends softly, with a dying fall, and the cheering is led by an over-eager APPLAUSE LEADER. One often wishes that some other way could be found: perhaps silent bowing, as in Japan. On the other hand, there is nothing more depressing than an orchestra shuffling off the stage in silence, the silence possibly punctuated by audible remarks like 'Soprano wasn't too hot, was she?' or 'Did you notice my DOMINO in the *Agnus Dei*?' Times have changed however, and even churches and cathedrals now permit applause. The overture to vw's *The Poisoned Kiss* contains a note by the composer: 'The Audience is requested not to refrain from talking during the Overture, otherwise they will know all the tunes before the opera begins.'

Nobilmente

An indication of expression and mood associated with Elgar's GOD IS AN ENGLISHMAN music. He first used it in *Cockaigne* (1901) but not in his *Falstaff*, the ENIGMA, the coronation Ode or the *Pomp and Circumstance* marches. When others have used it since, e.g. vw, they have always done so with a nod in Elgar's direction. The word in Italian denotes not only nobility of spirit but also rank and birth.

'Nobody knows the Traubels I've seen'

Saying attributed to the Austrian-born opera administrator Sir Rudolf Bing (b.1902), who worked at Glyndebourne, Edinburgh,

and the MET. The quip is a combined reference to a negro spiritual*
and the Wagnerian singer Helen Traubel (1899–1972) whose
performances at night-clubs and other low establishments led to
many disagreements with Bing and others, and over which she
left the opera house.

* The song is catalogued in the BBC Gramophone Library as *'Nobody knows the
Troubles I've Seen* – see under *Nobody knows De Troubles I've Seen'*, demonstrating
what sticklers they are for accuracy at the BBC.

Note/tone

A transatlantic confusion perpetuated by German-speaking refu-
gees. In English a *note* is a musical sound; and a *tone* consists of
two semitones. But in German, *ein Ton* means *a note* as well as *a
sound*. So when Schoenberg (or Hauer, as some say) invented a
system of composition using twelve notes, he called it *Zwölfton
Komposition*. Those of his friends and colleagues who fled to
English-speaking countries mistranslated it as 'Twelve-tone . . . '.
If anything it should be 'Twelve-semitone' music.

Nun's trump

An instrument known by various engaging names, including
Nun's Fiddle, Tromba Marina, Marine Trumpet (in German
*Nonnengeige, Marientrompete, Trummscheit, Trompetengeige, Schnarr-
geige*; French, *trompette marine*, etc.) but seldom heard. It is a tall,
narrow instrument with a single string and a 'loose' bridge which
vibrates against the belly when the string is sounded, producing
a kind of piercing, snarling sound. Unlike other string instruments
only the natural harmonic series is used, thus giving rise to the
'trumpet' nomenclature. But its etymology is mostly obscure and
many reasons have been suggested for the instrument's curious
names – from marine signalling to ways of allowing nuns to make
trump-like noises without loss of feminine decorum. It appears in
many old prints and had music written for it by Lully, Alessandro
Scarlatti and others. Although many instruments survive, few
players persevered with it in the face of small artistic reward for
considerable effort, and it died out. Even the authentic music
movement, which normally stops at nothing in its relentless
pursuit of primitive old sounds, has largely ignored this musical
dodo.

Obbligato

Italian for a passage or PART that must be played or an instrument that cannot be dispensed with, from *obbligare*, to oblige, to bind. In practice it denotes a specially prominent part ('Aria with Oboe Obbligato') for which an additional fee may be payable to an orchestral musician: a form of 'danger money'. The double-b is obligatory in English usage.

Punch, 1860

"Thy voice, O Harmony!"

Conductor: *"Heasy with them Bones, Bill!"*
Bones: *"But I'm a playin' Hobligarter."*
Conductor: *"Well, I didn't say you wasn't; but you needn't go and drownd my Tremoler!"*

'The oboe is an ill wind that nobody blows good'

A much quoted saying which is as untrue as it is ungrammatical. For a similarly ill-informed comment, see CLARIONET.

Ocarina

See SWEET POTATO

Off-key

See OUT OF TUNE

Offstage music

French: *Dans la coulisse*, German: *Hinter der Kulisse*. Music directed to be played behind the scenery, or, when referring to a concert performance, in an adjoining room or corridor. The practice is fraught with pitfalls, and mishaps abound. Even when an assistant conductor relays the beat (or closed-circuit television is brought into use) there remain difficulties of intonation, as offstage music presents the listener with the aural illusion of sounding flatter than the ambient intonation closer at hand. For that reason the offstage trumpeter in Beethoven's *Leonora* overtures PUSHES IN his tuning-slide a little more for the first call than the second, for which he moves nearer to the orchestra. Offstage work is a desirable kind of engagement, as a full MU fee is paid for a few moments' work and no dressing-up is required. Only the poorest orchestras send an on-stage player off during a performance and then expect him to tiptoe back to his place, thus destroying all illusions sought by the composer (especially in a work like Berlioz's *Symphonie fantastique* in which some unnamed disaster befalls the offstage shepherdess, when she fails to reply). The most famous offstage story is probably apocryphal, and concerns the trumpeter who had rehearsed in the ideal spot for the *Leonora* trumpet calls, just inside the stage-door – only to be forcibly restrained by the door-keeper at the performance: 'You can't play that thing here; there's a concert going on inside!' On two other occasions things went wrong in the same piece. Once the trumpet call failed to materialize at all, as the player had got lost in the labyrinthine corridors of the hall on the way to his place. In the other performance, the offstage player's location was quite different at the performance from the one agreed earlier. 'Why didn't you play where you were before?' asked the conductor. 'I'm sorry, but there was somebody in it.' In Holst's *Planets* Suite the wordless chorus of women's voices which concludes the work, intended to convey impressions of cosmic infinity, on one occasion suddenly got louder again. It turned out that the ladies of the Liverpool Philharmonic Chorus, who were walking away as they sang, had got beyond the halfway point in the semi-circular corridor behind the platform and were actually coming closer again. And when Sir Thomas Beecham conducted a production of *The Boatswain's Mate* by Ethel Smyth (1858–1944) in 1916, the composer was meant to relay his beat to an offstage chorus of 'lusty sailorboys', which she did by peeping through a little hole in the scenery. Things went wrong time after time; and when Beecham called impatiently, 'Ethel! Where is your chorus of lusty sailorboys?' she replied, 'I'm sorry, Sir Thomas, I can't find my little hole.' Beecham bellowed, 'Stage Manager! Come here and show Miss Smyth where her little hole is.' See also FOGHORN.

On Cooking the First Hero in Spring

Inadvertent spoonerism sometimes repeated as a facetious nick-name for Delius's well-known piece.

One-work composers

Composers *known* for only one work, not for having *written* only one. Among such best-known least-known composers is Christian Sinding (1856–1941), a Norwegian who wrote two operas, many overtures, symphonies, cantatas, string quartets, piano sonatas and countless songs, but is known to most music-lovers only for his *Frühlingsrauschen*, or 'Rustle of Spring', Op. 32, a tinkly piano piece. At one time there was hardly a piano stool that did not contain a copy under the seat. No wonder a frustrated piano teacher (who?) called the composer 'More sinned against than Sinding'. And it would be interesting to have the opportunity of hearing the *Scenes from Faust*, one of the half-dozen operas or five symphonic piano concertos by Henry Litolff (1816–91). But all we ever get is the *Scherzo symphonique* for piano and orchestra wrenched from one of the concertos.

On the Night

The performance, even when this takes place at 10 a.m., e.g. a children's concert. From the well-known saying 'It'll be all right on the night.'

On tour with VW

Sir Thomas Beecham's wife, the pianist Betty Humby, died at about the same time as R. Vaughan Williams. A newspaper reporter who had not heard of her death asked, 'Will Lady Beecham be playing a concerto on your tour?' Beecham replied, 'No, she's gone on tour with VW.' It became something of a standard sick joke among musicians. For example, a well-known London FIXER who died in 1967 was said to have 'gone fixing for FLASH.' See SCHRAMMEL.

Oom-cha-cha(s)

'Playing the oom-cha-chas' is the derisive reference to those players – the second fiddles and violas and also often horns, trumpets, etc. – who play the second and third beats in Viennese waltz-time. It should really be the 'cha-chas', the 'ooms' being played by the bass instruments. It is as boring a job as may be found in the musical profession, but not an unskilled one: oom-cha-cha-ists are the custodians of the VIENNESE LIFT. See also SCHRAMMEL.

Oom-pah band

Onomatopoeic word for the characteristic sound made by the brass when playing the 'oom' in the bass on the first or strong beats, and the 'pah' on a weaker beat of the bar. See also GERMAN BAND and above.

Orchestra Manager

In most orchestras he is a kind of works foreman, a GEIGER COUNTER (sometimes CONCERT MANAGER) who sees to it that everyone is present, for it is easy for a conductor to start a piece without noticing that an important player is missing. The Orchestra Manager may be a playing member himself, but if so his instrument will be one that is seldom heard or not missed if absent. He also has to signal the end of that hallowed English industrial tradition, the tea break (TAKE FIFTEEN) or the concert interval (although the drink is more likely to be coffee now), which he does by clapping his hands, like an Arab potentate calling for his slaves. Wally Jones, for many years Orchestra Manager of the HALLÉ, had his favourite catch-phrase: 'Come on, you famous people. They are all waiting for you!'

Orchestra porter

The man who carries the larger instruments on and off the platform, and not only the piano and drums; even the rarest Amati double bass may be entrusted to him, for players in contract orchestras get their instrument transported for them and expect to find it ready for them, either on the platform or the nearest corridor to it. Fiddles travel in big, communal skips or wicker baskets, placed there by their owners after the show and removed by them before the next one. The drums, etc. are stowed in percussion boxes, usually owned and fitted out by the individual players. It should be added that many orchestral players refuse to entrust their best instrument to porters and drivers of furniture vans and may use their 'other' fiddle on tour; but in either case are likely to carry a precious bow, itself possibly worth thousands of pounds, separately in a slim wooden case. Orchestra porters also arrange the platform seating and have to know the requirements for various works in the repertoire.

Organology

A confusing word meaning the study of musical instruments in general, now much used by musical scientists and especially members of the Galpin Society (founded in 1946 to further such studies). The word does not mean the study of organs in particular, as might reasonably be supposed. Its first musical application is credited to Canon F. W. Galpin (1858–1945), who devoted his life to the collection and study of musical instruments: a strange lapse on the part of this learned man to take an existing word listed by the *Oxford English Dictionary* (*Organology*: the department of biology which treats of the organs of living beings . . .) and wilfully give it a new meaning. Only the latest Supplement to the *OED* admits organology in its musical sense.

Orpharion

See POLYPHANT

Orpheus in the Underground

Jocular nickname for Offenbach's opera *Orpheus in the Underworld*.

Ossia

Conductors may be heard at rehearsal telling players 'to play the ossia'. The word means *rather, that is to say, in fact*, etc. in Italian; but in music is an indication that an alternative version may be played. This is often printed on a separate line, and the line or passage is simply and without further explanation marked *ossia*. The *ossia* suggestion may be the composer's or the editor's; either an easier alternative or a more difficult one; it may contain fewer or more ornaments, trills, etc.

L'ours

Also 'The Bear': Haydn's No.82 in C major. Some have imagined a few growling justifications in the score.

Out

As a brief indication at the head of a movement, it means that the number so marked is not performed. But when someone is described as 'out' during a performance, the singer or player in question has lost his place but may not be aware of it; or may be manfully battling on in the hope of getting back *in*.

Out of tune

Never 'off key', as often heard from music critics and laymen. Only if someone is so out of tune that he is actually singing or playing wrong notes can he be described as off key.

Ovation

Enthusiastic applause, especially when preceded by 'standing'. From Latin *ovare*, to exult; not connected with *ova*, eggs – rotten or otherwise.

Over-arm/under-arm bowing

Not a cricketing controversy but one concerning the double bass. Some players prefer to hold the bow with the wrist underneath, palm facing upwards, others hold it the other way round, like violinists. The proponents of under-arm bowing (also called the Dragonetti method, after the famous player) say it makes a better sound, as the weight of the arm is not pushing down on the string. It is certainly more authentic, going back all the way to the viols. Thanks to the AUTHENTIC music revival their number is constantly growing, but in most orchestras both methods now co-exist. Conductors tend to prefer the over-arm way, as it tends to get more noise out of the bass section.

Overblowing

In wind instruments, the method of achieving second and subsequent octaves. It does not mean blowing *harder*, for otherwise playing higher would inevitably mean playing louder. Over-blowing means letting the same amount of air pass through a smaller aperture in the lip or reed, making the air travel faster. A good analogy is a hosepipe that squirts water further if one squeezes the end of the nozzle, although the water pressure at the other end remains constant.

Over the top

During the First World War the dreaded moment when troops left their trenches and engaged the enemy. But the term was soon demobilized and taken up by performers, both theatrical and musical. A musician whose performance is said to be 'over the top' indulges excessively in his particular mannerisms: exaggerated vibrato, rubato, portamento, etc. 'Every Note a Pearl!' is the customary sardonic comment on orchestral PRIMA DONNAS, sometimes varied to 'Every Pearl a Swine'.

The Oxford

Haydn's No. 92 in G, intended to be played when he got his honorary degree from that university.

Pachelbel's Canon

A piece which shot into prominence in the 1970s. Like ALBINONI'S ADAGIO or BOCCHERINI'S MINUET it is but one of probably hundreds of canons by Johann Pachelbel (1653–1706). 'Pachelbel's Canon' is like 'Beethoven's Sonata', 'Bach's Fugue' or (as some still say) 'Tchaikovsky's Piano Concerto'.

Pads (1)

The folders in which each player's PARTS are kept (or one for each pair of string players sharing a DESK). On tour, when different programmes may be played in rotation, there is a separate pad for each programme, and it is the orchestra librarian's job to make sure the correct pad is put out and contains the right pieces for the night. On rare occasions it has been known for a conductor to begin one piece while the orchestra starts another. There was an occasion (comic only in retrospect) when Gordon Green was engaged to play two works for piano and orchestra with the RLPO. One (perhaps Beethoven's G major Concerto) began with piano solo, the other with the customary introductory orchestral TUTTI. Conductor and soloist made their entrance, the pianist sat down, adjusted his stool, and nodded to the conductor that he was composed and ready for the orchestral tutti. The conductor, thinking the pianist was beginning on his own, nodded back that he, too, was composed and ready – for each thought the other started the piece. So they nodded to each other like a couple of over-polite Japanese prize-fighters until the orchestra realized what was happening, and the LEADER (to a chorus of titters) reminded the conductor of the correct order of programme.

Pads (2)

The skin or leather-covered felt discs attached to the underside of the keys that help to close holes on wind or brass instruments.

The Paganini of the Alps

Nickname of Louis Jullien (1812–60), when he was an alleged boy-prodigy violinist. See PROMS.

The Paganini of the Piano

See THE BEETHOVEN OF THE FLUTE, THE JOACHIM OF THE HORN and other cross-references.

Pallets

The leather-covered valves that admit air to the pipes of an organ which, when they stick, cause a CIPHER.

Papa Haydn

See FATHER OF THE SYMPHONY

Papering the house

Giving away COMPS for a concert which has attracted too few paying customers. The German word for 'papered' in this sense is *wattiert*, i.e. padded out.

Paradiddle

Also sometimes Taradiddle: a side-drum stroke in which the left-hand and right-hand sticks alternate in the following manner: LRLLRLRRLRLLRLRR, etc. There are also the Double Paradiddle, Triple Paradiddle and various other drum strokes with charming, onomatopoeic names: Flam, Flamadiddle, Drag Paradiddle, Ratamacue and Ruff. See also MUMMY-DADDY.

Part

See SCORE AND PARTS

Particell

A 'short' score. Short, not in length or dimension, but a compressed score, with details such as harmony, orchestration,

etc., perhaps only cursorily indicated, as in a composer's preliminary sketch, or with several instruments or even groups of instruments sharing a stave. The French call a particell or short score
by the paradoxical name *monstre*.

Passage work

Any musical tune or part thereof may qualify for the description
of 'passage', possibly with a qualification such as 'bridge passage'
(i.e. one that leads somewhere, as in sonata form), or 'fugal
passage'. But 'passage work' is the musician's description of rapid
or showy fingerwork (often in a concerto) designed to give an
impression of bravura and difficulty. This does not mean that such
passage work is necessarily intended merely for showing off and
therefore musically worthless. In some of Mozart's concertos, for
example, the passage work is an integral, melodic and harmonic
part of the design.

Passenger

A player who does not pull his weight; and sometimes one who
does not play at all. When the Busch family orchestra, headed by
Wilhelm Busch (father of Adolf, Fritz, Hermann, etc.) was engaged
for dances and receptions, and paid per head, the youngest player,
as passenger, was given a greased bow – purposely silenced so
that he would be seen to take part, but not heard. There are also
passenger-conductors, who 'ride' on the orchestra's sound and
merely perform a kind of ballet to the music.

La Passione

Haydn's No.49 in F minor, also called *Il quakuo di bel'umore* (The
Good-humoured Quaker). This was probably the title of a play or
opera (not necessarily Haydn's) for which the symphony was used
as an overture. The modern Italian word for a Quaker, incidentally, is *quácquero*.

The Pathétique

Always means Tchaikovsky's Sixth.

Patter

Orchestral players' derisive word for a conductor's habitually repeated spoken requests and instructions at rehearsal. All conductors have some kind of musical bee in their bonnet – about certain kinds of bowing, about misplaced stresses; even about the way people hold their instrument or sit in their chairs. They therefore tend to utter the same cries, such as 'On the bridge!' or 'At the point!' or 'Don't move in the GP!' Some conductors, like Hermann Scherrchen or Sir Henry Wood, would write the patter (and sometimes even jokes) into their scores at the appropriate place. Wood's music was bequeathed to the RAM, where these memoranda may still be seen. John Amis assures me that at a certain point in Beethoven 5 Wood wrote (and always shouted), 'Like a cavalry charge!' and in Tchaikovsky's *Romeo and Juliet*, 'Onward rushing to its doom!' During a rehearsal Hermann Scherrchen repeatedly said, in a certain passage of Brahms's TRAGIC Overture, 'Ze oboe *begging*!' Afterwards I looked at the score of one of his pupils who followed him about, and the relevant place had the laconic annotation, 'Oboe begging'.

Pause

One of the most confusing musical terms. One *pauses* by temporarily ceasing to do what one is doing. Yet in music a pause sign over a note indicates that one goes on doing it longer, i.e. holds the note for an unspecified time; and when a pause sign is placed on a rest, the silence is prolonged. In German, *Pause* is the word for the interval or break in a rehearsal or concert; and what we call a pause is their *Corona*. The Americans call this *fermata* – which again is not the same as the German *Fermate*, which is what the English call a full close or a final cadence. Then again, when the French speak of *une pause*, they mean a semibreve rest, a bar's rest, or a rest of unspecified duration. The Italians' pause is called *punto coronato* or (heaping confusion on confusion) *punto d'organo*. This in turn is *not* the same as the German *Orgelpunkt*, which has the same meaning as the English *pedal point* or *pedal*. That should make it clear.

Pearlies

See PURLIES

Pearshaped notes

Notes (played or sung) which have a bulge in the middle, either because of the player's or singer's imperfect control or, in authentic performances, through a misunderstanding of the eighteenth-century *messa di voce* effect (for which please see an ordinary musical dictionary).

Penguin suit

A man's 'full' evening dress now consisting of white shirt, white bow-tie, white waistcoat and black tailcoat and trousers. Orchestral players formerly wore black waistcoats (as waiters do still) which, when enclosing a starched white shirtfront or DICKEY, gave rise to the penguin comparison. Nowadays a certain laxity of dress is acceptable: the shirt is no longer starched, the collar wingless and soft; the bow-tie may be coloured and ready-tied; the waistcoat has shrunk to a cummerbund, little more than a narrow bandage or a sort of bra slipped down from the chest; and the silk-faced lapels replaced by plain ones. Many orchestral players buy their evening suits at waiters' outfitters, who supply harder-wearing garments than those sold by ordinary stores and intended to be worn only once or twice a year for social functions.

Penny whistle

See TIN WHISTLE

Pensato

The Hungarian painter George Mayer-Marton, active in England in the 1950s and 1960s, told me that he was present when Anton Webern supervised the rehearsal of one of his works. A violinist pointed out that he had a note he could not play – a G flat marked *pensato*, a semitone lower than the lowest string of his violin. Webern said, 'You do not *play* it. You *think* it.'

Perfect pitch

Few things in life are perfect. See ABSOLUTE PITCH.

Perks

The nickname of Percy Grainger, inventor and proponent of BLUE-EYED ENGLISH.

Persimfans

Acronymic abbreviation of *Pervyi Simfonichesky Ansambl*. This was the result of a Soviet Russian experiment instigated by some Committee of Culture Commissars in 1922 who hoped to apply the principles of socialist equality to musical performance. They decided that the symphony orchestra was a western-style reactionary bourgeois assembly (or 'ansambl?') in which comrade worker-musicians were subjugated into hireling lackeys by a single capitalist imperialist hyena, known as a conductor, who took undemocratic decisions without first consulting his comrades on the shop floor. So the conductor was liquidated and the orchestra run like a collective farm. Each freedom-loving worker-comrade, instead of looking at his PART and following the beat, was now required to have an intimate knowledge of the SCORE and gain full awareness of the dialectical implications of each bar and every semiquaver. Each man or woman had an equal voice at rehearsals, which in effect became committee meetings (with a sub-committee, or 'caucus', for each section?) and were presumably expressed in the proper pseudo-political jargon. 'Comrade Principal Bassoon, may I suggest that your bottom B flat has a certain revisionist, counter-revolutionary loudness, a quality incompatible with my melody on the tuba . . . . ' Music-making now took ten times as long and cost a lot more of the state's money, and it was soon found that a symphony orchestra with 75 conductors was an infinitely less efficient body than it had been under a single one. Also, the LEADER still filled the same musical role as he had done in capitalist orchestras; more and more responsibility devolved upon him, and in no time things had turned full-circle – just as in Orwell's *Animal Farm* when the pigs started to walk on two legs. After ten years of orchestral socialism the experiment was quietly dropped. Prokofiev said of Persimfans that 'its principal difficulty lay in changing tempo' – a comment which just about sums up the whole political system.

Le Petomane

The nickname (also *le Ventomane*) of a celebrated French music-hall artist who between 1892 and 1900 took Paris by storm with what today's newspapers would inevitably have described as a whirlwind success. He had, said a contemporary report, 'perfected an unique act which shook and shattered the Moulin Rouge'. So great was his fame that on a single day he took 20,000 francs for one performance, whereas Sarah Bernhardt, then the greatest French box office draw, took only 8,000. His real name was Louis Baptiste Pujol (1857–1945) but he performed under the *nom de guerre* of *Petomane*, from *peter*, to fart. For he had developed such an extraordinary control of the muscles of his anus that (provided

Le Petomane performing at the Moulin Rouge. Cartoon from Paris qui rit *1892*

he trained on a suitable diet) he was able to perform amazing musical feats with it, playing tunes both *au nature* and with the help of 'a little flute with six stops (on which he) could render tunes like *Le roi Dagobert* and, of course, *Au clair de la lune*'. As far as can now be ascertained his act, which caused as much outrage as mirth, was perfectly genuine, and appears to have been verified by medical evidence. It is a pity he was not able to sustain his powers into old age, or he could have played against the Boche during the occupation of France, or better still, used his unique gifts for DONKEY MUSIC, for which they were eminently suited. The above information comes from *Le Petomane, a Documentary Biography* by Nohain and Caradec (English translation, Souvenir Press, 1967). See also FARTOPHONE.

The Philosopher

Haydn's No.22 in E flat. The unusual presence of two ENGLISH HORNS has been said by some programme note writers to make the work 'sound philosophical' (whatever that sound is) but the title is more likely to refer to a now forgotten stage piece.

Pianino

See MINIPIANO

Piano

The instrument is always so called by professional musicians, never 'pianoforte', which, like 'violoncello' now has an old-fashioned ring about it.

Piano conductor

A SHORT SCORE or PARTICELL containing CUES which, when used by a conductor directing from the piano, may take the place of an ordinary SCORE, the cues enabling him to fill in for, or help out, players who are less than competent, or absent. See also AUBREY WINTER.

Piano duet

The term always denotes two pianists at one keyboard, not those playing a piano each, which is a 'two piano' combination. Piano duettists, who are able not only to see each others' hands but can actually touch, have fewer KERDOINK problems of ENSEMBLE than two piano partnerships. As with the HOSENROLLE, the musico-sexual aspects of piano duet playing have not yet been fully explored. At the end of the eighteenth and during much of the nineteenth centuries, the heyday of the piano duet, and when Schubert and Mozart (to name but two) were taking the form to new heights, men and women were not normally allowed to sit in such close physical proximity. Only engaged persons could decently have hand-contact apart from the formal handshake; and sitting cheek-to-cheek on the same stool, their bottoms touching, was something only a married couple could do; and even they would seldom do it in the presence of others. With this in mind, composers writing piano duets for themselves and a desired female partner would naturally go to great lengths to include passages requiring crossed hands. Conversely, for a well-brought-up Victorian lady the accidental touch of a man's thigh and leg would probably have brought on a swooning fit.

Pianola

Trade mark for a specific kind of self-playing piano patented by an American called Votey in 1897. He may or may not have been pleased to know that it was to become the generic name for any player piano, liké Hoover for a vacuum cleaner.

Piano stool fiddlers

Piano soloists who take a long time to adjust the height and position of their seat before they are ready to play. The slightest suggestion of unevenness in the floor and consequent rocking of the legs of the stool can bring on a display of artistic TEMPERAMENT. One soloist refused to start a concerto until an attendant had placed a single sheet of paper under one chair leg. Perhaps this is why older piano stools had only three legs. Why do the modern ones not have individual height adjusters in the legs as well as the seat?

Piano trio/quartet/quintet, etc.

Just as Beethoven's Harp Quartet is not for four harps, nor Schubert's TROUT Quintet for five trout, the *piano trio* is not for three pianos but piano with two string instruments (usually violin and cello); the *piano quartet* for piano and string trio (usually violin, viola and cello); and the *piano quintet* generally for piano and string quartet. There it stops. 'Piano sextet' is not a standard musical term. *Flute quartet* means flute and string trio, the flute usually taking the place of the first violin of a string quartet; but 'flute quintet' is rarely used: 'flute and string quartet' being more likely. The same goes for other wind-and-string chamber music combinations. *Horn trio* always means the Brahms trio for horn, violin and piano (and its companion pieces;) but *horn quintet* means only one work: Mozart's Quintet in E flat, K407, for horn and string quartet, in which the customary second violin is replaced by a second viola. However, none of the foregoing prevents composers of, say, quartets for four horns (and there are such works) from describing these, too, as 'horn quartets'. When the London Horn Trio, which specializes in performances of the Brahms work mentioned above, arrived at a music club they found that there was no piano in the hall. 'Oh but we thought you were a horn trio,' the organiser said.

Pièce(s) de rechange

One or more alternative sections supplied with eighteenth- and nineteenth-century woodwind instruments to enable the player to adjust the pitch to varying standards, the sections being of different size. This was necessary before pitch was standardized to a nominal A=440 cycles per second. In the flute the extra pieces were middle joints; in the oboe the entire top joint was interchangeable. The French term seems to persist, although there is nothing wrong with 'extra joints'.

Pinhole

A small hole near the top of the bassoon CROOK, covered with a key. It is designed to help the sounding of some notes of the scale. The invention dates from the third quarter of the eighteenth century and has been in general use since the nineteenth.

Pizz

Abbreviation of *pizzicato*, the plucking rather than bowing of a string. In Italian the word has wider meanings. *Pizzicare* is to pinch, nip, tingle, prick, prickle and bite (of insects); *sentirsi pizzi-*

care le mani means an itching palm – not for money, as in English, but feeling the need to slap or hit someone; and *un pizzicato* is a man with a pock-marked face. In music the opposite of *pizz* is *arco*. This, too, has non-musical meanings – an arch (as in architecture); and *arco di stomacco*, the effort of retching or vomiting.

Platform etiquette

Certain commonsense rules have evolved over the years on how to behave on the concert platform. For example, the LEADER gets precedence in leaving the platform after a performance (but not at rehearsal). The other players hang back with what may be feigned respect until he is through the door. Non-observance of this has been known to lead to unpleasantness and, in one case, fisticuffs followed by dismissal. But the most important platform rule is 'Eyes Front' when someone makes a mistake. The temptation to look round at the perpetrator of a wrong note or DOMINO (spot the red face!) has to be resisted. It merely draws attention to what might otherwise have gone unnoticed by the audience. Waving to members of the audience, or even having a chat with them from the platform, is considered the mark of an amateur; and to communicate with the audience, if only by a wink or a nod, during the concert an unpardonable lapse. (Yet there is a picture showing Mozart during the *performance* of one of his operas leaning against the rail of the orchestra pit and having a chat with a fiddle player, who has put his instrument down.) One young player in an orchestra tried to flirt with a pretty redhead in the front row, and after the concert rushed round to chat her up; only to find she was the wife of the new principal trumpeter. However, many of the time-honoured rules go by the board at informal or only partly musical occasions, such as the PROMS. Other rules are laid down by concert managements. Some ask women members not to display too much distracting bare flesh, or wear items of jewellery that catch the bright lights. Occasional attempts are made to control the pre-concert jumble of noise made by players warming up, known as PRELUDING; or to get some order into the TUNING procedure so that the oboe gives the A to one section after another, rather than trying to make himself heard through the noise. Leaders and conductors prefer to make their entrance to a respectful silence from the orchestra so that they can hear the first clap or two of applause; and it is considered bad manners for players to continue tuning or last-minute practice while others are making an entrance.

Player piano

See PIANOLA.

'Play it again, Sam'

Cliché derived from the film *Casablanca* (1942), used *ad nauseam* ever since, especially to players called Sam, although no one actually says it in the film.

Plinky-plonk music

The pianistic equivalent of vocal or orchestral DONKEY MUSIC.

Plumbing

Brass players' reference to the tubing on their instruments.

Plunker boy

American jazz term for a guitarist.

Pocket score

Also miniature score or study score. Small-format scores pioneered by the three firms of Payne, Donajowsky and Eulenburg. They first came into use at the end of the nineteenth century, after advances in photo-engraving by which full-size lithographed, engraved or even hand-written scores could, for the first time, be photographically reduced on small printing-plates. A player who has forgotten to bring his PART may be obliged to play from a pocket score – a near impossibility; although conductors often manage to conduct from the small-size score, probably because they do not actually have to *read* the music they conduct. The last of the great pocket-score publishers, Dr Kurt Eulenburg, died on 10 April 1982 aged 103 in London, whither he had moved his firm in 1939 to escape from the Nazis and which then became the world centre of pocket score publishing.

Podium

American for what the English prefer to call the conductor's *rostrum*. Germans prefer the teutonically polysyllabic *Dirigentenpult*, or 'conductordesk'.

Polyphant

This charmingly named and now obsolete, seventeenth-century English instrument suggests some sort of polyphonic elephant. But a manuscript in the British Library describes it as being 'of forme called a polygon . . . an hollow yet flat kind of instrument containing three dozen of wier strings to be played upon . . . there is on the belly a crooked bridge and three small sound holes.' John Evelyn's *Diary* (14 August 1661) describes it as a 'Polyphone', of which 'polyphant' may be a corruption. The instrument appears to be connected with another instrument of the period, the orpharion.

Portamento

The Italian meaning of this word is deportment, demeanour, bearing, behaviour, etc; also the management of the voice in singing or the hands in playing. But in musical performance, especially when said by Englishmen, it now refers exclusively to a sliding effect between one note and another. It should not be confused with a GLISS(ando). *Portamenti* are subtler than *glissandi*, cover a smaller part of the scale, and are a form of expression (often used to excess) rather than an 'effect'.

Porterage

Fee charged by players for carrying their own instrument to a rehearsal and/or concert. Under MU rates only the larger instruments qualify for porterage, among them cellos and basses, contrabassoons and drums. Violins, bass clarinets and bassoons do not. But percussionists are apparently able to 'swing' porterage on even the smallest instruments.

Positive organ/portative organs

A *positive* organ is one whose pipes are exposed, not enclosed in a case; a *portative* one, an organ (whether positive or not) that can easily be carried. The two descriptions are sometimes used interchangeably. There is no 'negative' organ, but worse things have been said of electric instruments that produce the sound synthetically.

Positive organ with direct wind supply. Eighteenth-century engraving by Guélard after Huet

La Poule

Haydn's No. 83 in G minor. Some programme note writers claim to be able to hear in this symphony (as in Mozart's SPARROW Mass) 'pecking' quavers in the strings. If that were so, every eighteenth-century work with staccato string passages would qualify.

Practise/rehearse

Musicians *practise* alone but *rehearse* with others. One speaks of *band practice* but orchestral *rehearsals*. Church singers have choir *practice*, but cathedral, chamber and symphonic choirs *rehearse*. This is merely to record current parlance as it has developed, not to lay down laws. Americans *practice* rationalized spelling.

Prelude and Liebestod

These two BLEEDING CHUNKS from Wagner's opera *Tristan und Isolde* are sometimes called 'the Biggest CUT in the History of Music,' as the excerpt consists of the opening and closing portions of the opera played in one continuous piece but with the rest of the work omitted. In the *Liebestod* there may be a soprano soloist, but it is often heard with the voice part omitted.

Preluding

The jumble of noise made by an orchestra warming up is *preluding* – not tuning, with which it grossly interferes. Preluding is like something between the revving of an engine on the starting-line of a motor-race and the systematic checking of controls before taking-off in a plane. There is also an element of concert nerves in preluding, perhaps with the repetition of some difficult passages that need practice (though this may come under the heading of platform etiquette, for it draws the audience's attention to the technical problem of whose existence they might otherwise not have been aware). Near-neighbours among the principal players may compare notes for intonation or try some tricky DOVETAILING. Most players have their own, personal preluding or warming-up passage which they stick to throughout their career. It may be a flourish of great brilliance ranging from the top to the bottom of the instrument's register. Percy Hatton, for many years second clarinet of the RLPO and a member of the family that produced John Liptrot Hatton (1809–86), would unfailingly introduce into his flourish a sardonic quotation from 'Happy Days are Here Again'. Preluding breaks out at rehearsal, too; and conductors dislike it with good reason as it spoils their concentration while they are dealing with some point elsewhere. And before the start or re-start of a performance they prefer to walk onto the stage in the respectful silence they feel is their due. Barbirolli always insisted on this mark of respect (even at rehearsal and in the shabby drill-hall that was the HALLÉ's rehearsal room). On several occasions, as he was about to make his entrance, he could be heard shouting from the wings at one or two players who were still preluding, 'Shut up, you buggers, will you!'

Preparatory beat

'A-one, a-two, a-one-two-three-four' is the traditional and audible jazz method of 'counting in', possibly accompanied by the rhythmic snapping of fingers and thumb. In orchestras such things are done more subtly (if at all) and with one or more preparatory beats (see also (BAR) FOR NOTHING) that silently set the tempo; and in chamber music the merest UPBEAT of a bow or a wind instrument is enough to set the pace.

Prepared piano

A piano which has had nasty things done to it – i.e. nuts, paper-clips, etc. put into the works – so as to alter the tone of its strings; an outrage for which any respectable piano is totally unprepared. The American self-publicist John Cage (b. 1912) has claimed responsibility for this particular outrage

Pretzel bender

American slang for a horn player – because of the PLUMBING found on that instrument.

Prima donna

In Italian opera houses, the name for the leading female singer – by tradition always a soprano. There were also other grades and kinds of operatic rank, e.g. *prima donna assoluta* (highest degree prima donna), *seconda donna*, and *primo* and *secondo uomo*. Maria Jeritza (pre-1887 – 1982) became known as *la prima donna prostrata*, supposedly for the way she could sing *Vissi d'arte* in Puccini's *Tosca* lying on the stage floor. That was *her* story. The real reason is said to be related to a Beecham story: 'Sir Thomas, how do you expect me to perform properly while lying flat on my face?' — 'Madam, I have given some of *my* best performances in that posture.' In the orchestra, however, the term prima donna is applied to players thought to be conceited, self-important or always eager to draw attention to themselves. They may do this by affecting exaggerated body movements while playing, or by throwing rehearsal tantrums of one kind or another ('My lip is sore, maestro . . . '). Some prima donna wind players wear ostentatious rings that catch the light; they may even wobble a finger or two on a salient note of SOLOS in imitation of a string player's vibrato. In a more insidious manner, the orchestral prima donna may lend a phrase that has has just been played normally by a colleague a subtly unsubtle degree of extra RUBATO or VIBRATO; or indulge in one of several other possible ways of exaggerated, OVER THE TOP showing off.

Principal second

An apparent oxymoron: the title of the LEADER of an orchestra's second violin section.

Principal, sub-principal, rank-and-file

The main ranks and degrees of precedence in a symphony orchestra, though the distinctions may be more loosely applied in smaller orchestras (where the one double-bass player is principal, sub-principal and rank-and-file rolled into one) and are not used at all in chamber music. Only the strings have rank-and-file; and in the wind and brass certain anomalies exist. The first flute is a principal (in some orchestras in effect the LEADER of the wood-wind), the second a sub-principal, but the third flautist is the principal piccolo and counts as one of the orchestral soloists. But, of course, he plays third flute as well.The same goes for other second, third or fourth players of the bass clarinet, saxophone, cornet (as opposed to trumpet) and double-bassoon, etc. If an orchestra has four horns, the first and third are principals, the second and fourth sub-principals, a throwback to the days when horns were still NATURAL and therefore worked in pairs pitched in different keys. When a principal flute, oboe, clarinet, etc. is absent, his place is usually taken by the third player SITTING UP. That is partly for practical and partly financial reasons. No sitting-up fee is payable, and only one player takes a possibly unfamiliar part, which would not be the case if all moved up one seat.See also REPET.

Professor(e)

Italian publishers who send advertisements to British musicians will address even the humblest BACK DESK player in the grandest terms ('Professor Joe Bloggs'), much to the amusement of his colleagues. In Italy anyone who wields a musical instrument is called *professore*, but the title does not translate well. Foreigners are more free also with the title MAESTRO, using it as one might call the master of any small boat 'Captain'. But in recent years teachers at the bigger English colleges of music have taken to adopting the title 'Professor', perhaps because such colleges have university status.

Programme

Apart from the obvious meaning, i.e. the printed sheet of paper or booklet sold to the audience at a usually exorbitant price without necessarily giving much useful information, the 'programme' of a composition is the story the music is said to convey. This may be the composer's own, in which case the work qualifies for the description of 'programme music'; or it may have been fancifully foisted on it by posterity. Orchestral players are seldom aware of what they are supposed to be portraying. Either they do not care, or else nobody tells them: certainly few conductors bother. Barbirolli would occasionally say that the first *sforzato* in the Prelude to Wagner's *Tristan und Isolde* represented the first physical consummation of their love; and similarly, the whooping horn GLISSANDI during the orchestral introduction to Strauss's *Der Rosenkavalier* are supposed to illustrate what takes place on the sofa on stage before the curtain rises. However, Strauss is said to have answered a critic who claimed to be able to discern the musical representation of specific sexual activity in the tone poem *Don Juan*, 'Yes, and did you notice that the girl had red hair?'

Proms

This old-established English institution was in fact imported from France, hence its French name. Promenade Concerts began in 1833 on the Champs-Élysées in Paris, the invention of the showman-musician, Philippe Musard (1793–1859), and were further developed by the even more publicity-seeking Louis George Maurice Adolphe Roch Albert Abel Antonio Alexandre Noé Jean Lucine Daniel Eugène Joseph-le-brun Joseph-Barême Thomas Thomas Thomas-Thomas Pierre Arbon Pierre-Maurel Barthélemi Artus Alphonse Bertrand Dieudonné Emanuel Josué Vincent Luc Michel Jules-de-la-plane Jules-Bazin César Jullien* (1812–1860). Jullien (his friends called him 'Louis' for short) was a successful rival to Musard, and of course tried to out-do him in showy splendour.

Because bankruptcy forced Jullien to flee to England he transferred the concerts to London, where (starting at the Drury Lane Theatre in 1840) they were at first called 'Concerts d'été', and established

Kissing Polka: Philippe Musard, founder of the Proms, carried shoulder-high by 'Musardines'

the conductor as a popular cult figure. As the *Musical World* said of him in 1853, 'Jullien was the first who directed the attention of the multitude to the classical composers . . . broke down the barriers and let in the crowd.' The crowds are still let in each summer at the Royal Albert Hall, London, although the Proms under Sir Henry Wood (see TIMBER) had more in common with

Musard's and Jullien's than with today's: enormously long, with light music and the occasional musical joke interspersed with first performances by serious contemporary composers. It was Wood who threw out the sillier conventions, like Jullien's of conducting Beethoven with a jewelled baton handed to him on a silver salver and in white gloves (changing to black for the funeral march of the Eroica). Since 1927 the Proms have been run by the BBC, and have reflected the personal taste and idiosyncrasies of successive Heads of Music, occasioning sometimes acrimonious comments from those who think the job should be done differently. In some ways the Proms are the musical equivalent of football matches, at which a minority of hooligans is more noticed that the many genuine fans, and the unbridled behaviour of a few make the well-behaved forget some of their decorum. At the Proms this does no great harm, except when on semi-musical occasions like the Last Night the high spirits often spoil the enjoyment for everyone else, especially radio listeners who cannot see what is going on. Exhibitionists abound at the Proms (as at football matches, where the massed singing is less tuneful but far more rhythmical, especially when promenaders attempt to clap in time to the music). Like football supporters, promenaders sway in great human waves, packed together like MUSARDINES. But unlike them they also indulge in a curious form of knees-bend, like elderly gentlemen 'adjusting their dress'. However, the football fans' ironic cheers (as for a miskick by an opponent) are reserved merely for the attendant's lifting the piano lid. The Proms are for many young (and a few not so young) people their first introduction to good music, but for others more of a social than a musical occasion.

" Jullien's many forenames were given to him because his father, a bandmaster, did not wish to offend any of the 36 members of his band by asking only one to stand as godfather, so he invited them all – thus anticipating the modern football fanatics who name their children after all the members of their favourite team.

Protest song

A musical form developed in America during the early 1960s by left-wing entertainers with one eye on social injustices and the other on record sales figures. The appropriate accompanying instrument for protest songs is the guitar, strummed in a rudimentary, inexpert fashion. In the twenty-odd years that have elapsed since the protest song emerged, most of the erstwhile protesters have retired on the proceeds of their protests; and one is a born-again Christian.

Prussian Quartets

Haydn's Quartets, op. 50: a set of six composed in 1787 and dedicated to King Friedrich Wilhelm II of Prussia, composed for him in gratitude for 'a beautiful ring' the king had sent to the composer. The name is also given to the last three quartets Mozart wrote (K575 in 1789, and K589 and 590 in 1790) because they were written for the same king, a gifted cellist. Both Haydn and Mozart wrote especially grateful and prominent cello parts for him.

Pudding stirrer

Also 'stirring-the-pudding conductor'. A conductor whose beat consists largely of unclear, circular movements. See STICK TECHNIQUE.

Pulling out/pushing in

'Would you mind pulling out/pushing in a little?' when said to a wind or brass player is as good as saying 'You are playing sharp/flat.' The player then lengthens/shortens the sounding part of the instrument. The adjustment is made on the flute by moving the position of the head; on the oboe, bassoon, etc., the staple or CROOK; on the clarinet, the BARREL; and on brass instruments the requisite slide.

Pull-through

Like gunners and riflemen, clarinettists and bassoonists use this to clean the bore of their equipment. A typical pull-through consists of a small bundle of absorbent cloth strips tied to a length of twine, at the other end of which is tied a small brass or lead weight. The weight is dropped through the tube and the cloth pulled after it. Many players are nervous about getting WATER into vital keys during a performance and constantly dry their joints. Sir Malcolm Sargent used to object to the way Reginald Kell (1906–82) used to fuss and fidget with his pull-through. 'It is distracting both to me and the audience,' he said. Kell, who did not suffer conductors gladly, thereupon instructed his colleagues to go through the routine in unison with him several times during the following performance – dismantling the clarinets, bending down to pick up the pull-through from the case at their side and, together, wipe the instruments dry. Sargent looked daggers at them each time they performed this improvised ballet, but said no more. There are some battles conductors can never win. Flautists do not use a pull-through but a wooden or metal stick with a piece of cloth threaded through its perforated end, as their headjoint is closed at one end, and it is impossible to pull anything through it. Oboists traditionally use a pheasant's feather to dislodge droplets of moisture. See also CIGARETTE PAPERS.

Pump-handle conductor

Debussy's description, in a letter (22 May 1909) to Paul-Jean Toulet, of the conductor Campanini (1860–1919) who he thought made awkward and ungainly arm movements: 'The conductor answers to the name of Cléofonte Campanini; he beats time in a most curious manner which resembles . . . the action of a pump handle.' Debussy was writing from London, where he was attending the final rehearsals before the Covent Garden première of *Pelléas et Mélisande*. See also GRECIAN-URN CONDUCTOR.

Purlies/pearlies

A temporary inability to keep the bow steady on the string, due to nervousness: a rapid chattering results instead of a continuous note. The spelling varies, and the word could come either from a 'purler', which is an accident, like a 'cropper'; or from the diminutive of pearls, i.e. a row of regularly repeated sounds; or from 'pirl', which is an old English word for a slight, regular ripple, as on water.

Pushed-up

Derogatorily said of a soprano or tenor: 'She's a pushed-up MEZZO', i.e. a singer whose natural range has been unnaturally raised by training and practice.

Push pipe

American musicians' slang word for the trombone. See also under SLUDGE PUMP.

Quadraphony

An expensive but short-lived electronic fad devised in the late 1960s on the false assumption that music lovers had four ears and liked to hear music from the same position as the fifth viola player in a symphony orchestra. Quadraphony (later joined by other systems such as Ambisonic Sound and Surround-Sound) seems to have disappeared as suddenly as it came, like the FLEXATONE, MUSIQUE CONCRÈTE, QUARTER-TONES and other ideas. 'Quadraphony' was in any case a bastard word: half Latin, half Greek – which in itself is no bad thing – but the electrician who coined it unerringly hit on the one uneasy formation: *quadrophony, quadruphony* or *quadriphony*, yes. But 'quadraphony' betrays him (whoever he was) as a man who spells saxophone 'saxaphone' and accordion 'accordian'. The first recorded instance (1969) is given in the *OED* as 'quadriphonic'.

'Quantz says . . .'

A frequent preamble to a statement about the performance of eighteenth-century music. The reference is to *Versuch einer Anweisung . . .* by J. J. Quantz (1697–1773), which was nominally a flute tutor but contains much important general information about contemporary performing methods. Although it was published in the middle of the eighteenth century, it went through many editions and much of it may be applied to later eighteenth-century music. For example, the English version* appeared as late as c.1778 and is in some respects updated. Other sources that are quoted by proponents of authentic performance include treatises by Leopold Mozart and C. P. E. Bach ('Leopold says . . . ' and 'C. P. E. says . . . ')

---

* 'Easy and Fundamental Instructions' (reprinted as *Quantz Says*, ed. Spiegl, Liverpool Music Press, 1976).

Quarter-tones

These were the newest, trendiest thing of the 1920s and 1930s musical avant garde, and although they were still occasionally mentioned in the 1940s have now been forgotten. Even composers like Bartók and Ives for a time experimented with quarter-tones but they, too, soon abandoned them. Who loves them now? The trouble is, of course, that even the moderately trained musical ear is unable to tell the difference between someone trying to play quarter-tones and someone who is playing IN THE CRACKS. For a time, 'He's playing quarter-tones' was heard by way of sardonic comment on bad intonation but after a time the joke, too, died a natural death. *Sic transit gloria musicae* . . .

Queen in G

Three words when passed round an orchestra just before a concert signify that the National Anthem is to be played in its standard key of G major. However, some conductors prefer it in the 'brighter' key of B flat, in which it is also played by military bands. The anthem is seldom rehearsed. Everyone stands for its performance (except the harpist and cellists, and the Queen if present). The anthem is, of course, always played from memory, unless one of the many special arrangements is used. They include one by Elgar (with a notorious DOMINO trap at the beginning), the FAIRY QUEEN, and a preposterous version by Benjamin Britten, first (and probably last) performed in Leeds in 1961 by the Leeds Festival Chorus and the RLPO, under John Pritchard. This has a curious, three times reiterated supplication, 'Go-od save the, Go-od save the, Go-od save the Queen', as if the deity were hard of hearing. Some conductors give no instructions as to DYNAMICS, simply beating a perfunctory three-in-a-bar as if to get the thing over and done with. Some (as Beecham used to do and Norman Del Mar still does) treat it like the first item on the programme, with full histrionics. Some like it fast, some slow, and a few go so far as to attempt to observe faithfully the 1933 British Army Order approved by George V: 'The first bars will be played *pianissimo* at MM 60 crotchets . . . the brass [instruments] will be brought up smartly into playing position on the third beat of the fifth bar . . . ' (and I should like to see *that* bit enforced in the LSO) '. . . side drum will be added on the second beat of the sixth bar, the four quavers being slurred, making a rubato' (what can that mean?) 'at the tempo of MM 52 crotchets. The last eight bars will be played *fortissimo* as broadly as possible . . . . A *rallentando* will be made in the second-last bar.' In recent years, with the revival of interest in old music, attempts have been made to find suitably authentic versions. That by Thomas Arne is probably the most faithful version of a tune whose origins have yet to be discovered. *God save the King*, as it then was, was the direct inspiration for Haydn's EMPEROR hymn.

Queer flute

Hobson-Jobson mistranslation of the German *Querflöte*, i.e. transverse flute. See FLUTE/RECORDER.

Rabbit principals

Principal singers in oratorio who instead of sitting in their place throughout a performance, ready to sing, make a special entrance for each aria or group of arias and then leave the stage again. This practice went out when applause began to be given at the end of each half rather than for individual contributions. The nickname first occurred in an article in the *Musical Times* in 1874 deploring the habit. They were, says the writer, 'popping up and down on either side [of the stage] like rabbits in a warren'.

Rach

Pronounced 'rack'. Familiar abbreviation of Rachmaninov, as in 'Rach Two' meaning that composer's second piano concerto – not his second symphony, which would be more fully described.

Rache aria

See REVENGE ARIA

Rage over a Lost Penny

Spurious title of Beethoven's *Alla ingherese, quasi un capriccio* ('a kind of caprice in the Hungarian style') which was his own, cumbersome name for an early (pre-1800) piano piece though he later pencilled in the title, 'Easy Caprice'. 'Rage over a Lost Penny' was someone else's later joke: doubtless a reference to Beethoven's notorious, penny-pinching meanness. He used to count the slices of bread and measure the wine on the side of the bottle. When Schumann saw the piece in 1835 he wrote, 'There is hardly a funnier thing than this prank. When I played it through for the first time recently I had to laugh all the way through.' The remark is puzzling, for although the work is cheerful and lighthearted there is absolutely nothing in it to laugh at – except perhaps the absurdly exaggerated speed at which modern pianists take it – usually about twice the *allegro vivace* Beethoven intended.

Racket

See KORTHOLT and SAUSAGE BASSOON

RAM

The Royal Academy of Music, London, founded in 1822.

Rank-and-file

Those members of a string section who are not PRINCIPALS, SUB-PRINCIPALS, or in some orchestras also 'third players' who, because of their proximity to the front DESK, are given extra status (and money). Wind, brass and percussion do not have any rank-and-file players.

Rasumovsky

When a string player announces 'I'm playing the third Rasumovsky quartet on Friday' he uses the recognized abbreviation for Beethoven's Quartet in C major, op. 59, No. 3. It is the last of three dedicated to Count Andreas Kyrillovich Rasumovsky (1752–1836), a Russian diplomat who – to put it in modern terms – defected in Vienna after serving there as ambassador. He was a patron of the arts and an accomplished violinist who kept (and played second fiddle in) a resident professional string quartet, led by Ignaz Schuppanzigh. A spare second, Louis Sina, took Rasumovsky's place when he wanted to be a listener. It was this group which first performed many of the string quartets of Beethoven. Not only op.59 but also the Fifth and Pastoral symphonies are dedicated to him. At dawn on New Year's Day 1815 Rasumovsky's palace in Vienna was burnt down, and with it perished a great collection of books, manuscripts, furniture and instruments. By way of small consolation the distraught count was elevated to the rank of prince at the scene of the disaster. Counts and princes are two a penny on the continent, but Rasumovsky's name is honoured because of his constant and faithful support of Beethoven. And incidentally, the modern string player's statement at the head of this entry is an exact translation of what Schuppanzigh said to Beethoven (Conversation Books, November 1823): *'Freitag spiele ich das 3e Rasumoffskische Quartett.'*See also THE RUSSIAN.

Ratamacue

See PARADIDDLE

Rave notice

See CRIT

The Razor

Haydn, it is said, once cursed his razor while shaving and exclaimed, 'I'd give my best work for a decent, sharp one.' Tradition has it that the prize in question was his op.46 in F minor, now known as 'The Razor Quartet', and that the man responsible for the anecdote was the London publisher John Bland. It sounds plausible. Haydn spent the first night on his arrival in London in 1791 at Bland's house in Holborn. England was then the source of all things desirable and excellent, as is shown by numerous references in composers' letters and diaries. Haydn might have dropped a heavy hint to Bland, and would have been delighted by the gift of a pair of razors of finest Sheffield steel.

RCM

The Royal College of Music, London, founded in 1883. See ROOM 99.

Realize

'Realize/realise – to make real' (*OED*). But in music this has a special application which the dictionaries ignore. It dates from about 1950 and the rise of the BBC Third Programme (now Radio 3) and is a rather stilted term meaning making a musical arrangement or transcription of (usually old) music. At first it was used for filling out (i.e. 'making real') the shorthand of a figured or unfigured THOROUGH-BASS; then widened to include free arrangements and reorchestrations, such as Britten's realization of the *Beggar's Opera* (reorchestrated and reharmonized) and Stravinsky's of choral works by Gesualdo (reconstruction of two missing vocal lines).

Recit

The almost invariable abbreviation of *recitative* – a form of singing in free, natural speech rhythms, like talking, first used in the middle of the seventeenth century (although rudimentary forms occur earlier). It arose because stories that are sung take longer to tell than those that are spoken, and are harder to understand. Recits therefore save time and aid clarity – a form of early *Sprechgesang*. They come in two kinds, *secco* and *accompagnato*. However, both are accompanied: the first by keyboard and/or supporting bass instruments, the second with larger forces. *Accompagnato* is usually slower, more melodic and dignified. In Mozart's operas it is the weightier recits (e.g. Donna Anna in THE DON, in Bach's Passions the part of Christ) which are *accompagnato*, the chirpy, fast-moving dialogue in the first, and the Evangelist's utterances in the second, *secco*.

The Recitative

Haydn's Quartet No.22 in G major.

Rehearsal letters/figures

Reference points in orchestral SCORES AND PARTS that enable performers quickly to find their place at rehearsal. Thus when a conductor says, 'We'll go from fourteen bars after figure 16', or 'Letter P without wind', everyone knows where to begin. In well-organized music the first bar of each stave is numbered, and reference points come at salient points: a notable solo, a sudden *fortissimo*, a change of mood, key, tempo or orchestration, all save players a great deal of COUNTING BARS (as do CUES) and help to avoid DOMINOES.

Rehearsal syllables

In order to convey their ideas of phrasing and general shaping of melodic lines to the orchestra, conductors are obliged to sing. Very few can actually do so, but even a tuneless croak can often make their intentions understood. Of conductors within living memory,

Toscanini's 'singing' was easily the worst, leading a brave player to mutter, 'Maestro, if you're not careful we'll play it like you sing it.' Conductors invariably resort to a well-established system of onomatopœic nonsense syllables, like *rat-ta-ta, yat-ta-ta, YAH, titty-tum*, etc. which always strike the non-musician as comic or even suggestive, but orchestral players think nothing of them. Some conductors may be seen to mouthe them silently during performances. German conductors are very fond of *schrumm, bumm*, and similar teutonic sounds. The Swiss conductor Ernest Ansermet (1883–1969) was once heard exhorting an English orchestra to play the opening quavers of Mozart's G minor Symphony (K550) with 'Not short, gentlemen, *tick-e-tick-e-tick-eh*, but soft: *bug-ger, bug-ger, bug-ger*.' It is one of the mysteries of the profession that foreign maestri who have for decades resided in English-speaking countries continue throughout their lives to speak in fractured English, delivered in thick continental accents. One would have thought that their musical ear would help them to acquire speech patterns which, like music, are learnt by listening to, and imitating, one's betters.

La reine

Haydn's No. 85 in B flat, also 'La Reine de France' and 'The Queen of France'.

Relative pitch

See ABSOLUTE PITCH

Répétez!

French for ENCORE.

Repet(iteur)

The French word for what the English call an assistant school-master, private coach or crammer is *répétiteur*. In British opera houses, however, he is a pianist who helps singers to learn their part, and acts as general factotum, rehearsal accompanist and assistant conductor when required. Numerous well-known conductors started their career as repetiteurs. In English orchestras, however, the repet (never repetiteur in full) is the violinist who sits on the 'inside' of the LEADER and acts as his deputy – although the word is more common in the North than the South of England, and more in theatre and opera than symphony orchestras: 'I hear Jim's got the repet at the GARDEN.' The tradition goes back to the old days, when the leader acted as conductor or STEHGEIGER, and helped with the training of the stage artists.

Resting

When an actor does this he is using the accepted euphemism of his trade for being out of work. Musicians 'rest' on the platform: either when COUNTING BARS or, more literally, when leaving the TUTTIS to their BUMPER-UP.

Revenge aria

German *Rachearie*: an old operatic stock cliché, like the CURTAIN ARIA, drinking-song, LAUGHING-SONG, MAD SCENE and SOLDIERS' CHORUS. Osmin's *Ha, wie will ich triumphieren* in the third act of Mozart's *Die Entführung aus dem Serail* is probably the best-known *Rachearie*.

Revolutionary Study

Spurious nickname of Chopin's op.10, No.2, which is supposed to reflect a bout of Polish patriotism that overtook the composer during one of the recurring spells of trouble his country had with its Russian neighbour. Like many another fervent patriot, Chopin spent as much time as possible at a safe distance from his unrestful homeland.

Richard II

German nickname for Richard Strauss, Wagner being considered the undisputed Richard the First. Gustav Holst (1874–1934), however, felt no such qualms. In a letter to VW (1903) he writes: 'As I told you once before, Richard II seems to me to be the most "Beethovenish" composer since Beethoven. Perhaps I am wrong, but anyhow, you will agree that, whatever his faults, he is a real life composer. As far as I can make out, his training seems to have been: (1) Bach, Mozart, Beethoven. (2) Schumann and Brahms. (3) Wagner. Mine [adds Holst] has been: (1) Mendelssohn. (2) Grieg.

(3) Wagner. This alone speaks volumes.' True Wagnerians admitted no second, for they maintained that their idol could have no successor. But there were also those who rallied *against* Strauss, saying 'If it must be Richard, let it be Wagner; if it must be Strauss, let it be Johann.'

The Rider

Haydn's Quartet No. 74 in G minor is called both *Reiterquartett* (Rider Quartet) and *Ritterquartett* (Knightly Quartet), from its bouncing equestrian rhythms in the first movement.

Rimshot

A loud noise like a gun-shot, made by striking the rim of a side-drum rather than its skin or head. It is used in PROGRAMME music, musical comedy, MUSIC-HALL and in the circus to give emphasis to what is happening on the stage, e.g. a pratfall; which is why drummers (like trumpeters) of circus bands get higher MU rates than other musicians.

Rimsky

The customary abbreviation of Nikolay Andreyevich Rimsky-Korsakov (1844–1908): not one in a thousand music lovers is likely to know his full name. He was one of HE MIGHTY HANDFUL and, like them, really an amateur: 'an officer-dilettante who occasionally enjoyed playing or listening to music . . . ' he modestly described himself, although, of course, there is nothing 'amateurish' about his music. Rimsky had a most remarkable musical handwriting: all his notes sloped to the right – perhaps the only composer to write italic notes.

The Ring

In both English and German this is the universal abbreviated name for Wagner's four-part music-drama *Der Ring des Nibelungen*, consisting of *Das Rheingold*, *Die Walküre*, *Siegfried* and *Götterdämmerung*. The French name for the *Ring* is *La Tétralogie*.

The Rite of Spring solo

Once a dreaded thing for bassoon players – the top C which opens the solo introducing Stravinsky's *The Rite of Spring*. In 1913 this note was considered unsafe if not unplayable by most bassoonists and, when they did manage it, always conveyed a great sense of strain and effort. In some performances it gave the impression that Stravinsky's primeval rites were initiated by a sick cow. At one time you would always encounter, just before any performance of the work, the anxious PRINCIPAL standing in a corner of the BANDROOM and playing the short solo over and over again. But as bassoon technique improved, so the solo came to sound more and more 'comfortable'; which, of course, is contrary to the composer's intentions. It has been suggested that in order to preserve the implied sense of discomfort in the face of ever-improving technique, the solo should be transposed a semitone up every ten years.

Rits and ralls

The abbreviation of *ritardando* and *rallentando*, respectively: instructions telling players to slacken or slow down the tempo. Pencilled reminders of such markings may take the form of a WIGGLY LINE.

RLPO

The Liverpool Philharmonic Orchestra, founded 1840. Max Bruch was its conductor 1880–3, followed by HALLÉ, Sargent, Rignold, etc. It got the 'Royal' prefix in 1957 after its municipally-appointed (Labour) chairman, with characteristic Scouse 'chutzpah', wrote to the Queen and asked for it. Soon afterwards he himself was given a knighthood.

Robbie

Affectionate nickname given by colleagues and associates to both Stanford Robinson, the veteran BBC conductor (OBE 1972) and H. C. Robbins Landon, the Haydn scholar.

Room 99

The RCM was built towards the end of the nineteenth century with 98 teaching and practice rooms. When a professor could not be found because he was having a quiet drink in the nearest public house, the hall porter would tell the enquiring student, 'He's in Room Ninety-nine', which in due course became the accepted euphemism. When the College was later enlarged, the tradition was respected, and the additional rooms began with Room 100, leaving 99 its alcoholic connotations. See also GLUEPOT.

Roratorios and uproars

Oratorios and operas. This facetious definition is given in Grose's *Dictionary of the Vulgar Tongue* (1823).

Rossini crescendo

Nearly all the popular Rossini Overtures have this device in common: a repetitive passage of growing excitement, starting softly, getting gradually louder and culminating in a fortissimo. It works almost to a formula: four-bar phrases, usually harmonized in thirds or sixths, are repeated over and over again in a SCHUSTER-FLECK sequence; and at each repetition further instruments join in. It is therefore a crescendo of quantity as well as volume. At the climax the melodic interest is always transferred to the bass instruments, usually with trombones added, while the upper instruments play rhythmic figures reminiscent of the MANNHEIM style, from which Rossini got the idea. It was also used by Donizetti: there is a splendid example in that composer's opera *Emilia di Liverpool* (1824). Nor are Rossini crescendos necessarily restricted to instrumental passages in overtures: they occur also in vocal versions in the operas themselves.

Rotarian

An instrument called for by Ernst Toch (1887–1964) in his Symphony No.4 (1957). What the composer specifies (without further elucidation) is a mysterious object called 'A Rotarian with Wooden Balls'.

La Roxelane

Or, in Italian, *Roxolana*. Haydn's No. 63 in C major.

The Royal Family

In the Hallé Orchestra, during Barbirolli's conductorship, the name for some of the older members of the orchestra with whom he had long-standing, special friendships and who had both his ear and his confidences. But in spite of the often underhand politics carried on in orchestras, there was no intrigue and nothing sinister about this particular group.

RPO

The Royal Philharmonic Orchestra (to which 'of London' has been added on foreign tours), founded by Sir Thomas Beecham in 1946. He got its Royal prefix by what was almost a confidence trick. Beecham obtained an agreement from the Royal Philharmonic Society (founded in 1813 but not declared Royal until George V awarded it the title for its centenary season 1912/13) nominally to provide the society's orchestra. But when the arrangement lapsed, Beecham was told that his orchestra was no longer able to use the prefix. However, he persisted, and after a little unpleasantness, including veiled threats of litigation, the good old British capacity for compromise prevailed: in 1966 the Queen officially conferred the Royal prefix on the orchestra – thereby giving Beecham what he had already appropriated. On the other hand, Sir Henry Wood's mistress lived for many years under the name 'Lady Jessie Wood', which she adopted by deed poll, but her title was never legitimized. For the story of how the RLPO got the handle to its name, see under that heading.

Rubato

The proper term is *tempo rubato*, 'robbed time' in Italian. It means a subtle way of playing out of time, but in such a way that the general pulse of the music is not disturbed. The effect is often overdone by pianists playing romantic music, especially Chopin; and by opera singers seeking added expression and characterization. Mozart in a letter (24 October 1777) says '. . . they are all astonished that I play strictly in time. They simply can't understand that in an adagio *tempo rubato* the left hand knows nothing about it. With them, the left hand gives in.' Some jazz pianists are especially good at this kind of free playing with the right hand while keeping an iron rhythm going with the left. See also VIENNESE LIFT.

Ruff

See PARADIDDLE

Rum-ti-tum music

Derisive, onomatopoeic description of a certain kind of light music, inconsequential but less bland than MUZAK. Keats writes in a letter dated 15 April 1817, 'I hope one of you will be competent to take part in a Trio . . . when you have said Rum-ti-ti you must not rum any more.' See also REHEARSAL SYLLABLES.

The Russian

Nickname for Haydn's Quartets No. 29–34. The Germans also call them *Jungfernquartette*, or 'Virgin Quartets', presumably in the Holy, not sexual, sense. To add to the confusion, the Italians know the set as *Gli scherzi*, 'The Jests', but that is probably because their minuets are more in the nature of scherzos. 'The Russian Quartets' is, however, the best description, for they are dedicated to the same Prince RASUMOVSKY whose name belongs to Beethoven's op.59.

Rute

The German word for a bundle of twigs, or a switch, such as German schoolmasters use(d) to chastize their pupils with. Mahler asks for one in some of his symphonies, and CLASSICAL composers like Mozart and Haydn use it in their TURKISH MUSIC, where a certain kind of notation for the bass drum implies alternate use of stick and *Rute*. The word is pronounced to rhyme with 'boot-eh', although British percussionists usually say 'root'.

Sackbut

See SHAGBUT

Sardines

Facetious name for a mute, from Italian *sordino*, French *sourdine*.

The Satz

When string quartet players talk about 'doing the Satz' they mean Schubert's *Quartettsatz* in C minor, D703. *Satz* simply means movement, and the work in question is a movement from an incomplete string quartet. There is also a little-known earlier *Satz* in C minor, D103, dating from 1814.

Sausage bassoon

The racket(t) or KORTHOLT. It is not a modern nickname but a translation of the German *Wurstfagott*. For another musical food term, see PRETZEL BENDER.

'Save your lip'

A conductor's exhortation to brass and wind players to take it easy and reserve some of their strength for the performance. They do not usually have to be told; but it is an important point of rehearsal communication. For conductors must ascertain whether the sounds they hear when rehearsing are those they are likely to get ON THE NIGHT, thus enabling them to balance the DYNAMICS.

Schmaltz

Schmalz is the German word for dripping or lard; and its slightly anglicized spelling (sometimes also *shmaltz*, adjective *shmaltzy*) is used in music to describe a performance or work imbued with excessive sentimentality, e.g. a violinist who uses too much rubato, portamento or other tricks of exaggerated expression.

The Schoolmaster

Haydn's No.55 in E flat. Not to be confused with THE PHILOSOPHER.

Schrammel music

A kind of Viennese café and tavern music of long tradition and classical antecedents but slightly lower social standing than the music of the WALTZ KING – and certainly a little more *schmaltzy*. It has its own authentic and characteristic instrumentation: usually a special kind of squeaky piccolo clarinet in G, nicknamed in Vienna *Das picksüsse Hölzl*,* or 'sickly-sweet little wooden stick', two violins and a bass guitar – the old, non-electric kind, of course, and a descendant of the old *chitarrone* or bass lute. The origins of Schrammel go back to the entertainment trios favoured by Schubert's contemporaries such as Wenzel Matiegka (1773–1830) who (being a guitarist himself) specialized in trios for flute, viola and guitar. Schubert himself arranged and augmented one of Matiegka's trios. The first Schrammel music began as a trio, formed in 1878 by the brothers Johann and Josef Schrammel and the bass guitarist Anton Strohmayer. They were later joined by the clarinettist Johann Danzer, famous for his sweet tone, who died on his way home from a successful appearance at the Chicago World's Fair in 1893 and was replaced by an accordion player. Johann and Josef died in 1893 and 1895, respectively, to be replaced in the Schrammel group by different fiddlers, but their name was retained. The original quartet gained the recognition and support of musicians like Bruckner and THE THREE JOHNNIES: Hans Richter, Johannes Brahms and Johann Strauss, the last-named in no way considering them in competition to his own music. Echoes of the Schrammel style can frequently be detected in the music of Mahler. When Bruckner died in 1896, Brahms in 1897 and Strauss in 1899, it was said in Vienna that God had called the brothers Schrammel to heaven ahead of them so they would FIX a decent fiddle section for the giants: something of a stock joke among musicians (see ON TOUR WITH VW). Modern Schrammel music comes in various combinations loosely based on the original group: often both clarinet *and* zither take part, and occasionally a zither is heard in addition to or in place of one or other instrument. This kind of music is now considered an essential part of the *Heurigen* wine lodges of Vienna and is supported by the tourist industry, which has thus helped slightly to stem the tide of blaring electronic pop music from Viennese places of entertainment. The elder Schrammel was both the leader and business manager of his band, and also composed or arranged the music. His march, *Wien bleibt Wien* (1887), roughly translatable as 'Vienna Never Changes', is still in the repertoire of every Austrian band or orchestra. The brothers' business acumen led them to copy the advertising practice of displaying the piano maker's name in large letters; and their fiddles carried, for a consideration and in large letters, the legend 'MADE BY CARL ZACH, VIENNA', on the ribs (the part turned towards the audience). Out of gratitude Zach carved on each of the violin scrolls the portrait heads of their owners.

* The nickname adjective *picksüss* given to the small G clarinet had a double meaning. It was a pun on both the *Piccolo* (the German word for this instrument is *Pickelflöte*) and *pickig*, which is the Austrian slang-word for 'sticky'. Compare this with the various English nicknames for the Clarinet, including LICORICE STICK. The Schrammels' name should not be confused with *schrumm*, which is a kind of onomatopoeic noise for strumming sounds in German, and one of the favourite REHEARSAL SYLLABLES of German-speaking conductors.

Schusterfleck

In German it means a cobbler's patch. Beethoven described the theme sent to him by the publisher Diabelli for his *Variations*, op.120, as 'the theme with the cobbler's patch'. This is usually interpreted as a criticism, a derogatory way of saying it was a feeble, patched-up job on which he was expected to write variations. The description is, however, factual, for *Schusterfleck* is a German technical term denoting the repetition of a passage at different degrees of the scale, usually but not necessarily higher, called a *sequence* in English. The Italian equivalent is *rosalia*: said to come from a song *Rosalia mia cara* ('Rosalie, my dear') in which sequences occur. But is it not equally plausible that it is related to *rosario*, a rosary, comparing melodic repetition to the telling of beads? Further confusion is caused by the German alternative name, *Vetter Michael* – 'Cousin Michael' – another song incorporating the device. As indeed *Schusterfleck* probably refers to a now forgotten tune. Diabelli's little minuet certainly employs a cobbler's patch. So do Handel's *Hallelujah Chorus*, Mozart's JUPITER and the

DIES IRAE, to name only three. For a modern, lazy equivalent of the cobbler's patch see SEMITONE UP.

Schwammerl

One of the nicknames given to Schubert by his close friends. Documents show that at the age of twenty-one he was disqualified from military service on account of his height, given as 4 ft 11 ins. This, together with his stout body and curly-topped head rather too large for it, accounts for the name *Schwammerl*, which is Austrian dialect for 'little mushroom'. See KANEWAS.

Big Michael Vogl and 'Little Mushroom' Schubert. After a contemporary drawing (c. 1825)

Scordatura

'Were you playing the scordatura?' a colleague might ask a viola player anent his performance of Mozart's Sinfonia Concertante in E flat K364. The word comes from the Italian *scordare*, to mistune; and in the instance quoted the mistuning would have been intentional. Mozart, who played the viola himself, left the violin tuned as normal in K364 but instructed the viola player to tighten his strings so that they sound a semitone higher (i.e. C sharp, G sharp, D sharp and A sharp). Then he has to play the piece from a PART written in D, and the result is once more E flat. The intention behind this is to obtain a little extra brilliance from the tauter strings. The *scordatura* effect was used also by J. S. Bach and Heinrich Biber (1644–1704) and others, though for different purposes, e.g. to achieve different DOUBLE-STOPPING possibilities. Haydn's No. 60 turns it into a joke; Saint-Saëns's *Danse Macabre* and Mahler No.4 use a detuned fiddle to make the figure of death sound more frightening (see TOTENTANZ).

Score and parts

'Music is said to be in *Score*, when all the *Parts* are distinctly wrote and set under each other, so as the Eye, at one View, may take in all the various Contrivances of the Composer.' This definition by the Newcastle organist and composer, Charles Avison (1709–70), in his famous *Essay on Musical Expression* (1752) can not be bettered. Some non-musicians are unaware that each orchestral (or for that matter chamber music) player has only his own part in front of him, containing (apart from the occasional CUE) only the music he himself plays. Listening to, and hearing, the other parts as he plays his own is only one of the skills of co-ordination he must develop. When he is not playing but RESTING, he must COUNT BARS (unless, of course, he knows his entries by heart and long experience) and hope for a cue from the conductor. He, on the other hand, has all the music in his *score*, although he 'reads' it in a different way, as outlined in SCORE-READING.

Score order

'Room numbers will be given out in score order' may be an announcement heard as an orchestra on tour arrives at an hotel. Or, 'Line up in score order for your handshake' when certain players are presented to royalty. The term refers to the order in which instruments traditionally appear on a score, i.e. (reading downwards) flutes, oboes, clarinets, bassoons, horns; then the other brass, the percussion, piano, harp, etc., followed by the strings: first violins, second violins, violas, cellos and double basses. The arrangement came to be standardized early in the nineteenth century. Before that time, many scores (including some of Mozart's) were published in any order according to the whim of the composer, publisher or printer.

Score-reading

A term with a wide range of meanings, some of them misunderstood. The orchestral player is expected to *read* his PART. That is, he identifies each note, its pitch and duration and the accompanying instructions as to DYNAMICS and expression; and having done all that, he instantaneously translates that information into the required configuration of lips, arms, hands and fingers so as to produce the intended musical sound. Not all scores are printed, or even written legibly; and to absorb all this information and put it into split-second practice is often a considerable feat (see SIGHT-READING). Conductors, on the other hand, may read the SCORE in several different ways. Some develop an astonishing facility for translating even the biggest scores into sound on the piano and can thus sight-read the salient contents of some thirty lines of music, including a proliferation of strange clefs and different TRANSPOSITIONS; and give some sort of keyboard approximation of it. If they are opera scores they may even add some more or less approximate vocal effects as well. Reading a score as one silently reads a book, however, is a different matter. Some musicians, especially those with ABSOLUTE PITCH, can *hear* in their mind's ear what they see on paper: both individual sounds and those produced in combination of complex harmony and counterpoint. To do this they must, of course, draw on previous aural experience, combined with a well developed memory. How else could stone-deaf composers like Beethoven and Smetana have continued composing music? They could not have read, let alone *written*, the simplest common chord had they not developed through much practice the capacity of relating the written to the heard; and when their hearing failed, the memory remained. (The non-musician to whom this appears like magic might care to look at the words, 'A handbag?' and then imagine Edith Evans's well-known recorded rendering of it in Oscar Wilde's play, *The Importance of Being Earnest*; and her inflexion, intonation and enunciation will immediately come to life.) The conductor who can do all this is indeed lavishly endowed with musical gifts. Unfortunately he is also very rare. Many of today's glamorous maestri with household names, although they may have other fine qualities, do not possess this largely God-given talent – and conversely, many humble musicians do, who lack the personality as well as the opportunity of becoming conductors. But instead of 'reading' his score, the conductor can fortunately learn its content from a record (many conductors practise with the gramophone, though few admit it). And while conducting they in any case have no need to decipher and identify the notes. The players do it for them, though his ear should, of course, make the conductor aware of any discrepancies between the written notes and what is played. Some of a conductor's strength and superb qualities may lie also in his ability to shape phrases by his hand movements, to control the speeds and their relationships to each other, to see to the internal balance, give CUES where needed, express his ideas to the players, gain their total co-operation and generally keep the performance on an even keel – none of which should be under-rated or belittled. Greatness can take many forms.

Scotch snap

A rhythmical musical device consisting of a short note played on a strong beat followed by a longer one held for the duration of that beat. Sing the word 'butter' quickly, with explosive emphasis on the first syllable, and you have a Scotch snap. It is a characteristic element in the strathspey, but is not of course, unique to Scottish music. Purcell was very fond of it, especially in his songs and RECITS, and it also features strongly in the folk music (and related art music, e.g. that of Bartók and Kodály) from Hungary, where it is made all the more common because in that language all words are heavily stressed on the first syllable. In the 'snap' context 'Scotch' is for once acceptable in preference to 'Scottish'.

Scratch orchestra

An orchestra 'gathered together promiscuously, hastily assembled' as the *OED* defines the word; but it is not necessarily a reflection on the sound made by its string players. There are semi-scratch orchestras, e.g. touring theatre, opera or ballet companies which may bring with them certain key players but pick up others from the freelance pool of each place they visit. There was also *the* Scratch Orchestra, a group of crypto-musicians assembled by Cornelius Cardew (1936–81), who believed in Marxist 'free' expression but not in the hard work all true artistic accomplishment requires. He asked of them no previous experience, or even that they bring an instrument. His views are expounded in his book *Scratch Music* (Latimer Press, 1972), which also contains much of his music, consisting mostly of doodled GRAPHIC SCORES. Some have no 'music' at all, only verbal instructions. For example, Cardew's 'String Piece' goes like this: 'A piece of string is stretched from one side of the room to the other. Audience are on one side, players on the other. To play, a person must cross from the audience side to the playing side. To join the audience, a player must re-cross to the audience side. Players read the score from one side to the other. Embellishments can be attached to the string. . . . If the string breaks, or is cut, the piece ends.' This is the kind of rubbish some composers produce (note well, in all seriousness!) when mixing politics with what they think is music. Cardew, to the amazement of many in the profession, appeared on the prospectus as an alleged Professor of Composition at the Royal ACADEMY of Music and was elected a fellow of that institution. (This in spite of his definition of *arpeggio* in *Scratch Music* as 'Three or more related or unrelated sounds played in quick succession'!) He was for a long time one of the most articulate high priests in the phoney art of musical INDETERMINACY, though like most extremists he later recanted, whitewashing his ideas in the best Stalinist tradition, and returned to writing something not unlike real music, including a *Vietnam Sonata* (and for all I know a *Grunwick Concerto*). Cardew met an untimely death in a road accident in December 1981.

Screamer donna

Nickname for a woman engaged by a PRIMA DONNA to scream for her on stage, as too much screaming is detrimental to the singing-voice. The English soprano Rita Hunter (b. 1933) once told me that her operatic screams were performed for her by her dresser, who stood in the wings. Mozart relates in a letter his dissatisfaction with the quality of Zerlina's scream in *Don Giovanni*, when she is indecently assaulted by the DON offstage. Her scream was never loud enough for him, so, he says, he crept up behind her and at the appropriate moment pinched her bottom, merely to obtain a realistic scream. That was his story, anyway.

Screamer Donna: Sophia Schröder-Devrient as Isabella in Meyerbeer's Robert the Devil

Scrubbing

String players' name for a TREMOLO i.e. the rapid and regular reiteration of a note by means of a quick to-and-fro movement of the bow. It may be done in two ways: either by playing at the point of the bow, with a fully-extended rigid bow-arm and only the wrist in a cramp-like, trembling motion (which is the best way for an atmospheric, *pianissimo-tremolando*), or using as much of the bow as possible, with the whole arm in motion and bending at the elbow (best for *forte* or *fortissimo tremolando*) which lends a feeling of excitement to the music. *Scrubbing* is more often applied to the latter sort, and *tremolando* to the former.

Seating (orchestral)

The manner of arranging an orchestra on the platform is fairly constant today, although minor variations are dictated by the individual taste and preference of certain conductors. Some like first and second violins seated antiphonally, others prefer the cellos at the front and to their right, in the belief that the bellies of fiddles should face outwards and project the sound towards the audience (which is why LEFT-HANDED violinists make ideal second fiddles in a string quartet). Although early orchestras were positioned in all kinds of ways (and usually stood, incidentally) before the end of the nineteenth century, woodwind players now always sit in the middle of the orchestra, with brass behind and to either side of them. Kettle-drums always seem to be at centre-back, as if presiding over the proceedings. A few conductors like to string out all the double basses in a big semi-circle at the back of the platform, and STOKEY at times indulged in various, highly eccentric, seating plans, with woodwind in long lines rather than in banks of players, to the detriment of ENSEMBLE. Whatever the foibles of conductors, certain conventions of string seating are universally observed. For example, the 'outside' players (i.e. those nearest the audience) have precedence of rank over the 'inside' ones. And when it comes to turning the pages, it is the inside player's job to perform the chore, even if he sits nearer to the left page and has to reach across his colleague to do so (although some outside players sensibly ignore protocol and turn the page themselves). In the wind and brass, principal players sit together, e.g. the first flute with the first oboe on his left, and behind them and adjacently, the first clarinet and first bassoon, respectively, their SUB-PRINCIPALS to their right or left of them. Harps are usually at the extreme edge of the platform, not in the middle, where the swaying top of their instrument interferes with the sight-line of players behind them.

Seating rehearsal

See SITZPROBE

Secco

See RECIT

Second horn concertos

Strictly, 'Second-Horn Concertos'. In the eighteenth century horn players came in two sorts: those who specialized in playing the higher parts and those whose EMBOUCHURE was specially developed for the lower notes. First-horn players would naturally deal with the higher parts, second hornists (also fourth players, as the NATURAL instruments came in pairs) with the lower. The latter became known in German as *Sekundhornisten*, and concertos written for their register as *Sekundkonzerte*. Wenzel Stich (1746–1803) was a noted player and composer of such concertos, a friend of Mozart's and the man for whom Beethoven wrote his Horn Sonata, op. 17. Mozart wrote of him 'Punto blows magnifique' and tailor-made for him the horn part of the *Sinfonia Concertante* K297b. Stich also specialized in the production of chords on the horn, by means of simultaneous humming and playing and used them in his own compositions for the instrument. He italianized his name to Giovanni Punto – Punto being the Italian translation of *stich*, a point or sting.

The Second Viennese School

The movement embracing the music of Schoenberg, Berg and Webern, who worked in that city at the end of the nineteenth century and the earlier part of the twentieth. The First Viennese School is the CLASSICAL period of Haydn, Mozart and Beethoven, but seldom if ever so called.

Securicor

Name of a security firm and nickname of the big-bore HORN, because it is safer in performance than the old FRENCH HORN.

'See you at the double bar!'

Sometimes said when players embark on a very modern or difficult work – in the hope of at least finishing together.

Segue

Italian for 'follow'. When a conductor or player says, 'We'll play the next movement segue' it means there is little or no break between it and the previous one. For an amazing example of segue playing, see ENCORE.

Selection

The English word for a *potpourri*, or musical medley of (usually) light CLASSICAL music.

Semitone up

The pop musician's substitute for modulation. Modern pop songs do not usually modulate, i.e. change key, like real music, but consist of a MIDDLE EIGHT sandwiched between tedious repetitions of what is usually a meagre idea in the first place. So when things get too boring the manufacturer of pop has a simple answer: 'Semitone up!' That is, the whole thing shifts upwards by half a note, without warning or preparatory harmonies. It is, in some ways, the modern equivalent of the SCHUSTERFLECK.

Serialism

A form of TWELVE-NOTE MUSIC hedged about by even stricter mathematical rules than DODECACOPHONY. Serial music is also sometimes called 'Snap Crackle and Pop Music' (pun: serial/cereal) as well as DONKEY MUSIC. When Richard Strauss was told by a serial composer that he had laboured for many years on a certain work, he is said to have replied 'If you find composition so difficult, why do you bother?' But opinions about serial music do vary. As the anonymous poet said:

> Here's to Music, joy of joys:
> One man's Music – another man's Noise.

Sessions

Short for recording-sessions for gramophone records, television or radio jingles etc. They are usually extremely lucrative, involving a minimum of effort for disproportionately high fees. Because they take place in private, without an audience, they attract some of the most illustrious musicians, including orchestra LEADERS and distinguished soloists who would otherwise consider it a loss of status to be seen playing in humbler positions than normal. The same applies to off-camera television work, where half the leaders of London orchestras may be seen playing RANK-AND-FILE.

Sevenfold Amen

See DRESDEN AMEN

Shagbut

The delightful old English name for the sackbut, which to all intents and purposes is a small-bore trombone. But see also the mythical KANOON, and FLAT TRUMPET.

Sheet music

Practising musicians never use the term (still less 'music sheets', invented by journalists) unless referring to songs. They prefer to be precise: SCORE or PARTS, or less specific, 'the MUSIC', e.g. 'I've left my music at home'. DOTS is for pop musicians, though the word is increasingly heard elsewhere.

Shepherd Boy Étude

Nickname of Chopin's Étude No.1 in A flat, op.25. Percy Scholes says that it is authentic so far as Chopin is said to have 'told a pupil that he had imagined a little shepherd taking refuge in a grotto from a storm and playing the melody on his flute.'

Ship's piano

In specialized and probably now outmoded sailor's slang this means not a piano but a piano accordion, from the German *Schifferklavier*.

Shlep

To drag, either oneself or a heavy weight; the same as 'drag', as in 'it's a bit of a drag'. It comes from the German word *schleppen* which, while adapted as a slang word into American/Jewish usage, has gained further currency in orchestral speech because it often appears as one of the NEGATIVE MARKINGS in German scores. But see also ORCHESTRA PORTER for the man who really has to do the 'shlepping'.

Shop stewards

See MU

Short score

See PARTICELL

Shuffle

A kind of private form of applause. 'Getting a shuffle' at rehearsal denotes approval for a solo, when colleagues shuffle their feet to show appreciation. String players may gently tap their music with their bow instead. A conductor's speech of thanks may also produce this muted applause. But the loudest shuffles result from his announcement of a cancelled rehearsal. Real applause on the platform is sparingly used – for special conductors or really spectacular solo achievements.

Sib

VW's nickname for Sibelius (in a letter to Mrs VW, 1948).

Siffleur(-euse)

A whistler. The art of whistling is seldom used in any but the lightest of light-music scores. But in continental CLAQUES *siffleurs* were (and probably still are) paid to express disapproval of a rival artist. It should, however, be remembered that applause customs vary from one country to another. To be 'whistled off the stage' on the Continent is the worst thing that can happen to an artist, whereas in Britain whistling is a sign of approval.

Sight-reading

A 'good reader' or 'sight-reader' is one who can play a piece of music reasonably accurately without having previously seen or practised it. The Germans use the macaronic *prima vista spielen*, i.e. playing at first sight, whereas the English term implies the same without labouring the point. This is illustrated by an anecdote about Handel (printed in Townsend's *Account of the Visit of Handel to Dublin*, Dublin 1852). The composer was waiting in Chester for a fair wind from Parkgate, and organized there an impromptu performance of *The Messiah* in preparation for its Dublin premiere. Mr Janson, a local printer and amateur bass singer, came to grief during the trial of the chorus *And with His stripes we are healed*. Handel 'burst into a rage' (and if *that* is true he was a ruder man than is generally thought, for after all he was a guest at Chester and the locals were doing him a favour), saying in a broken English which Townsend attempts to record phonetically, 'You schauntrell! Tit you not dell me dat you could sing at soite?' 'Yes, sir,' replied the unfortunate basso, 'and so I can; but not at *first* sight!' Which made it Chester 1 – Handel nil. Many extraneous difficulties may conspire to make a normally good sight-reader into an indifferent one: bad light, poor copying or printing, incorrect spacing of the notes (both vertical and horizontal), DOUBLE PARTS, other players' misleading annotations, etc. But few complaints will be heard, lest they be taken for excuses. The essence of good sight-reading is looking ahead; and its skill lies in the fact that the fingers (or voice) are performing what the eyes saw a bar or two (or three or four) earlier. Conversely, by the time the notes are heard, the eyes are already deciphering and identifying the notes ahead. This may be compared to the driver of a car, who looks at what is coming, not the piece of road the wheels already cover. The last two or three decades have seen enormous improvements in sight-reading, especially among singers (who call it sight-singing). The poor sight-reader's promise 'I'll take it home and look at it' is seldom heard nowadays. But it should be said that among great opera singers there are still many who cannot read at sight; and some who are household names cannot read music at all but have to learn everything by ear. This is not the disadvantage it may appear to be. Indeed, some conductors and producers positively prefer it; for they know that such singers will do exactly what they and their REPETITEURS have drummed into them.

Sinfonias and sinfoniettas

Sinfonia: The Italian word for a composition known as a SYMPHONY. But in the last few decades the word has been used in the naming of symphony orchestras. The fashion was started by Walter Legge, who got the idea from the attractively-produced POCKET SCORES that were published between the wars by the Vienna Philharmonic Publishing Company under the 'Philharmonia' trade mark belonging to the publisher Alfred Kalmus (1889–1972). Until Legge started the Philharmonia Orchestra in 1945 there were symphony orchestras, philharmonic orchestras and chamber orchestras. Soon, however, philharmonias began to proliferate, and brought in their wake sinfonias and sinfoniettas; and the fashion coincided with the misleading American craze for calling a chorus a 'chorale'. Thus a sinfonietta is now no longer a small symphony but a chamber orchestra. If the fashion is carried further we may soon have TRIO SONATA groups called 'The Sonata of London' or, if duet partnerships, 'The Sonatina of Newcastle', or wherever; for it is lately fashionable also to add an ensemble's place of origin: The Northern Sinfonia being now 'The Northern Sinfonia of England'. Presumably to make it clear that it is not an Alaskan orchestra.

Single-tongueing

See TONGUEING

Singspiel

In German this literally means 'a singing-play' but is used to describe an operatic work in which sung arias and ensembles are interspersed with spoken dialogue. However, what the English usually call an operetta is not necessarily called an *Operette* in German. For example, Mozart's *Die Entführung* is called an opera by the English but a *Singspiel* in German; whereas Strauss's *Die Fledermaus* an operetta/*Operette* in both.

Sitting up

One would expect all musicians who play seated to do this, and not to loll back in too relaxed a manner. But in its jargon sense sitting up means playing in a higher position than one is contractually obliged to do. That is, a SUB-PRINCIPAL may sit up as a PRINCIPAL; a RANK-AND-FILE string player as sub-principal, or a BACK-DESK fiddler as REPET or even LEADER. For such temporary promotion a 'sitting-up fee' is payable.

Sitzprobe

German for both a seating rehearsal and a seated rehearsal. Orchestras have *seating* rehearsals. These are convened (e.g. on tour when the same programme is repeated in a strange hall) not usually for playing but to see that all musicians are present, have room to play and can see the conductor. They may, however, include STOPS AND STARTS. Opera companies, on the other hand, use *Sitzprobe* in the sense of a *seated* rehearsal, i.e. a rehearsal that takes place early in the production process and at which the singers may sit and probably still sing from their vocal scores. (Only at later rehearsals will they sing from memory and – still in their ordinary dress – begin to take up their positions on the stage or a marked area of the rehearsal-room.) In spite of the fact that the native terms make these useful distinctions, English musicians prefer to use *Sitzprobe* for both kinds of rehearsal; and moreover generally mispronounce it as if it were an English word, to rhyme with 'Kit's robe', with the false plural 'sitzprobes'.

Skins

Orchestral drummers mean by this the skin (now often plastic) covering of drums; whereas jazz and pop drummers use the word for the drums themselves.

Skip

From theatrical use: the padded wicker basket or box in which smaller orchestral instruments and the players' dress clothes (and on foreign tours, souvenirs and contraband) may be carried. See also ORCHESTRA PORTER.

The Sleep of the Last Virgin

A probably intentional mistake sometimes made by Sir Thomas Beecham when announcing one of his favourite LOLLIPOPS, Massenet's *The Last Sleep of the Virgin*.

Sleeve

The outer covering of a record or ALBUM. Record sleeves are the modern equivalent of the often beautiful, coloured lithographed songs published in SHEET MUSIC in Victorian times.

Sliver-sucker

American orchestral and jazz name for a clarinettist, from the way they lovingly suck their reed before fixing it on the mouthpiece. Oboists, on the other hand, give a preparatory CROW on their reed.

Slow bicycle race

'It's a real slow bike race today', said by a player, means the speed chosen by the conductor is excessively slow. From the children's game which consists of trying to see who gets to a certain point last by riding his bicycle as slowly as possible without falling off. See also LIGHTNING CONDUCTOR, WHERE'S THE FIRE?

Slow handclap

Abroad this is a mark of approval for a performance – but in Britain it can be the equivalent of booing, especially when an audience is kept waiting by a delay on the stage or platform.

Sludge pump

Also *slush pump*: orchestral and jazz players' name for the trombone. See also TAILGATING.

Smear

Another word for a GLISS(ANDO) or sliding passage on the trombone.

Snap, crackle and Pop music

See SERIALISM

Snorkel

Nickname for the bassoon: from the way the BELL, which to some suggests the air-tube of diving-apparatus, sticks up in the air. It is noteworthy that German orchestral players use *Schnorchel*, which is the original name used for the breathing-tube by U-boat men, later anglicized into *snorkel* by British submariners and divers (*Schnarchen* = to snore).

Soldiers' Chorus

Like the CURTAIN ARIA, LAUGHING-SONG, etc., a stock ingredient of opera.

Solo

In printed orchestral PARTS this word is shown in two ways. As *solo*, with a small *s*, it indicates that the passage so marked is a solo played by the player in whose part it occurs. When, in the parts of a concerto, it appears as *Solo*, it means the soloist enters at that point. This is effectively a place-finding device, as explained under REHEARSAL LETTERS/FIGURES. The practice probably was pioneered and certainly followed in the orchestral material of BREITKOPF. See also TUTTI.

Song writer

The term needs redefining in the light of popular modern usage. Schubert was a song writer. That is, he took the work of poets and set it to music, or occasionally set his own words. Today's song writer may be responsible for either the words ('lyrics') or the music, or both, or neither. Paul McCartney ('the greatest song writer since Schubert' – a music critic, c.1966) and other entertainers of his kind do not 'write' songs, as they are usually unable to write music. They may, however, hum a few notes, or pick them out on a piano, to be taken down and processed by a real musician like George Martin. Or experiment with multi-track tape-recorders. Had it not been for Martin and his like, phenomena like the Beatles could not have happened.

The Sorcerer's Apprentice

The customary nickname (from the well-known TONE POEM by Dukas after Goethe) for a young conductor employed by an orchestra and, in effect, apprenticed to a more experienced one. Zubin Mehta briefly occupied this position under John Pritchard in Liverpool after winning the RLPO Conductors' Competition in 1958. Such aspirants, like the sloth and Sydney Smith's well-connected curate, 'spend their life in a permanent state of suspense', half hoping that some illness, calamity or other disaster would befall their master – in order that they might step into his shoes at short notice and show how much better they can do the job. It is remarkable how many great (or at any rate famous) conductors do indeed owe their first appearance to such circumstances.

Soubrette

The French word for a serving-wench or young girl-in-waiting. But in both English and German (*Subrette*) operatic and theatrical jargon it stands for a stock character in opera from the seventeenth century onwards. Serpina in Pergolesi's *La Serva Padrona* is an archetypal soubrette; and part of the soubrette's function is to introduce into plots some of the master-servant relationships (Don Giovanni/Leporello, Countess/Susanna, etc.) so common on the stage. They know their place, but also use it to offer sly or philosophical observations and asides. Soubrettes are always sopranos with a light (sometimes even 'twee') voice. In Mozart's *Cosi fan tutte* Despina not only fills that part but is instructed by the composer to make herself sound even sillier: to say of a soprano 'She'd make the ideal Despina' is tantamount to an insult. There is no male vocal equivalent of the soubrette, but servants are seldom tenors. That voice is the hero's preserve: see HELDENTENOR.

Sousa

John Philip Sousa (1854–1932), the 'March King' (see WALTZ KING); famous American bandmaster and composer, for many years suffered from the rumour that he was really of Japanese descent, originally Mr So, who added the letters USA to his name on his American naturalization. This is as much a fiction as the supposedly 'Scottish' descent of Donizetti from one DONALD IZETT. But Sousa did once shave off his beard in the interval of one of his concerts, which is a better joke than either. Imagine Sir Thomas Beecham re-emerging after the interval without moustache or goatee, or André Previn without his Beatle-cut . . . .

Sousaphone

One of the most delightful musical inventions of the nineteenth century and an addition to the already huge family of new brass instruments – many of them named after either their inventor (like the saxophone and the sarrusophone) or, like the sousaphone and the Wagner tuba, after the composer who specified them in his orchestra. The player of the sousaphone both plays and wears it. Tuba players call a smaller tuba a Verdi Tuba.

Sparrow Mass

Mozart's Mass, K220, the nickname derived from some pecking, staccato violin figures in the *Sanctus*. It is called *Spatzenmesse* in German; and *Spatzen* is the German nickname for choirboys (see below and also CANARIES), which could be another explanation of the name.

Sparrows

Austrian and German choirboys are nicknamed *Spatzen*, i.e. sparrows, just as choral scholars at Eton College (and presumably singing-boys in other schools and in cathedrals) are known as CANARIES. If German *Spatzen* are attached to a cathedral they become *Domspatzen* (*Dom* = minster; though the fact that *Spatz* is a juvenile penis in colloquial German is probably coincidental). The nickname may contain some forgotten reference to the occasional appearance of sparrows in the Bible, where they are mentioned as appearing in church to compete with human voices and which exhorts us to tolerate them (e.g. St Luke XII:6). Unfortunately there was an occasion in 1979 when the Austrian guitarist Konrad Ragossnig was giving a guitar recital in a church: a solitary sparrow perched on a beam and decided to join in. 'It was absolutely impossible', the vicar was reported in the popular press (which made much of the occasion and doubtless exaggerated some of the detail); 'the artist just could not start. He is a true professional, and you know what these chaps are like . . . .' So the vicar's son was called, and with his air-rifle summarily executed the little sparrow. This is in contrast with Debussy's account of a performance of Schubert's UNFINISHED given by Arthur Nikisch (1855–1922), during which a whole flock of sparrows alighted on a high window-sill and joined in the music. 'He had the grace not to demand their expulsion,' writes Debussy. Nikisch was also a true professional.

Speak

The action of an instrument or organ-pipe sounding. Reeds also speak, either well or badly.

Spectacles

See WARNING SIGNS

Speed merchant

Derisive name for a player or conductor who habitually chooses speeds that are too fast, either for comfort or the sense of the music. Also LIGHTNING CONDUCTOR, WHERE'S THE FIRE?

Spiegel-kanon

German for mirror-canon, a contrapuntal device consisting of a piece of music that can be played by two or more players, forwards

Spiegel-Kanon, or Mirror-Canon, by Haydn (Harmonicon, 1823)

or backwards simultaneously. Various ingenious variations and refinements have been devised by great contrapuntists like J. S. Bach and others. TABLE MUSIC is a variant. The example here can also be read through the paper, both right way up and upside down.

Spike

The adjustable telescopic metal support protruding from the bottom of a cello or double bass which enables the instrument to be held at a comfortable playing-height. Its proper name is endpin, but this is seldom used in informal speech. The spike also helps to transmit the sound to the floor and, if sharp and pointed, spells instant injury to carpets and other floor-coverings; you can always tell by examining a concert platform where the cellos sit. A 'slipping spike' is an event dreaded by players, who habitually make a good and proper hole to avoid the horrid grating and rumbling noise that is produced as an instrument skids away, not to mention the accompanying shock and loss of concentration. Many cellists now use an angled spike, which meets the floor at a more obtuse angle and is less likely to slip; and some carry a special, floor-protecting, anti-slip device which is hooked round the player's chair-leg. The viola da gamba is played without a spike, merely gripped between the knees; and until the second half of the nineteenth century so were cellos. Some bassoonists now use a spike in place of the customary sling.

Spike   *No spike*

Spinet

For a reasoned definition of this type of harpsichord, see an illustrated dictionary of music. It appears here as a misnomer often used by antique-dealers when they want to make a Victorian square piano appear more antique and desirable.

Spinettl

In spite of the foregoing, the term spinet survived into the nineteenth century, as *Spinettl*, which is the Austrian diminutive and in this context means a small piano, sometimes also known as a 'pedestal piano' or 'conductor's piano'. It was a kind of large music-stand with a small keyboard and piano action, on which a conductor could both rest his score and play the odd passage to demonstrate musical points to his players. Beethoven had – or was offered – one for the first performance of his *Choral Symphony*.

The Spring

Although many composers (Vivaldi, Haydn, Glazunov, etc.) wrote descriptive music about the four seasons, 'The Spring' is usually short for Beethoven's Violin and Piano Sonata, op. 24, in F. The nickname comes from the German *Frühlingssonate* but is spurious. Beethoven simply called it 'Sonata seconda', and the only extraneous remark he added, in bold red pencil, to a copy of the sonata reads: 'N.B. The copyist who put triplets and sextuplets here [i.e. in place of quavers] is an ass!'

Squeeze horn

The IRON HORN, or jazz player's trumpet.

Stadler Quintet

Spurious name for Mozart's Clarinet Quintet in A major, K581, derived from the fact that Mozart called it 'Stadler's quintet', i.e. 'the quintet I wrote for Stadler' (letter, 8 April 1790). This he did merely to identify, not to christen it. The Concerto K622 and the KEGELSTATT Trio K498 were also written for the clarinettist Anton Stadler (1753–1812).

Staff

Another word for the *stave* – the five lines on which DOTS are written, hence *Staff Notation* as opposed to TONIC SOL-FA.

Stage dust allergy

When the Duke of Edinburgh, visiting some African ruler, was invited to join a big-game shooting party, he suddenly discovered that he was suffering from what his equerry described as 'a whitlow on his trigger finger'. He was therefore unable to take part, and could thus spare the feelings of both his host and wildlife preservation societies. In the early 1980s a world-renowned singer found himself unable to meet his contractual obligations because he had developed a distressing condition his physicians diagnosed as stage dust allergy. Instead, he went on holiday with his secretary, and soon recovered. Doctors believe that this kind of allergy is caused by the same virus as the royal whitlow.

From La Silhouette, *1882*

Stagione

The Italian word for a season, as in Vivaldi's ever-popular *Le quattro stagione* (a bogus title anyway), and also to describe that part of the year (usually the autumn and winter) in which opera performances are given. The word is used by opera lovers all the world over to describe a certain seasonal repertory system followed at some opera houses.

Stand

The music-stand, or DESK. Also used for 'one-night stand', as in other entertainment professions.

Stehgeiger

See FIDDLER ON THE HOOF.

Stick

Musicians in general prefer this word to BATON, perhaps subconsciously translating from the German *Taktstock* or *Dirigentenstock* (literally, 'tempo-stick' and 'conductor's stick', respectively). Such sticks have not always been the thin twigs (with or without a cork handle and painted white for better visibility) that are today's batons. In the seventeenth and eighteenth centuries batons (if used at all) were more like the big, ornamental staves now twirled and tossed by bandmasters, and were employed audibly as well as visibly: thumped on the floor to keep time. Poor J. B. Lully (1632–87) stabbed his foot with one, which caused blood-poisoning and his premature death. In the nineteenth century the stick shrank to a length of about 2 ft but lost none of its ornamental qualities. Many, like that of early PROMS showmen like Jullien, were made of ivory, some of them jewelled and bound in gold or silver, objects for presentation as well as time-beating. When Mendelssohn and Berlioz met at Leipzig in 1841 they exchanged batons rather like today's footballers swap jerseys after a match. Berlioz's gift was accompanied by a letter (which incidentally reveals that he, like Schubert, was addicted to the Red Indian novels of Fenimore Cooper): 'Au chef Mendelssohn. Grand chef! nous nous sommes promis d'échanger nos tamahawcks; voici le mien! Il est grossier, le tien est simple; les squaws seules et les visages pâles aiment les armes ornées. Sois mon frère!' And when Mendelssohn conducted in London on 29 May 1844 he had occasion to confess his forgetfulness to the orchestral librarian, Mr Goodwin: 'Please to send me immediately the Score of my music to the Mid Summer Nightsdream, and the Conductorstick which I left Monday on the desk (if you found it).' Goodwin was the founder of the famous firm of Goodwin & Tabb Ltd. (now part of Novello & Co.), who for many years provided a comprehensive service to musicians, from the hiring of SCORES AND PARTS to copying, arranging and orchestrating their customers' music. Nearly all famous conductors used their batons, which were offered in various shapes and sizes, and given appropriate names ('The Foil', 'The Rapier', 'The Bulb', etc.). Their advertisement ended with the cryptic words: 'Our Batons are suggested by, and modelled upon, actual examples of Sticks used by world-famous conductors who leave their mark on the orchestras of today.'

Stick technique

Sir Adrian Boult once said conducting was 'the only job whose technique could be learned in an evening'. He was referring to the stick technique, which is the mechanical side of conducting, not to the musical skills, which take a little longer to acquire. A conductor does not simply perform a graceful ballet in time to the music (see LATE PLAYING) but with his beat shows the players what he wants them to do and also where they are in each bar. The first beat is always a DOWNBEAT; intermediate beats go sideways or diagonally (to the left or right, according to certain rules), and the last beat must necessarily be an upbeat so as to get the stick into position for the next downbeat. That more or less describes the conductor as traffic policeman. The conductor as artist is another matter: genius cannot be described, nor the various degrees of it assessed. Besides, many conductors have risen to eminence without having much stick technique, by using only the most rudimentary gestures. Beecham's were often either wild blandishments or vague twitches; though, of course, he *could* beat properly when he wanted to. But Stokowski (see below) went through his long life giving *two* downbeats in six-eight time instead of one (i.e. beating two lots of three-eight, and I witnessed some mistakes he thus caused an English orchestra to make). Furtwängler's beat was little more than a snaky, nervous wiggle; and some of today's famous conductors beat so badly that certain ENSEMBLE problems have to be solved by private discussion among the players themselves. Yet even conductors who cannot (or will not) use a clear stick technique often obtain superb performances. Some musicians argue that it is the very *lack* of clarity that makes players listen more. Many a KAPELLMEISTER (or 'bandmaster'), on the other hand, gives clear, easily followed directional beats – but the music means nothing and the performance sounds as square and wooden as their movements look.

Stirring-the-pudding conductor

See PUDDING STIRRER

Stokey

Nickname of Leopold Stokowski (1882–1977), He is sometimes accused of having adopted that name in preference to his family name Stokes, because of the once current fashion for English musicians to adopt foreign-sounding names. The facts are that Stokowski was born a British subject, in London, the son of a Polish father and an Irish mother; and that the family did indeed change its name: *from* Stokowski to Stokes, so as to escape the strong xenophobic agitation and riots in the East End of London during the First World War. The conductor's change back to Stokowski was therefore merely a proud readoption of his family name. Whether he would have been less successful as Mr Stokes is open to conjecture, but he was undoubtedly one of the great conductors of the twentieth century, although his STICK TECHNIQUE was not impeccable. Nor was his approach to his players. If they gave him a hard time at rehearsal, he would try to get his own back; and his sense of humour had a wicked streak. For example, he might invite the musicians to bring their families to a rehearsal, an opportunity resisted by few who had seen him in Walt Disney's *Fantasia*. Then, with the hall full of visitors, he would make a point of picking on the men who had offended him, making them play on their own and vehemently criticizing their playing – to humiliate them before their families. At the age of 95 he signed a ten-year recording-contract but, alas, met his own recording angel soon afterwards, at Nether Wallop, Hampshire. Conductors tend to live long, perhaps because they get plenty of exercise. He was not alone in his aspirations to long life. Pierre Monteux (1876–1964) accepted a contract in 1961 with the LSO only on condition that it was for twenty years. He died after fulfilling three years of it. Sir Malcolm Sargent was struck down by illness at 71, but he remained a lithe and active conductor almost to the end. Barrie Hall relates an incident when (as Publicity Officer for the BBC) he was invited for a drink at Sargent's residence after a PROM. With them was a younger conductor who was then rather short of engagements. As the three entered the hallway of the Albert Hall Mansions, where Sargent lived, the lift-doors were about to close and they all sprinted along the corridor to get it. Safely inside, the portly young conductor, rather out of breath, panted, 'I'm afraid I'm not in such good trim as you, Sir Malcolm.' To which Sargent replied, 'You should do more conducting, Mr ——, you should do more *conducting!*'

Stop

To organists this means both a rank of pipes and the wooden knob which, when pulled out, brings them into play. For a list of the many strange names for organ stops, see the appropriate textbook. Organ-builders often show a curious sense of humour in naming their stops after instruments ('cello', 'tenoroon', 'gemshorn', etc.) to which their tone bears not the remotest resemblance.

Stops and starts

Also 'tops and tails': a cursory form of rehearsal involving only the beginnings and endings of movements or parts of these where RITS AND RALLS, upbeats, etc., may cause problems of ENSEMBLE. These manoeuvres, like take-offs and landings by aircraft, are often the most difficult and accident-prone, whereas much of the rest of a performance (or flight) may take its course on automatic pilot. Stops and starts may figure in a SITZPROBE.

Strad

The normal professional abbreviation for products from the workshop of Antonio Stradivari (1644–1737). He was a pupil of Nicolo Amati (1596–1684) and they, together with Guarneri (and their respective families), represent the peak achievements of the Cremona school of FIDDLE-making which, of course, also produced violas, cellos and double basses, in addition to harps, guitars, mandolines and all but forgotten instruments like the NUN'S TRUMP. The superior quality of Cremonese string instruments is indisputable and factual, i.e. not related to their price and rarity. It is also mysterious and indefinable (possibly connected with the choice of either wood or varnish, or a combination of both, which are matters of endless discussion and argument). Their quality is, however, chiefly discerned by the player: e.g. by their 'feel' and ease of speaking. Listeners making a 'blind' test of instruments played behind a screen are rarely able to tell a Strad or Amati, etc., from another fine instrument, though they may be aware of the player's greater comfort and ease of tone-production. Identification of instruments may also be a matter of argument. Although each maker had his own characteristic fingerprints (some of them minute, others, like the way of cutting the F-holes, easily apparent) many of the best fiddles are without labels, or TICKETS. These may have been removed by unscrupulous dealers and put into inferior instruments, for a good instrument will be accepted by the professional on its own merits, with or without a ticket, whereas a good label may lend to a bad fiddle a false promise of quality. The Latinized ending Stradivari*us* is derived from the manner in which old fiddle-makers signed their labels, e.g. 'Antonius Stradivarius Cremoniensis Faciebat 1710' ('Made by Antonio Stradivari of Cremona in 1710'), which leads to occasional enquiries from hopeful finders who claim to have an old instrument 'made by Faciebat'. Of the 600 or so Strads known to have survived, at least 1000 are in the United States alone; and only a handful of the genuine ones are in anything like original condition. Most have been strengthened to take the increased string tension (from ca. 60 to about 90lb) demanded by modern pitch, which is higher than that contemporary to the instruments; have had longer necks grafted in accordance with modern playing technique (such graft joins always distinguishes an old fiddle from a modern one) or suffered more or less extensive repairs, for instruments are fragile things that easily suffer damage to both wood and varnish (see THE UGLIER THE FIDDLE). Most great fiddles have names (*The Messiah, The Lady Blount, The Betts*, etc.) as well a pedigree that can trace previous owners back to players like JOACHIM and Paganini. One of the saddest things about Strads and other instruments is that they deteriorate when not played on, and that many are in the ownership of either rich amateurs or investors waiting for their value to increase.

'*Straight on!*'

Instruction given at rehearsal (or sometimes whispered through clenched teeth, *sotto voce*, during performances, when it usually comes too late) for the non-observance of repeat marks. Its opposite is the laconic but meaningful YES.

Stretch

Generally the distance a player's fingers have to stretch in order to reach certain KEYS, either on the piano or a wind instrument. On the latter such difficulties are overcome by the judicious placing of the keys, which with the help of levers enables holes to be opened and closed that would otherwise be out of reach. Pianists with 'a good stretch' may be able to play the interval of the tenth (e.g. from C to the second E above it); others find it difficult to stretch an octave. Robert Schumann (1810–56) had a very small stretch, and foolishly allowed a quack to cut the tendons between thumbs and first fingers in the hope of enlarging his stretch. He never really recovered from the operation and had to have a piano made with the keys closer together.

Stretto

See HOME STRAIGHT, and CABALETTA. The stretto is also an ingredient of the FUGUE.

Striding bass

A certain kind of bass-line which has greater movement than the 'tunes' above it. Much of Elgar's NOBILMENTE music is characterized by such a bass, among other things. But basses need not stride; sometimes they merely stroll, e.g. in Bach's AIR ON THE G-STRING. See also TROMMELBASS and the MANNHEIM effects.

La Stupenda

Nickname admiringly applied either to the late Maria Callas or Dame Joan Sutherland, according to taste, context or preference.

Sturm und Drang

German for storm and stress, which is a perfectly acceptable translation when applied in a general sense. However, when the context is specifically German, note should be taken of its origin. The term was invented in 1776 by Christoph Kaufmann (1753–95) when the German playwright Maximilian von Klinger (1752–1831) showed him a play he had written, called *Wirrwarr* ('Hubbub'). Kaufmann did not like the title and ventured to suggest a more euphonious one, *Sturm und Drang*, which Klinger accepted. It immediately became a fashionable expression, 'much bandied about', Klinger later wrote, 'and enjoyed by many a halfwit'. *Sturm und Drang* (capital letters should be used) is typified in music by certain eighteenth-century symphonies (e.g. by Haydn and Mozart) usually in the minor key; and much of the late eighteenth- and early nineteenth-century LIEDER output comes under this heading, often combined with stormy expressions of unrequited love, romantic pessimism and teutonic self-pity.

Sub-principal

See PRINCIPAL

Suck

Charles J. Suck was an eighteenth-century English oboist and composer of foreign origin; a colleague (possibly pupil) of J. C. Fischer (1733–1800), the foremost oboe virtuoso of his day (and also the painter Gainsborough's son-in-law). Suck was probably a Bohemian – certainly Central European – immigrant who anglicized his name from Suč, Suk, Suck or Zuck, sensibly capitulating to the inevitable mispronunciation he would have met in England. He might have arranged, say, a concerto by John Blow for MOUTH ORGAN, but unfortunately musical chronology is against it. Otherwise the delightful juxtapositon 'Blow-Suck' might have appeared on concert programmes.

Sugar plum fairy

Posthumous nickname for Tchaikovsky, whose homosexuality was a badly-kept secret for nearly a century except in Soviet Russia, where the culture commissars still try to deny it, suppressing what evidence they can. As David Brown convincingly postulates in his monumental study of the composer, it was the threat of exposure by his 'friends' that forced him to suicide and is the true PROGRAMME of the PATHÉTIQUE.

The Suggia position

From the celebrated portrait by Augustus John of the cellist Guilhermina Suggia (1888–1950). The position she takes up in the picture shows the bow arm fully extended, the body proudly erect and head thrown back. Cellists, for some reason, tend to indulge in a greater and more spectacular variety of extravagant postures than other string players (perhaps because they do not have to hold their instrument up) and the Suggia position is adopted by many. It sometimes looks a little posed and mannered. Suggia

used to snort and sniff audibly when she played. See also CELLISTS'
FACES, thumb position.

Suitcase

American jazz players' nickname for a drum. When there is no
real drum to hand, drummers traditionally practise their PARA-
DIDDLES on a suitcase.

The Sun Quartets

Haydn's String Quartets Nos. 23–28. See below.

The Sunrise

Haydn's Quartet in B flat op. 74, No. 4, so called because of the
rising nature of its glorious opening tune – which could equally
describe THE LARK. Not to be confused with THE SUN QUARTETS, a
set named after the watermark of the paper.

The Surprise

Haydn's No. 94 in G. Surprisingly enough it was first given *without*
the 'surprise'. Haydn apparently added it (a loud chord of G major
occurring soon after the piano/pianissimo opening of the slow
movement) as an afterthought, because he wanted 'to give the
ladies a fright'. All Haydn's great late symphonies contain some
wonderful surprises, just as they all deserve the sobriquet
MIRACLE. The Germans call this the 'The Symphony with the Drum
Beat', thereby risking confusion with the DRUM ROLL.

Swallow tail

A kind of key on old instruments, shaped like a swallow's tail
so that it could be played either in the normal manner or LEFT-
HANDED.

The Swan of Pesarro

Rossini's nickname, after the place of his birth.

Sweet potato

Nickname for the ocarina (Italian for 'little goose') – a small wind instrument made of clay, terracotta or china, which was invented in the middle of the nineteenth century and has a sweetly cloying sound. Ocarinas come in various sizes, and some have elaborate tuning-slides.

Swordstick

When used in an orchestra, this will be wielded harmlessly by a percussionist. It is not a weapon but a kind of short sword fitted with jingles like the JINGLING JOHNNY. Not to be confused with threatening lyre or FLEXATONE.

Symphony

A confusing but increasingly common American abbreviation of 'symphony orchestra', like SINFONIETTA. When an American musician says 'I played in a symphony last week' one does not know whether he means an orchestra or a work played by one. Symphony is also an old-fashioned name for the instrumental introduction of a song.

Tablature

An old form of notation (e.g. for the lute or recorder) which uses a kind of pictorial representation of the instrument to which it applies, not unlike modern guitar symbols.

Table music

Music so composed and written or printed that it can be played simultaneously by two persons seated opposite each other at a table. Not to be confused with the German *Tafelmusik*, which is to be played at table during meals. See also SPIEGEL-KANON.

Tacet

Latin for 'it is silent' (i.e. there is nothing to play), but used and pronounced ('tasset') as though it were an English word: 'You're tacet in that bar.' If a player has no more to do in a movement or work, and is obviously absolved from further COUNTING BARS, his PART simply bears the verbal information 'Tacet al fine', without showing the remaining numbers of bars' REST. One of the most surprising tacets in the history of music occurs in the Violin Concerto, op.34, by Hans Pfitzner (1869–1949), in which the soloist is marked tacet throughout the slow movement.

Tactical errors

Tactics and strategy do not usually enter the musical profession but there is one kind of tactical error which must be explained. As the hand of the clock moves towards the end of an orchestral recording-session, with only a small amount of music yet to be taped, a small coughing-fit, an inadvertently dropped bow or a cracked note are sure to be heard – thus necessitating a retake and the payment of overtime for the whole orchestra. Some attribute this phenomenon to the musical equivalent of MURPHY'S LAW but there are other explanations.

Allegro Moderato. Duet for two violins, composed by NICOLO MESTRINO, 1720-1790.

Table music

285

Taffy-teffy conductors

The name for choral conductors who are temporarily put in charge of symphony orchestras (especially in the North of England, where choral societies hire orchestras on a self-drive basis, supplying their own conductors). Many of them were trained on the old French system of note-durations called *langue des durées*, which is admirably explained in GROVE. Such conductors speak not of quavers, minims, semibreves and hemidemisemiquavers but 'te-fe-ta-te', 'te-re-li-li', etc., causing amusement and consternation among the uninitiated.

Tailgating

A 'dirty' way of playing music, especially on the trombone. It comes from early jazz usage, when bands used to play on top of open waggons (later presumably motor trucks); and the trombonist would naturally have to be stationed at the tailgate so that his slide would not impede his colleagues but emerge from the back of the vehicle. See also SMEAR.

Take fifteen

When announced by the ORCHESTRA MANAGER during a recording session, this means 'Take fifteen minutes' break,' a time-honoured joke referring to the numbered takes and retakes of a recording session which are then edited into a performance. See also ROOM 99.

A talker

He's a *talker* is said derisively of a conductor who spends much time at rehearsal talking instead of conducting, and attempts to explain in the minutest detail his philosophy and general approach to the work under rehearsal and music in general. The commonly expressed view is, 'If he can't do it with his stick he can't do it at all.' One player, treated to a long dissertation about how he should play a certain passage, deflated the *maestrino* with the seemingly innocent question, 'Do you want it *louder* or *softer*?'

Tambourin

Without the final e this denotes the French diminutive for *tambour*, a drum. It is sometimes misunderstood, by both conductors and players, in the *farandole* of Bizet's *L'Arlesienne*, where a drum is called for, not a tambourine.

Tapeworm

A very long orchestral piece or opera.

Tappers, nodders and time-beaters

Members of the audience who feel the need to participate in a performance by tapping their feet, nodding their head or helping the conductor beat time. They may distract or even infuriate their close neighbours in the audience, but they have no idea how much more distracting and visible they are from the orchestra. Even solo singers do it on the platform. See also CHOCOLATE RUSTLERS, COUGHERS.

Tarantella

The myth that Southern Italians poisoned by the bite of the tarantula could cure themselves by furiously dancing the tarantella was probably raised in Carl Engel's *Introduction to the Study of National Music* (1866). His assertion has been much repeated but never proved: and a simple experiment is open to any musicologist willing to conduct it. Just as the Krakoviak comes from Krakow, the Pavane from Padua and the Lambeth Walk from Lambeth, so the Tarantella doubtless comes from the town of Taranto in Italy.

Tárogató

A Hungarian folk instrument (pronounced and stressed like 'tar, oh gateau') with a single reed like a clarinet, oboe fingering and a sound like a COR. It was used effectively in the opera house by Gustav Mahler when he conducted Wagner's *Tristan und Isolde* (the Shepherd's Tune in Act 3; see also HECKELPHONE).

Tchaik

Professional abbreviation. As in 'Tchaik One', which could be either Tchaikovsky's first symphony or his first piano concerto.

Teeth

These are important to wind or brass players: their EMBOUCHURE and lip technique depend on them. A few decades ago a player's career would have come to an end, or have been severely prejudiced, by the loss of even a few teeth. Today, thanks to the skill of modern orthodontists, musicians can and do have casts made of their teeth while they still possess them, so that in the event of an accident they can be precisely copied.

Temperament

There are two kinds in music. One is supposed to show itself in the self-willed display of a musician's inflated ego (and can usually be dismissed as a sign of nervousness or bad manners) and the other refers to a system of tuning that produces (by means of a subtle compromise amounting to slight mis-tuning) a musical scale acceptable in all keys. This was effectively demonstrated (though not invented) by J. S. Bach in his 'Well-tempered Clavier', known also as THE FORTY-EIGHT.

Tempora mutantur

Haydn's No. 64 in A. The suggestion that the opening of the last movement fits the rhythm of the Latin tag (which means 'The times they are a-changing') is probably far-fetched. The full quotation is *Tempora mutantur, nos et mutamur in illis*: 'All things are changed and we are changed with them.'

Tenor

To singers, the tenor voice; to recorder players, the instrument pitched in C one octave below the descant; and to jazz musicians, the tenor saxophone in B flat. And there are other kinds of tenor, including the inaptly named HELDENTENOR.

Tenorino

Italian diminutive for a tenor; not one who is short in stature but with a very high voice. In the eighteenth century it was a euphemism for a castrato or CAPON.

Tenoroon

Tenor bassoon pitched a fifth higher than the ordinary bassoon, a portmanteau word made from tenor + bassoon. The Germans, who like to make up words that contain their own definition, call it *Hochquintfagott*, literally 'fifth-higher-bassoon'. Organists think of the tenoroon as the name of a STOP. There is also a tenor oboe, which the Germans might have called a 'fifth-lower-oboe' but decided to name HECKELPHONE instead.

Tenoroon

The tenor thumb

A famous picture of Brahms by W. von Beckerath shows clearly what was known as 'Brahms's tenor thumb' – because of the way he was able to bring out with it any tenor parts in the harmony.

Tessitura

The range or predominant 'lie' in which a musical PART or line is written, usually for the voice. One with many high notes is said to have a 'high tessitura'. Critics love this word, but there are plenty of English ways of describing what it means. In Italian it is the ordinary word for texture.

'That's all'

Some musical educators, e.g. introducers of children's concerts, put these words to the commonest two final chords, i.e. the dominant followed by the home chord as exemplified by the conclusion of Beethoven's Violin Concerto. Haydn turns the cliché into a joke by five-fold repetition at the *beginning* of a movement in one of his string quartets.

Brahms's 'Tenor Thumb' portrait by W. von Beckerath

Thematic catalogue

Catalogue of works listed in chronological order, together with information such as number of bars and pages, date of composition, first performance, extant manuscripts or copies and their location or ownership, publication date, arrangements, literature, etc. What makes a catalogue 'thematic' is the inclusion of the INCIPIT of each movement in musical notation. The most famous catalogue, and the one which set the standards for all others, is that of Mozart's works compiled by KOECHEL, under which heading a number of other notable thematic catalogues are listed.

Theremin

An early electrical musical instrument, used in a few compositions by Martinu, Varèse, etc., but now largely forgotten. It was made by Louis Thérémin (b. 1896), a Russian of French extraction, and is unusual among musical instruments in that the player does not touch it. He merely waves his hand at it and, by disturbing an electrical field with what is, in effect, controlled interference (such as one gets when walking past a badly-tuned radio or tv set) changes the pitch of the (otherwise constant) note it produces. It therefore makes an unattractive, whining or whooping sound. The player looks rather like a magician trying to cast a spell, and the skill lies in his sense of pitch, by which he governs the notes produced.

Thermometer

American orchestral and jazz musicians' nickname for an oboe – from the way the reed is held in the mouth.

Third stream music

GROVE says 'The term *third stream music* was coined by Gunther Schuller (b. 1925) in 1957 to describe amalgamation of jazz and art music, and gained wide currency.' Many composers have dabbled in this mixture, with more or less success. Stravinsky in his Ebony Concerto, Joseph Horovitz in a Jazz Harpsichord Concerto, Peter Maxwell Davies and others. There appears to be no TWELVE-NOTE jazz by members of the SECOND VIENNESE SCHOOL, but some of Schuller's own third-stream compositions do attempt to bring serial principles to jazz.

'This is where the lightning strikes the sh**house'

Said in orchestras to describe a sudden, loud and dramatic moment of climax in the music. A politer saying is used in German orchestras: 'They're burying a horse here' – which probably comes from some obscure Prussian army joke that sounds better in the original. But see also LIGHTNING CONDUCTOR.

'This is where they always clap'

Sarcastic comment sometimes heard during avant garde music when the music comes to a sudden but temporary halt. See also CLAP TRAP.

Thorough-bass

See FIGURED BASS

Threefold Amen

See DRESDEN AMEN

The Three Johnnies

In German, *Die drei Hanse(ln)*: Johannes Brahms, Johann Strauss and Hans Richter, all their forenames being diminutively *Hans* or *Hansel* in German. The three were friends and often played cards together.

The Three Johnnies

Through-composed

Unsatisfactory translation of the even less satisfactory German word DURCHKOMPONIERT.

Ticket

The maker's label inside a stringed instrument See STRAD.

Till

Standard abbreviation of Strauss's *Till Eulenspiegel* op.28 (1895).

Timber

Nickname of Sir Henry Wood (1869–1944). He was one of the last conductors to use a really big STICK which would swish through the air to the accompaniment of rattling cuff-links. His players said that these sounds, together with a stentorian roar *'PIANISSIMO'* usually drowned the music. Wood's pseudonym 'Paul Klenovsky' was based on the Russian word *klen*, having association with the timber of the maple tree.

Timebeater

A conductor thought simply to beat time without bothering much about subtleties of expression. But see also 'HE DOESN'T GET IN THE WAY'.

Timps

Kettledrums or, if necessary, *timpani* ; not 'timpany' or 'tympany'. Timpano is Italian for a timbrel, drum or ear-drum: *rompere i timpani* means to deafen someone. Timps never come singly: always in pairs, threes or more.

Tin Pan Alley

The imaginary place where popular music is composed (usually manufactured), published, publicized and, its sponsors hope, turned into commercial success. The term dates from the early

Punch, 1868

Modest Appeal

Lady (to big drum): *"Pray, my good Man, don't make that horrid Noise! I can't hear myself Speak!"*

1920s, is American, of course, and comes from 'tin-pan shower', an American country word for a noisy serenade, or CHARIVARI. See also HIT.

Tin whistle

Like 'penny whistle', a misnomer for a legitimate folk-instrument on which many players attain remarkable skill. It is not made of tin, is not a whistle, and has long cost much more than a penny.

Tired lip

A complaint suffered by wind and brass players which may prevent them from playing as loudly, softly, or as much, as a conductor might want them to do at rehearsal. It can even incapacitate them in the same way as singers suffer STAGE DUST ALLERGY. See also BUMPER UP.

Tod

There are two meanings, each with its own pronunciation. Like 'toad' is the shortened form of *Tod und Verklärung* by Richard

Strauss; or, to rhyme with 'God', the nickname of the English conductor Vernon Handley (b.1930). He says it was given to him by his father when as a toddler he (Vernon) walked with a comic gait.

The Tolpuddle Martyrs

See the WOLF GANG

Tommy

Sir Thomas Beecham. None of his players called him Tommy to his face, of course, though many used the nickname to suggest they were on familiar terms with him.

Tommy Talker

See EUNUCH FLUTE

Tone poem

An uneasy but now accepted translation from the German *Tondichtung*. *Ton* means 'sound' in German, as in TWELVE-TONE music, not two semitones, as in English.

Tongueing

The action of propelling the air-stream through the EMBOUCHURE or into the mouthpiece when playing a wind or brass instrument – the tongue soundlessly pronouncing the letter T: single-tongueing by the repeated enunciation of T, double-tongueing by the alternation of T and K; and triple-tongueing with T-K-T. Methods of the eighteenth century recommend syllables such as DID-LL or TOO-TL, hence the onomatopoeic 'tootling'. Multiple tongueing is merely an expedient for making the tongue move faster, as there is a limit to the speed of reiterated T sounds (try it!); and it is up to the player to know when he has to change from single- to double- or triple-tongueing, and to make sure the listener cannot tell the difference. Few composers understand this. They think multiple tongueing, like FLUTTER-TONGUEING, is a special effect. There is an amazing example of this in Stravinsky's

Firebird, where the composer in the middle of a loud orchestral TUTTI suddenly alternates semiquavers TKTK, etc.

Tonic sol-fa

A complicated system of notation intended to make sight-singing easier and avoid the need for learning ordinary or STAFF notation. The most common form is that of John Curwen (1816–80) but there is also a French, and Italian, and even a Yorkshire Sol-Fa; Fixed Doh and a Movable Doh, the former obligatory in many music colleges abroad, where it is taught with ordinary notation. All are based on the teachings of Guido d'Arezzo (c.995–1050) – and all are, for practical music-making, inferior to standard notation. In the North of England, where

Tonic Sol-Fa tuition in c. 1500

Tonic Sol-Fa held its ground longer than elsewhere, orchestras are still occasionally confronted by conductors who think – and therefore rehearse – in Tonic Sol-Fa; and may even combine it with TAFFY-TEFFY. See also KLAVARSKRIBO.

Top line conductor

Conductors who are said to be chiefly interested in bringing out the 'singing' lines, the 'tunes', rather than the general texture of the music, whether these occur in the 'top' of the orchestra or the cellos, who can sing every bit as eloquently as the fiddles. Barbirolli was said to be a top line man; Sir Colin Davis could be described as an 'inner part' conductor. See also WAX CONDUCTOR.

Tops and tails

See STOPS AND STARTS

Torture chamber music

Name given by players to certain kinds of chamber music that are as unpleasant to play as to listen to. The music-lover sometimes forgets that professional musicians in general have to play whatever is put before them, whether they like the music or not.

Toscanono

Reference to Arturo Toscanini (1867–1957). Whatever his other qualities, he was also the rudest and most bad-tempered of conductors. He loved music deeply but gave no visible indication of this: his face always totally expressionless while he was conducting. 'Toscanono' is derived from the way he seldom let his musicians play more than a few notes before screaming 'No, no, NO, NO!' His temper was uncontrollable (a dubious quality for anyone in charge of important events – imagine a surgeon or airline pilot . . .) and he broke many a STICK before (never on) his musicians. He once tore his gold watch from his chain and, in a rage, flung it to the floor and stamped on it. Afterwards, the orchestra made a collection and bought a cheap nickel watch, which they left on his DESK. It was inscribed *To Maestro, for Rehearsal Purposes Only.* Recordings of his rehearsals bear witness to his bad temper, as well as the total submissiveness of his players. Today's musicians would either answer back or simply walk out. However, the best-known and most frequently repeated anecdotes about Toscanini concern not his temper but his phenomenal musical memory. He is said to have developed this because his eyesight was so bad that as a young orchestral cellist he was obliged to learn all his parts from memory. It sounds like an oversimplification: if your eyesight is so bad as to be beyond the help of spectacles you will not be of much use in an orchestra. The other favourite story, if true, is interesting – but more for what it does not tell us. Again, like so many anecdotes, it comes in embroidered and elaborated versions. Anthony Burgess writes in *The Spectator* (10 July 1982): 'A double bass player, whose E string had broken, asked, in the interval, to be excused playing in the rest of the concert . . . . ' Toscanini, according to Burgess, thought for a moment, and then said, 'You don't use the E string in this half. You can play.' A rum kind of band whose entire bass section is unable to muster a spare E string; and an even more extraordinary concert in which the entire second half avoids the lowest string of the double bass! The version I heard, which doubtless also comes from that prolific musical anecdotist, Ben Trovato, concerns a bass clarinet player. 'Maestro,' he says, 'I cannot play tonight. My E flat key has broken off.' Maestro closes his eyes and knits his brows for a moment in intense concentration: 'Yes, my friend, you can play. There is no E flat in your part.' If the story illustrates Toscanini's good memory it also reveals his ignorance of how wind instruments work. He must have thought that to play a note, one simply presses the requisite key, as on a piano, and the sound comes out; whereas, of course, a single broken key effectively puts almost the entire instrument out of action. It would be interesting to know what the bass clarinettist replied to Maestro.

Tost

The Tost Quartets are Haydn's Nos. 42–53, and the authenticity of the name is confirmed in Haydn's letters. They are dedicated to the Viennese violinist and merchant, Johann Tost.

Totentanz

'He played Totentanz', said of a pianist, means Liszt's work of that name. It means 'Dance of Death', French *Danse macabre*. Liszt's is unusual in being for piano and orchestra: most others, including those by Saint-Saëns and Mahler (in his Symphony No.4), follow the ancient tradition that Death was a fiddler with an out of tune instrument: see SCORDATURA.

Tracker action

On an organ, direct, mechanical linking between the keys and the sounding mechanism, not, as is now common, a system of electro-mechanical switches. Authentic organists demand direct action.

The Tragic

Schubert 4 in C minor and Mahler 6 in A minor share this name; as do other works. But care must be taken when translating such titles. Tchaikovsky's *Pathétique* sounds better in French than as 'The Pathetic Symphony'; and Zilcher's *Schmerzliches Adagio* is correctly but inadequately rendered in the catalogues as 'Painful Adagio'.

Punch, 1911

Nervous Performer at Country Concert: *"I 'aven't–never—sung to a pyanner bevore, but I dessay we'll get on all right if ye can just play the 'igh notes a bit low."*

Transposition

Reading one note and playing another. Some orchestral players, like horns, clarinets and trumpets, do it all the time, for theirs are transposing instruments. The original purpose of such instruments was to simplify their playing, e.g. so that clarinets in A would have fewer sharps to play (for an explanation of which please ask a clarinettist). But in effect, they usually play A clarinet parts on a B flat instrument and thus have to cope with a great many more ACCIDENTALS. Strings and other woodwinds are never expected to transpose at sight, but pianists who specialize in accompanying singers need to be able to do it.

Travale

The polite name for an unsavoury aspect of percussion playing – the soft tambourine roll. This is done by sliding a moistened thumb or several fingertips along the head of the tambourine, and the resulting half-lubricated friction makes the jingles vibrate to produce a trill or roll. 'Moisture' is unfortunately the euphemism for saliva: the spit soon dries up, so the unattractive action has to be repeated at frequent intervals.

Travesti

The Italian name for dressing-up parts – see HOSENROLLE. But also a form of late eighteenth- and early nineteenth-century operatic parody, in which well-known operas would be produced in send-up versions. In Vienna, for example, they had *Die travestierte Zauberflöte* and *The Two Figaros*, and in London, a travesty of *Don Giovanni* called 'Giovanni in London'.

Tremolo

The rapid reiteration of a note: achieved on string instruments by a certain action of the right wrist (see also SCRUBBING). On wind and brass, an effect like FLUTTER-TONGUEING; and in the case of singers, a fast WOBBLE masquerading as a VIBRATO.

GIOVANNI IN LONDON.

AN OPERATIC EXTRAVAGANZA. IN TWO ACTS.—BY W. T. MONCRIEFF.

Giov —" YOU ARE DRUNK, ROGUE."—*Act* i, scene 3.

Persons Represented.

DON GIOVANNI.	DRAINEMDRY.	CHARON.	MRS. DRAINEMDRY.
DEPUTY ENGLISH.	POROUS.	DEMONS.	MRS. POROUS.
LEPORELLO.	SIMPKINS.	PROSERPINE.	MRS. SIMPKINS.
FINIKIN.	MERCURY.	MRS. ENGLISH.	CONSTANTIA.
POPINJAY.	PLUTO.	MRS. LEPORELLO.	SQUALLING FANNY.

ACT I.

SCENE I.—*Infernal regions by fire and torch-light,*
DON GIOVANNI *lying on the ground, in the centre
of the stage,* FIREDRAKE *standing over him,
flashing his torch.*

DUET *and* CHORUS. FIREDRAKE, GIO-
VANNI, *and Demons.*

AIR—" Fly not yet."

Fire.   *Come along, 'tis just the hour,
        When Demons have the greatest power*

*To feed the libertine's desires,
And make him burn with real fires,
So bring your flambeaux near.*

*Enter Demons with torches, and female Furies with
wands twined with serpents.*

Giov.   *Oh pray! oh stay!
        No log am I. your flames restrain;
        Burn not yet, for oh! 'tis pain;
        Then take your links away.*

Dem.   *Nay! nay! Nay! nay!
        We are like earth's gas-lights here,
        We always burn when night is near,
        Make light of it, we pray.*

Triangle Concerto

Nickname for Liszt's first piano concerto, because of the prominent triangle solos used in interplay with the piano. Coined by Liszt's son-in-law, Hans von Bülow, and widely used ever since, especially by triangle players, who don't get many concertos to play.

Trio

The middle section of a work built on the ABA pattern, the Trio being B – i.e. the filling in the sandwich. It is not necessarily scored for three instruments (any more than a MIDDLE EIGHT must consist of eight bars). The Trio is also known as *Alternativo*, which is meant in the sense of alternating, not as an optional alternative. The Trio is usually the middle section of a minuet, but the term is also applied to the middle part of a march. The Trio of a *Gavotte* is usually a *Musette*, and that of a *Badinerie* a DOUBLE. Others may have names like *Forlane* or *Loure*. More extended movements, built on the ABACA pattern, have Trios I and II, at B and C.

Trio sonata

A source of confusion. Because of the conventions surrounding FIGURED BASS, the left-hand line of a keyboard part is often reinforced by one or more single-line bass instruments like the cello (gamba) and/or double bass or bassoon, occasionally even a bass lute. Thus a trio sonata may involve three, four, five or even more players. But conversely, J. S. Bach wrote trio sonatas for one organist: left hand, right hand and a pair of feet.

Triple paradiddle

See PARADIDDLE

Tritsch-tratsch

The name of the polka, op. 124, by Johann Strauss II, usually translated as 'Chit Chat': since *tratschen* in Viennese means chatting or gossiping. But from the musical evidence in the score (and from the accompanying eighteenth-century engraving it would appear that Strauss had in mind a toy rattle.

Fanciullo con Trich Trach

Tritsch-Tritsch: The origin of Strauss's polka

Trombone

In Italian the *-one* suffix denotes enlargement, as explained under VIOLA. Thus *trombone* literally means a big trumpet. In colloquial Italian it is also a blunderbuss or a type of wading-boot.

Trommelbass

The German word means 'drum bass' – a characteristic element of eighteenth-century style: repeated, drumming quavers in the bass line, and often other parts, e.g. viola. Mozart's and Haydn's music often features the effect (which is thought to have its roots in the MANNHEIM style, though J. S. Bach used it in some keyboard toccatas). In the hands of a master it lends tremendous rhythmic as well as harmonic momentum to the music. Beethoven achieved a glorious effect with it in two of his cello sonatas and in the first movement of his *Pathétique* Sonata. It also often figures in the ROSSINI CRESCENDO; and appears in operatic music by fast writers like Donizetti, Bellini and sometimes Verdi. Lesser composers, however, reduced it to an almost meaningless cliché, comparable to modern pop music drumming.

The Trout

Always Schubert's Quintet in A, D667, whereas the LIED on which it is based is generally given its German name, *Die Forelle*.

Tuner

Usually refers to the piano-tuner, though tuners are employed also for organs. Most harpsichordists learn to tune their own instruments, which are quickly affected by changing temperatures and the bumps and jolts of transport. Bach is said to have been able to tune a big, two-manual harpsichord in twenty minutes, a record against which others set their standards. Piano-tuning is a job often learned by the blind. Today's tuners could (in theory) be deaf: they are able to buy electronic devices that give a visual read-out of the correct pitch.

Tuning

It has never been established why the oboe is by tradition entrusted with the task of giving the A to the rest of the orchestra. Perhaps its sound carries better and further than that of the others. String players are liable to accuse oboes of giving a flat A, but then string players are always in search of brilliance and like to tune on the high side, calling their sharpness 'brightness'. Many orchestras now employ an electronic sound generator that produces an A of indisputable pitch. See above, and PRELUDING.

Turkish music

The generic name for a kind of music that became popular in Central Europe during the seventeenth and eighteenth centuries, as well as for a group of percussion instruments generally associated with such music, which is also known as Janissary Music. The Turkish influence arose from the frequent incursions into Europe by invading Turks, who got as far as Vienna and were not finally driven out until 1683. The 'Turkish style' has little or nothing to do with real Turkish music but was a kind of fashion superimposed on the music of the time. It manifested itself in a large number of operas, plays and other pieces on Middle Eastern subjects, with stories about sultans and harems, like Cornelius's *The Barber of Bagdad*, Weber's *Abu Hassan*, and, of course, Mozart's *Zaide* and *Die Entführung aus dem Serail*. Even Beethoven's *Die Ruinen von Athen* was considered close enough to Turkey to warrant the inclusion of 'Turkish' instruments. It was these that gave the music its distinctive colour, consisting of percussion instruments like triangle, side-drum, kettle-drums, cymbals, tambourine, big drum (played in a kind of OOM-PAH way, with a stick on one side and a beesom or RUTE on the other) as well as more specialized noise-makers such as the SWORDSTICK and JINGLING JOHNNY. Such instruments also found a place in military bands, and would therefore be included as a matter of course in works like Beethoven's 'Battle Symphony', which depicted an event totally unconnected with the Turks.

Tutti

Italian for *all*, *everybody* (masculine only – the feminine, presumably used in Italian ladies' orchestras, is *tutte*). When used in connection with an orchestral work or performance, *tutti* denotes a passage played by more or less the whole orchestra, as opposed to a SOLO. Conductors at rehearsal call out 'tutti!' when they have finished rehearsing a section of the orchestra and want the rest to join in.

Solo (Emil Sauer)   *Tutti (Arthur Nikisch)*

Silhouette by Otto Boehler

Twelve-note/twelve-tone music

A system of composing-by-numbers to whose invention Arnold Schoenberg (1874–1951) has laid claim, though this was disputed by others. For the NOTE/TONE confusion, see under that heading. Twelve-note music (also known by its Latin/Greek-based name DODECAPHONY) and its offshoot, SERIALISM, is based on the Orwellian principle that all notes are equal but some more equal than others. It met with fierce opposition during the 1920s and 1930s, in Austria and Germany as elsewhere. It is not clear whether the Nazis hated twelve-note music because Schoenberg was a Jew, because they disliked its sound, or because of the communist undertones inherent in twelve equal notes. But most orchestral players and singers dislike performing this kind of 'DONKEY MUSIC', because of its usually fragmentary nature, its lack of memorable 'tunes', and the large, unmelodic leaps they are often required to negotiate. It has been around for the greater part of the century, and although Schoenberg was a profound thinker, not a charlatan as his detractors tried to make out, and his influence on twentieth-century music has been immense, his own music is no more popular now than it was in 1925 (except to a small band of influential and highly vocal proponents). During the last decade or so most composers have indeed turned away from the limitations of both twelve-note and serial music. Schoenberg himself bravely risked a prophecy about his future, which has unfortunately not come to pass. It is a salutary story. In 1947 Thomas Mann published his novel *Doktor Faustus*, whose hero was a character who was obviously (but not admittedly) based on Schoenberg, and who had invented 'a form of composing with twelve notes'. Schoenberg threatened litigation and forced Mann to append a note in all copies admitting that he was the one and only begetter of the tone-row. This stated, 'The twelve-tone or -row system is in truth the intellectual property of a contemporary composer and theoretician, Arnold Schönberg.' This made the already touchy composer even more furious, who wrote, 'He has added a new crime to his first in his attempt to belittle me. He calls me "a (*a!*) contemporary composer and theoretician, Arnold Schönberg."' Of course, in two or three decades one will know which of the two was the other's contemporary.' Since he made that statement nearly four decades have passed, during which time Thomas Mann's novel *Death in Venice* (to name only one best-seller) was made into a successful film as well as an opera, both with music by contemporaries of Schoenberg – Mahler and Britten respectively. Mann, incidentally, slipped another barb into his carefully worded insult of an apology: by 1947 Schoenberg had officially Americanized his spelling in order to avoid the German *Umlaut*. Schoenberg changed his faith more often than his musical ideas, to which he remained true to the end of his life. He was born Jewish, brought up Catholic, became a Protestant at eighteen, and reverted to Judaism in 1933. He was also active as an expressionist painter, belonging to the Blue Rider school, and said that if he had failed to find success as a composer he would have turned to full-time painting.

'The uglier the fiddle the better the sound'

This is almost a proverb among violinists (who sometimes also apply it to female members of the orchestra). It is based on the observation that fine old string instruments may often look rather battered, patched and repaired, with the odd dent here and there, but are wonderful both to play and to hear. The precious old varnish, too, in spite of a usually good, rich colour, may be blotchy and blemished. Bernard McKey, one of the long-serving members of the RLPO, possessed a very fine old Italian cello which was uncommonly stained. He explained that when he was young he was a member of a circus band; and that one of the lions had expressed disapproval of some demeaning trick expected of him by lifting his leg (or however lions do it) all over the band. Several players put in for replacement evening suits, but McKey's cello was irreplaceable, still sounding well in spite of having had much of its varnish removed. At the end of his career he could wistfully recollect how he was lionized in his youth.

The Unfinished

Always means Schubert's Symphony in B minor, D759, although there are many other unfinished works in the repertoire, including, of course, Schubert's SATZ. If he failed to finish a work it was because he mislaid it or got bored with it. A man with his prodigious melodic gifts had no need to wrestle with a score that caused problems, real or imaginary. After writing a few bars of the third movement of D759 he laid it aside and composed the Wanderer Fantasy, D760, instead.

Urtext

The German word for 'original text', often used in English to describe editions that go back to the composer's AUTOGRAPH or some other authentic text and are without editorial additions or amendments.

Vamp (till ready)

Vamping is the playing of a repeated, simple accompaniment figure on the piano until the singer or soloist enters. It may be facetiously applied to occasions when someone has forgotten how the music should go and decides to improvise. In fact the word comes from the French term (probably first used in dancing) *avant pied*, anglicized and elided to 'vamp', and has been used in English for a long time: 'I remember very early in my musical life to have heard one of the waits at Shrewsbury vamp a base upon all occasions,' wrote Charles Burney in his *History of Music* (1789).

Vexations

See FURNITURE MUSIC.

Vibes

Short for the vibraphone, or vibraharp: neither a harp nor a phone, but a metal xylophone with an electro-mechanically induced WOBBLE.

Vibrato

An undulation of pitch in a note. Many authorities, including QUANTZ, have maintained that the human singing-voice has a natural vibrato (although boy trebles and proponents of the WHITE VOICE seem to manage without it). Singers and wind players make their vibrato with the action of the diaphragm, which alternately lowers and raises the air pressure and therefore the pitch of the note. String players produce theirs by rocking the note-finger to and fro, thus slightly flattening and sharpening the pitch. This makes a true vibrato only if done at a practical speed: too slow an undulation makes for a WOBBLE; and when it is too fast the effect is that of a TREMOLO. The non-stop vibrato in instrumental music is a fairly recent adjunct to a performance and a contentious issue in authentic performances, where it should be treated more as a special effect than a constant feature of performance. JOACHIM is said to have played without it. Vibrato helps to hide imperfect intonation (since the undulation touches both a higher and a lower pitch than the absolute, thus leaving the ear slightly uncertain). It also makes the sound of voices and instruments 'carry' a greater distance.

VI-DE

See CUT

Viennese lift

The traditional and characteristic way of playing the OOM-CHA-CHA accompaniment beats of the Viennese waltz. It is a subtle effect, and – like an English gentleman's well-cut suit – most successful when not noticed. You don't have to be Viennese to master the Viennese lift; and conversely, some Viennese conductors, including Willy Boskovsky, often vulgarly overdo it. It is impossible to convey in notation but may be described as follows: in three-four time, the second crotchet is played a little early, the third a little late – slightly hanging fire, as it were – but the first beat of the next bar occurs on time. Thus the RUBATO is kept within each bar and does not affect the overall pulse of the music. In orchestras it is generally only the 'cha-chas' of the inner parts that have Viennese lift problems; the 'ooms' are played by the lower instruments and remain in tempo. See RUBATO, SCHRAMMEL and WALTZ KING.

Viennese note

German, *Wienerische Note*: 'The unflattened seventh degree of the major mode when it resolves by step downwards in a subdominant context, that is, either as a 7-6 suspension over the tonic in parallel motion over the subdominant.' Thus says GROVE; and anyone who fails to understand that definition but sees, or hears, the music example quoted there will immediately recognize it as a familiar, characteristic effect in Viennese music from Strauss to Mahler.

Viola

Often looked upon as the Cinderella of the strings, as exemplified by the old orchestral players' riddle, 'What are the two coldest things in the world?' Answer: 'A polar bear's behind and a solo on the viola.' Those who know no better have been heard to accuse viola players of being 'failed fiddle players' and the instrument itself of being both too small and too big for its purpose. But the viola can claim to be, historically, the standard by which other instruments are measured and defined. *Violino* is the Italian diminutive of *viola* ; *violone* (with the Italian enlarging suffix *-one*) a large viola; and *violoncello* (with the added *-ello* or diminuting suffix), a small *violone*. There used to be more kinds of viola than any other string instrument: *viola da braccia* (viola for the arms), *viola da gamba* (viola of the legs), *viola d'amore* (the viola of love – see under D'AMORE) and *viola pomposa*. There was a little viola called *violetta*, and even, I regret to add, the *viola bastarda*. To make matters worse, the French word *violer* means to rape, and is used in that language for all kinds of unseemly puns.

Vivace

Contrary to general belief this is not a marking to indicate speed but, like *grave*, one of mood. In Italian it means flourishing, thriving, full of life. Beethoven uses *andante vivace*, as well as *vivacissimamente*.

Vocal range

The range of the voice is measured vertically, not by distance: see TESSITURA. So when you fill in a form for a summer school or music course and are asked for your vocal range, don't put 'approximately 3 ft 8 ins with a following wind'.

Voice leading

The American term for what in real English has always been 'part-writing', i.e. the disposition of separate PARTS in counterpoint. It is a clumsy translation of the German *Stimmführung*, brought to the USA by immigrant musicologists.

Vorspiel

German for *Prelude* – literally 'foreplay'; though the literal translation 'Wagner's Foreplay to Tristan' is not recommended.

V.S.

Short for *volti subito*, when written at the bottom of a page, tells
a player to turn it quickly.

VW

Not merely the abbreviation for a car, but also the composer Ralph
Vaughan Williams (1872–1958). Even German music-lovers have
been known to say 'Wee-double-u', because the full name usually
comes out as 'Worn Villiams'. VW's first name should be
pronounced to rhyme with 'waif', not 'Alf'.

Waldhorn

The German name (literally 'forest horn') for COR DE CHASSE or a hunting-horn. On the continent the hunt pursued edible quarry, not the fox, and took place in the woods rather than open fields. The horn has therefore always been the traditional sound used to evoke forest scenes. See also NATURAL HORN, SECURICOR, THE HUNT and other cross-references.

The Waldstein

Beethoven's Sonata in C, op.53, so called because of its dedication to his friend and patron, Count Waldstein (1762–1823). He was not only a nobleman but also a composer in his own right, diplomat, linguist, and a 'well-read man of great intellect'. In addition, Waldstein became an honorary colonel in the British army and in 1809 was entrusted with the recruitment in England of German expatriates to fight against Napoleon. When Beethoven was a young man, about to leave Bonn for Vienna, Waldstein presciently wrote in his autograph album 'With help of hard work you shall receive Mozart's spirit from Haydn's hands.' He died in poverty.

Wallala, wallala, la la leia leia la lei!

One of the less inspired lyrics Wagner wrote for his own music. This one opens his RING cycle, and is sung by the Rhine Maidens. See also HOHOJE!

Wallpaper music

See FURNITURE MUSIC

Waltz King

Title given to Johann Strauss II (1825–99). His death marked the end of the waltz era, the quickstep and two-step in two-four time (as exemplified in the music of SOUSA, the MARCH KING) bringing to an end the long reign of three-four time – from the minuet to the waltz – on the dance-floors of the world.

Warning signs

Pencilled into orchestral PARTS by way of reminder. They include:

eyes ◉◉

spectacles

warning triangles borrowed from the Highway Code

wiggly lines denoting a slowing-down of the tempo

reminders to take a breath ✔

or to take a specially big one

and, of course, verbal reminders, such as 'Watch', 'Look out', 'Follow second trombone commas', 'No vibrato', 'Don't drown harp', 'Wake Fred', etc. See COUNTING BARS.

The Wasps

Usually means the Overture of that name by VW, though it is part of a suite of five movements the composer wrote in 1912 for a Cambridge production of Aristophanes' comedy. The two best things about the Overture are the BIG TUNE, one of the glories of COWPAT MUSIC, and the noteworthy fact that *The Wasps* starts with woodwind trills on B's.

Water

The greatest enemy of the woodwind and brass. It is neither water nor spit, as commonly believed, but condensation caused by the player's breath. In the woodwind it causes sticking keys, in the brass, burbling and burping in the valves and tubes. Hence the constant and sometimes distracting use of PULL-THROUGHS (clarinet or bassoon), mops (flutes), pheasant feathers (oboes); and CIGARETTE PAPERS to dry sticking PADS. Also the frequent and compulsive emptying of water all over the floor out of the tubing of the horns. Hans Knappertsbusch (1888–1965), when musical director of the Vienna Philharmonic, used to object to Leopold Wlach, its famous First Clarinet, holding his instrument up so that it rested vertically on his knee. Players do this so that the moisture runs straight down the tube and not into keys; but Knapperts-busch presumably felt that if there was any implement sticking up in the air it should be his baton. Wlach replied (in German), 'Maestro, if you are going to tell me how to hold my clarinet when I'm not playing I shall tell you what to do with your baton when not conducting.' Wind and brass players are sometimes tempted to go through water-clearing motions after they have played a less-than-perfect or even wrong note. As John Clarke said as long ago as 1639, in his *Parœmiologia Anglo-Latina*, 'When a musician hath forgott his note/he maks as though a crumb stuck in his throte.'

Wax conductor

One whose fame rests chiefly or even entirely on his work in the recording studio, from the wax MASTERS formerly used for gramophone records. See also TOP LINE CONDUCTOR.

The Wells

Abbreviation for the Sadler's Wells Opera or Ballet, or the orchestra belonging to either. The Wells was named after a place where a Mr Sadler kept a well with allegedly curative properties. In about 1680 he erected a 'Musick House' to entertain Londoners who took his waters. The name was abolished in the current unseemly rush to reorganize and rename every historically inter-esting institution; although it has now been partly revived.

'When goes the next one?'

The punch-line of the best-known of all operatic anecdotes, often half remembered and attributed to a variety of singers. It belongs to Leo Slezak (1873–1946), the great Austro-Czech tenor famous for his witty pranks. He had the misfortune of making his English debut at the GARDEN on Mafeking Night. The news spread through the house while he was singing *Lohengrin*, and he was wondering why the audience was simultaneously weeping, laughing and cheering. The famous anecdote about Slezak's missing the *Lohengrin* swan that was being pulled across the stage on a string, and on which he was to have ridden, is told by his son, Walter Slezak, in *My Dear Boy: Letters of a Worried Father*. As the empty swan sailed down the stage without him, Slezak pulled back the sleeve of his costume, consulted his wrist and sang, 'Wann geht der Nächste?' What a pity Slezak lived before the age of television: he would have made the ideal chat-show guest. But when his voice began to give out he did the next-best thing and became a film star.

'Where's the fire?'

Sarcastic question sometimes heard from within the orchestra when a SPEED MERCHANT or LIGHTNING CONDUCTOR sets an excessively fast tempo at rehearsal. In such an event the orchestra can bring Maestro to his senses – not by trying to fight his tempo but by *hurrying even more*, so that the whole thing becomes totally unplayable. In German-speaking orchestras it is called *Affentempo*, i.e. 'monkey tempo', from the exaggerated action of monkeys flitting about the trees. In a SLOW BICYCLE RACE the idea is to SHLEP more than the conductor until the piece almost grinds to a halt.

Whistling

See SIFFLEUR, SLOW HANDCLAP

White voice

The sound of a certain kind of soprano voice exemplified by that of Dame Isobel Baillie (1895–1983), an ethereal, clear and rather sexless sound with little if any VIBRATO (and the very antithesis of the BOILED VOICE). It has lately become fashionable again in AUTHENTIC performances.

Wiggly line

See WARNING SIGNS

Williams

A partner in the well-known firm of concert AGENTS called Ingpen & Williams. The firm was originally run by Joan Ingpen with the help of a sleeping partner called Williams. What is not generally known is that Williams was her dog.

The Wireless Orchestra

See BBCSO

Wobble

A very slow and wide VIBRATO, the opposite of a TREMOLO.

Wolf

The name for a faulty note on, usually, a string instrument. Its cause is difficult if not impossible to establish. 'A slight mistake in the position of the sound-bar, a looseness, an inequality or roughness of finish, will produce that hollow, teeth-on-edge growl called "the wolf",' wrote H. R. Hawelis in 1884. String players talk much about their particular wolf note, but the effect is usually more noticeable and offensive to the player than the listener. But the phenomenon can occur on wind and brass instruments, too. Americans, who like the Germans refuse to distinguish between a NOTE and a TONE, cause confusion with their wolf note as well. They call it 'wolf tone' which must be annoying to Irish nationalists, one of whose heroes was Wolf Tone (1763–98).

The Wolf Gang

Nickname for the Amadeus String Quartet. It refers both to the fact that they take their name from Wolfgang Amadeus Mozart and that they have an eye – or eight eyes – for a pretty woman (or four women). In recent years they unwittingly gained another nickname. This came about when a team of students on University Challenge (a television quiz game), confidently answered the question, 'By what collective name are the following known: Norbert Brainin, Sigmund Nissel, Peter Schidlof and Martin Lovett?' with: 'The Tolpuddle Martyrs.'

WoO

Abbreviation often seen when reference is made to the works of Beethoven. It stands for *Werke ohne Opuszahl*, i.e. 'works without an opus number' and was devised for Kinsky's THEMATIC CATALOGUE of Beethoven's works. See also KOECHEL.

Woodles

Name for a characteristic accompaniment figure often given to clarinets in their lowest register: a kind of non-staccato ALBERTI BASS (though not necessarily a bass line, of course). The most beautiful woodles in the whole world occur in Mozart's great Wind Serenade K361 and are played in contrary motion by clarinets and basset horns: a sort of glorious musical sylvan rustling. The word is onomatopœic and is derived from the fact that they go 'woodle-oodle, woodle-oodle'.

Mozart's Woodles

Woofing-machine

Derisive nickname for the GERMAN HORN, especially from those who prefer the FRENCH HORN. Also 'Circular Trombone'.

Wop stick

See GOB STICK

Workshop

A fashionable modern term which, when applied to music-making, usually means a place where EXPERIMENTAL musical activities are carried on: perhaps with young people who, instead of being made to learn to play an instrument, are 'given something to bang' or invited to take part in SCRATCH MUSIC. In general, audiences prefer not to be experimented on.

Wozzeck/Woyzeck

The opera by Berg is *Wozzeck*, but the play by Büchner on which it is based was published under the name *Woyzeck*. The distinction is apparently based on a misreading by Berg (or someone) of Büchner's handwriting.

Wq

Followed by a number, refers to one of the THEMATIC CATALOGUES compiled by the unpronounceable Wotquenne. See KOECHEL.

Wrong-note finders

Every orchestra has at least one, a player who is constantly holding up rehearsals by questioning the accuracy of his and other PARTS 'Excuse me,' he says, just as the conductor's baton reaches the top of its initial upbeat, 'should I have a D sharp on the third beat seven bars after letter M?' The strings put their bows down and the wind release again the lungful of air they have just taken on board, and a general discussion ensues, perhaps with mutterings of 'We wanna get home.' Orchestral players are better placed than conductors to notice wrong notes, for they sit 'in the middle of the sound', whereas conductors must stand on the edge of it in order to get a balanced impression of the whole. It takes a certain kind of musician to be a wrong-note finder. He will have an abnormally acute ear and a willingness to study the SCORE as well as his own part. Wrong notes often remain undetected for years, even for centuries (as Norman Del Mar points out in his book, *Orchestral Variations: Confusion and Error in the Orchestral Repertoire*). Before the late Henry Datyner became an orchestra LEADER he was known as a prolific wrong-note finder as a rank-and-file member of the HALLÉ. Barbirolli said to him, after yet another ancient mistake had been corrected, 'What's the matter with you, Henry? Are you in touch with the composer's ghost?' Some conductors hear discrepancies better than others, without necessarily being better conductors for it. One maestro was so eager to be admired for his keen ear that he secretly got hold of the seventh double-bass part and pencilled an erroneous sharp into a *fortissimo* passage. Then, at rehearsal, he stopped the orchestra at that point and said, 'Seventh double bass! You played an F *sharp* there!' The player replied, 'No, I played an F *natural* as printed, but some bloody fool pencilled a sharp in front of it.'

Yes/No

When pencilled into SCORE or PARTS at the end of a section marked with a repeat sign, 'YES' means that the repeat is made, 'NO', that the player goes straight on. It appears obvious, but it is surprising how many accidents occur at such places through forgetfulness or failure to mark the part at rehearsal. 'YES' is in theory unnecessary, since printed repeat signs should automatically be observed unless countermanded. But orchestral material, especially when hired, goes through so many hands that it is full of contradictory pencillings. And some repeats are seldom if ever made (see FIRST-TIME BAR). Such essential arrangements are often the only things discussed at STOPS AND STARTS. The Austrian conductor Hans Knappertsbusch (1888–1965) was known for his laziness and reluctance to have more than a SITZPROBE. He believed, quite rightly, that familiar music sounds better when fresh, and that experienced players prefer to concentrate once a day, not twice. But there was an occasion when the Vienna Philharmonic begged him to rehearse the Eroica, as there were several new players in important positions. Kna (as he was known) reluctantly agreed and played through it in a perfunctory way. At the performance, some players made the repeat in the first movement, others went straight on. There was chaos; and after the performance Knappertsbusch stormed into the BANDROOM, angrily shouting, 'Now you *see* what happens when you rehearse!'

Yoof

Really 'Euph' – abbreviated nickname of the Euphonium.

The Yorkshire Messiah

In 1895 a Yorkshire composer offered to the publishers Novello & Co. a new version he had composed of the oratorio text: 'I feel sure', he wrote 'that the public would now like a change from Handel's music to my own.' It never caught on, and even the composer's name has disappeared from the Novello archives. The German composer A. J. Romberg (1767–1821) had no inhibitions about writing an oratorio called *The Messiah*, to words adapted by Klopstock.

YSO

The short-lived Yorkshire Symphony Orchestra, formed in 1947 and disbanded by a philistine Leeds City Council in 1955. Its chief conductor was Maurice Miles.

Zak, Pyotr

A fictitious 'Polish' composer of avant garde music invented by Hans Keller and Susan Bradshaw for a BBC broadcast of ultra-modern music. Some critics were taken in by the work (which was produced by random improvisation on a variety of percussion instruments), others correctly and courageously described it as rubbish. Would they displayed such courage more often! See also ESRUM-HELLERUP.

Zauber

The German word for magic, and a prefix element in the name of many German fairy-tale operas of the 'magic' movement that was so popular at the end of the eighteenth century and the beginning of the nineteenth, and in some ways anticipated the modern pantomime. Mozart's *Zauberflöte*, and Schubert's *Zauberharfe* are only two of them. The first Tamino in the *Magic Flute*, Benedikt Schack (who was a composer and flautist as well as a singer and therefore was able to play the 'magic' instrument himself on stage), also wrote an opera called *The Magic Island*, and another contemporary, Wenzel Müller, wrote an opera about a *Magic Bassoon* and a *Magic Zither*.

Zip fastener solo

Knappertsbusch's nickname for GLISS. He specifically used it for a certain solo violin passage in Strauss's TILL.

Zopf

Coloquial German for 'old hat'. The word really means pigtail, and 'Zopf style' refers to what is thought to be antiquated and no longer fashionable; or else is pedantically and self-consciously made to appear antique. Beethoven (who still wore the eighteenth-century pigtail when he was in his teens) would have considered

Leopold Mozart *Zopf*. In more recent times, Schoenberg scathingly dismissed as *Zopf* Stravinsky's neo-classical works, e.g. *The Rake's Progress*: see MODERNSKY.

Zuck

See SUCK

Zukunftsmusik

See MUSIC OF THE FUTURE